A GUIDE TO THE
MIDLAND & Gᵀ NORTHERN
JOINT RAILWAY

A GUIDE TO THE
MIDLAND & Gt NORTHERN
JOINT RAILWAY

NIGEL J. L. DIGBY

IAN ALLAN
Publishing

First published 1993

ISBN 0 7110 2187 2

© Nigel J. L. Digby 1993

Published by Ian Allan Ltd, Shepperton, Surrey; and printed by Ian Allan Printing Ltd at their works at Coombelands in Runnymede, England.

Frontispiece:

Although this view of Melton West Junction has been published several times before, it so encapsulates the M&GN in its golden days that it bears repetition. The Class A 4-4-0 No 23 was rebuilt with an MR type boiler in 1895, and received an extended smokebox c1910, and here sports the standard post-1904 lamp irons on which the express passenger code is shown. The train consists of two ex-Midland Clayton thirds, the second having been relettered in the standard mid-period style. The third vehicle is an ex-GN composite, followed by a 'new stock' third and a 'large stock' luggage brake, both four-wheel. There are two ex-GN vehicles on the Cromer siding. The signalbox is the M&GN type 1a opened in 1901, the small buildings in the foreground occupy the site of the first box. Note the check rails on the Cromer line and the train detector bar in the foreground, and the original 31½-mile post just above the engine's smokebox. This was replaced in concrete c1923 and moved to a spot in the vee of lines seen below the buffer beam.
Ian Allan Library

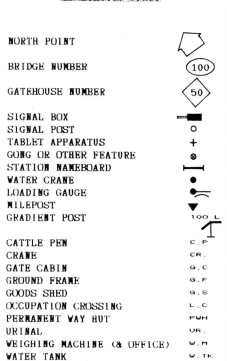

KEY TO SYMBOLS & ABBREVIATIONS
ON STATION PLANS

NORTH POINT	
BRIDGE NUMBER	(100)
GATEHOUSE NUMBER	50
SIGNAL BOX	
SIGNAL POST	O
TABLET APPARATUS	+
GONG OR OTHER FEATURE	⊗
STATION NAMEBOARD	
WATER CRANE	
LOADING GAUGE	
MILEPOST	▼
GRADIENT POST	100 L
CATTLE PEN	C.P
CRANE	CR.
GATE CABIN	G.C
GROUND FRAME	G.F
GOODS SHED	G.S
OCCUPATION CROSSING	L.C
PERMANENT WAY HUT	PWH
URINAL	UR.
WEIGHING MACHINE (& OFFICE)	W.M
WATER TANK	W.TK

Contents

Foreword

Sometimes I wonder how often an enthusiast whose interest has been aroused by a book or photo album is deterred from undertaking a model of a lesser-known railway by the lack of information. There may be dates of opening, some locomotive notes and few fuzzy photographs, but no real details on the architecture and operating or other facts essential for the construction of a layout, and so the interest wanes and the frustrated modeller passes on to another idea.

It is precisely to avoid these circumstances that this book has been written. I have intended in these pages to give enough information to enable any modeller who may be interested in the M&GN to build an accurate portrayal of the line, capturing the atmosphere both material and spiritual of this special railway.

Acknowledgements

Although much of this work is based on personal research and field-work there are many people who, directly or indirectly, were involved with the finished article. Of prime importance are the members of the M&GN Circle whose archives are probably the best collection of M&GN documents in existence. Former employees of the M&GN particularly helpful in their various fields were Messrs Bill Fulcher, Bob Loynes, Frank Morgan, Charlie Porter, Philip Porter and Alan Wells. In addition I have been able to build upon research undertaken at the PRO and elsewhere by Messrs Michael Back, John Hobden, John Horan and John Watling. Thanks must also be given to Mick Clark, editor of the M&GN Circle Bulletin, for his unfailing support, and to Graham Kenworthy whose selfless pursuit of priceless drawings made this book possible. On the photographic front invaluable assistance was to be had from Messrs Adrian Whittaker and Maurice Storey-Smith, the Circle photographic officers. It is also traditional to thank one's wife, but in this case it is well-deserved as Angela has wielded the measuring tape many times.

Biographical Notes

The Author was educated at the Paston School, North Walsham and attained a BA Degree in Architecture at Nottingham University. He has been constructing models for at least 20 years, professionally since 1987. The Author's father was a founder member of the M&GN Circle and so the Author can be said to be a lifelong devotee of the Joint.

Dedication

This book is dedicated to my mother and my late father Doug Digby who proposed a similar work many years ago.

The M&GN Circle

A prospectus and membership details can be obtained from Graham Kenworthy, 16 Beverley Road, Brundall, Norwich NR13 5QS.

1. Introduction to the M&GN

The Midland & Great Northern Railways Joint Committee was a main line joining the Midlands and the North to the Norfolk coast, over half of which happened to be single track, a proportion exceeding its close equivalent, the Somerset and Dorset Joint, and calling for even greater feats of operating efficiency from its staff than that distinguished and well-loved railway. This intensity of working, the atmosphere engendered by its locomotives and rolling stock and the great variety of countryside it traversed surely make this, the largest Joint Line in Britain, a worthy subject for any study. However, despite this worth, it still remains a largely untapped source. This is probably due to the fact that the majority of the system was closed in 1959, the first closure of a main line British railway, and failed to survive into the 1960s when its demise, like that of the S&D, would have made it a household name. Thankfully, a portion of the M&GN is preserved by the North Norfolk Railway, who are beginning to rescue M&GN stock, and there are still remains to be studied. But it is mainly due to the efforts of the M&GN Circle in saving countless artefacts, documents and precious first-hand accounts from the actual staff of the line that this book can be written today.

Any work of reference has it parameters and this one is no exception. As the title of this book suggests, I will be concentrating on the M&GN proper, that is the organisation in existence between 1893 and 1936, but some reference will also have to be made to the earlier and later periods. The history of the M&GN has already been covered exhaustively in books and magazines, and only enough to give a background knowledge to the newcomer will be included here. The controversy before and after closure and the reasons for closure will not be covered. What will be included are as many as possible of the elements from the smallest post to the surrounding landscape, which gave the atmosphere of the 'Joint'.

One of the Joint's most fascinating aspects is the richness of possibilities inherent in each distinct period and in each section and portion of the line. Some of the most apparent physical differences were between the so-called 'Eastern' and 'Western' sections, at least until system-wide features began to appear. This is because the M&GN was derived from two different railways, whose meeting point was King's Lynn. (Fig 1.)

The first line of what was later to become the M&GN was the ambitiously-named Norwich & Spalding Railway, virtually a branch of the Great Northern Railway, opened to Sutton Bridge by 1862. The N&S looked towards Wisbech but in the event it was the Peterborough, Wisbech & Sutton Railway, very much a Midland Railway branch, that got there. Arrangements were made to allow the N&S running powers from Sutton Bridge to Wisbech when the PW&S was complete. Meanwhile the Lynn & Sutton Bridge Railway was being constructed westwards from a junction with the Great Eastern Railway at Lynn, and was opened to a junction with the N&S at Sutton Bridge in 1864 (goods) and 1866 (passenger). The GNR agreed to work the line, along with the Spalding & Bourne Railway completed in 1866 from Spalding to an end-on junction with the GN's Bourne &

Essendine branch. Thus almost all the lines later to become the western section of the M&GN were in place by 1866.

The S&B and the L&SB proposed to amalgamate, lease the N&S and build a line from Bourne to the MR at Saxby, under the name Midlands & Eastern Railway. However, in the face of GN opposition the scheme was changed to incorporate MR running powers to Bourne over the Stamford & Essendine and Bourne & Essendine branches via a new junction at Stamford. It was agreed that the M&E was to be jointly worked by the MR and GN under the title Bourne & Lynn Joint. The PW&S opened later the same year, but was not included in the Joint arrangements. It was not until 1877 that the M&E formally absorbed the N&S and the B&LJt given statutory recognition.

In the east two nominally independent lines had been promoted: the Lynn & Fakenham and the Great Yarmouth & Stalham Light. Beginning at

Yarmouth in 1876 and Lynn in 1878 these two lines, faced with many GER obstructive tactics, slowly traversed Norfolk. The same contractor, Messrs Wilkinson & Jarvis, built and controlled both lines and the two railways can effectively be considered as one. The GY&S line, now under the title Yarmouth & North Norfolk, reached North Walsham in 1881 and the L&F line reached Norwich in 1882.

Having tried but failed to amalgamate officially, a separate railway Act was obtained for a link line between Melton Constable (destined to be the heart of the M&GN) and North Walsham and construction had begun when at last the amalgamation into the Eastern & Midlands Railway was sanctioned from 1 January 1883.

The E&M embraced all the lines east and west of Lynn but the working arrangements in force on the old B&LJt remained. Under the aegis of the E&M the link line to Melton was completed (1883) and a Lynn avoiding line built (1886) giving for the first time a direct main line from the Midlands to the Norfolk coast. A branch to Cromer was completed in 1887, having been opened only as far as Holt since 1884.

The E&M has been described as an 'aggressive' railway, in that it did not rest on its laurels, and promoted lines in many parts of the county, none of which were built, but succeeded in unsettling the GE. The E&M was also desperately short of

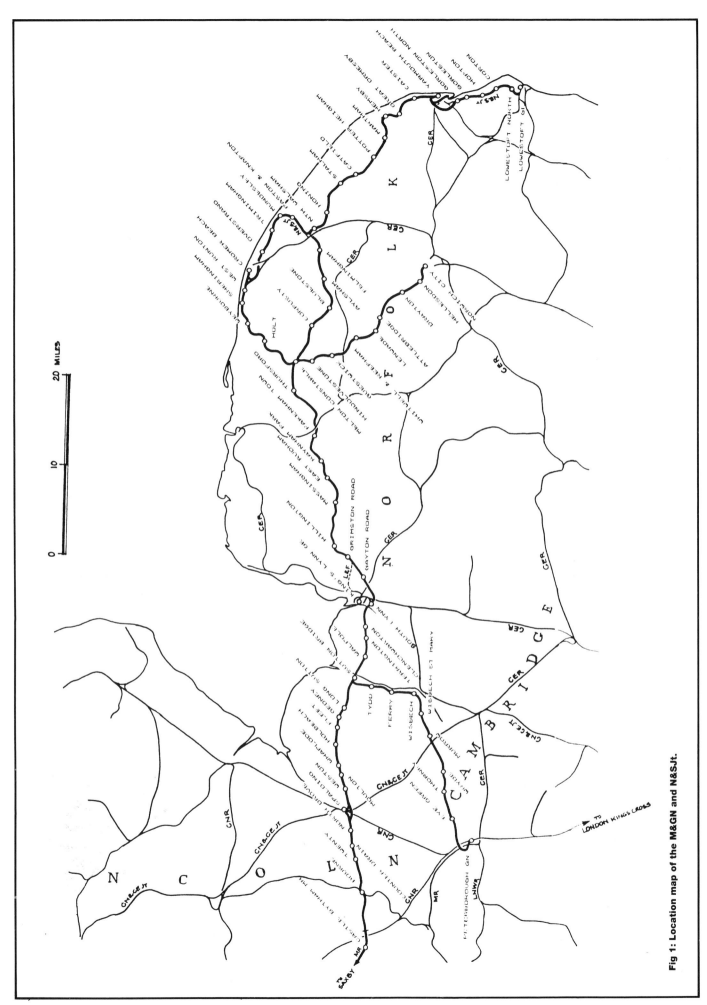

Fig 1: Location map of the M&GN and N&SJt.

Above:
Mr William Marriott, Engineer and Locomotive Superintendent 1883/4-1924, and Traffic Manager 1919-1924, on the occasion of his retirement.
M&GN Circle

being later the same month, incorporating the Mundesley line. Under this title lines were opened between Yarmouth and Lowestoft in 1903, and Mundesley and Cromer in 1906.

The Grouping of the railways in 1923 affected the M&GN very little. The Committee was still a joint one, but now with representatives from the LMS and LNER. The stock working on to the line from outside appeared in new liveries, but the M&GN continued very much as before. Mr Marriott became Traffic Manager in 1919 but retired in 1924. Mr R. B. Walker and Mr W. Newman were appointed Traffic Manager and Engineer respectively. Some modernisation in signalling and loco fittings and livery became apparent from the mid-1920s, and the use of Marriott reinforced concrete items became widespread.

Despite slight indications that the M&GN might be ceded to the LMS, it was in fact the LNER that took overall responsibility of the M&GN and N&SJt from 1 October 1936. The Joint Committee still met and owned the railway, but administration was passed to the Southern Area of the LNER based at Liverpool Street, and locomotive supervision was taken over by Stratford. The atmosphere of the line changed irrevocably as the old locos and carriages were replaced by GE, GN, GC and LNER types. Melton Works was effectively closed in December 1936 causing great hardship to Melton Constable village. Many M&GN men were transferred to other areas or left railway service altogether. However, the Joint still evoked loyalty from the staff and a family atmosphere managed to persist right up to the end.

Road competition had begun to bite in the 1930s and the M&GN was wise enough to introduce motorised collection services which staved off the worst effects, but after the 1948 Nationalisation road competition really began to tell. It would be depressing to catalogue the slow and perhaps avoidable decline of the M&GN. It seems clear that British Railways wrote the Joint off quite soon as a through line; nevertheless the closure at the end of February 1959 was quite a shock to the railway world, being the first closure of a major part of the railway system. Some lines remained, particularly for goods traffic, but most of these were picked off

Below:
The former Traffic Manager's office as it appeared from Austin Street in 1959. The building on the left was the Accountant's office.
M&GN Circle

Left:
'The Office' at Melton Constable where all the drawings were prepared, and from where the Engineer could keep an eye on things!
H. C. Casserley

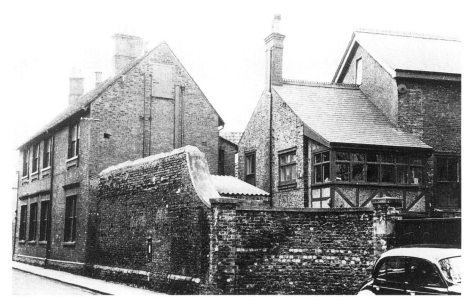

money. For some time after the Lynn loop had been completed the rails on the old alignment from Bawsey to Gaywood were left in place, in case they had to sell to the GE after all. However, it was hoped that if the deal was made attractive enough the MR might step in. It has been admitted that this was the reason the branch from Melton was built to Cromer rather than Blakeney, which was the bigger port at that time, in an effort to fulfil the MR's wishes for an outlet to a coastal resort. In the event, it was the MR and the GN who jointly took up the E&M from 1 July 1893, and the link line from Bourne to Saxby first proposed 28 years before was opened for passengers in May 1894.

The M&GN (known as the 'Joint', 'the Committee' and even the 'Midland') had its overall responsibilities divided: the MR supervised the loco department, the GN the signalling and track, but the day to day running continued very much as before, except that the Committee owned the lands, buildings and rolling stock and organised the running of the services. The western section was worked more or less as before, and the railway was only brought under one Traffic Manager's Office in Lynn from 1895. Midland engines assisted on the Eastern Section until the Committee owned enough engines to run the services itself. The Engineer of the E&M, Mr William Marriott (after a short period of uncertainty) was made Resident Engineer of the M&GN providing he gave up any private practice. Marriott was given very much of a free hand at his office in Melton Constable, and both he and the various Traffic Managers made sure the M&GN was run as a personal affair, with the staff on friendly terms with each other, their officers and the public. Before long the infant M&GN was able to 'pull itself up by its boot-straps' and by the 1900s become a really excellent railway, with what Ahrons called 'perhaps the smartest working on single line anywhere in the country'.

During the E&M period a branch from North Walsham to Mundesley was sanctioned, but this was not actually opened until July 1898. As a result of agreements with the GER, a new railway committee, the Norfolk & Suffolk Joint, came into

Above:
The fitting shop and the foundry in 1939. The drawing office is just off picture to the right.
H. C. Casserley

in the 1960s, and now only the Cromer Beach-Sheringham line is under BR control. Sheringham-Kelling, near Holt, was saved by the North Norfolk Railway.

The officers and staff were a very important factor in the atmosphere of the M&GN, both the local and the visiting public becoming familiar with station staff and train crew. Several M&GN officers will be mentioned in the following pages and it will be helpful here to give some biographical details.

The most outstanding figure in the history of the Joint was that of Mr William Marriott MICE MIMechE. There may be a danger in assigning too much mystique to the man, but there is an equal danger in trying to ignore him or belittle his achievements. He was an extremely gifted civil and mechanical engineer; reason enough for the M&GN often to be referred to as 'Marriott's Tramway'.

Born in 1857 at Basle, where his father was Professor of English at the University, he came to England in 1868 and took articles with Ransomes & Rapier Ltd of Ipswich from 1875-79. Returning as a draughtsman in 1880 it appears he was considering seeking his fortune in America but in 1881 heard of a vacancy as assistant Engineer with Wilkinson & Jarvis, then constructing the L&F and Y&NN lines in Norfolk. For a six-week unpaid trial period he assisted Mr Jarvis with construction at the Yarmouth end and was then offered a permanent post which he took, giving up all idea of going to America. Thus, in 1883, he found himself Engineer, and a year later Locomotive Superintendent, of the Eastern & Midlands Railway. At the age of 26 he was possibly the youngest Engineer of a public railway since the days of Stephenson and Brunel. He carried his dual role throughout the M&GN period and in addition became Traffic Manager from January 1919 until his retirement at the end of 1924. His many achievements include some of the first practical prefabricated concrete items, and design and construction of several locomotives, but perhaps his most difficult task was the efficient servicing of a railway on a shoestring budget. The M&GN was indeed fortunate to have Marriott as its Engineer as he was regarded with a kindly and indulgent eye from Derby, and what he asked for he usually got, except an increase in salary!

His relationship with the men was at first cordial; to them he was 'the young Guv'nor'. He was one of the old school; courteous and humane with that practical, unselfconscious Christianity which has become rare and old-fashioned in this century. Although being seen as a rather stern figure later in his tenure of office, he nevertheless remained popular with the majority of the men and officers and if a figurehead for the M&GN was sought then it would undoubtedly be William Marriott.

Mr Marriott's assistant and successor as Locomotive Superintendent was Mr William Newman who joined the E&M from the S&DJt in 1890. He was probably responsible for a great deal of the design work involved in the Melton-built locomotives. He retired in 1932 and was succeeded by Mr Albert Nash of the GW and latterly the LMS. Mr Nash was responsible for the variety of chimneys tried in the later years of M&GN motive power. He moved back to the LMS at Derby Works in 1937 when Melton Works were closed.

On the Civil Engineering side Marriott's assistant was Mr Graham Gribble who had also been with Wilkinson & Jarvis. Mr Gribble was instrumental in the successful design of Breydon Viaduct. He left in 1902 to be replaced by Mr Charles Slade, an old pupil of Marriott's and an assistant at Melton. His place was taken c1906 by Mr Albert Langley who succeeded Marriott as Engineer on his retirement.

Company Architect until c1913 was Mr George Ratcliffe, apparently coming from a practice in Norwich in 1892. His place was taken by Mr Arthur Roy who remained at Melton until the LNER took over.

At the Traffic Manager's Office, at Austin Street in Lynn, Mr George Curson at first continued as Traffic Manager (Eastern Section) as he had done since the former E&M TM, Mr Alfred Aslett, had left in 1891. From 1 January 1895 Mr William Cunning assumed the post of TM of the entire Joint line. Mr Curson, an old GE man who had joined the L&F in 1880, resumed his more usual post of assistant TM and Outdoor Superintendent based at Fakenham until his retirement in 1906. Mr Cunning had come from the Portpatrick & Wigtownshire Joint Railway (MR/LNW/CR/G&SW) but his health began to give way and from 1 July 1898 Mr Jonathon J. Petrie, of the Midland and the Severn & Wye Joint (MR/GW), was appointed Traf-

fic Manager. Mr Petrie was a man of great presence, dignified and kindly, and regarded as one of Lynn's leading citizens. It was he that introduced female clerks into the TMO for the first time. His death in office, in late 1918, was a great shock. He was succeeded by Marriott which put a few noses out of joint, there having been a healthy rivalry between Austin Street and Melton for many years!

Marriott brought with him as Chief Clerk Mr Robert B. Walker, who became Assistant TM in 1922 and Traffic Manager from 1 January 1925. 'RB' was a very popular figure, good-looking and upright, fond of sport. It was he who introduced the Staff Bowls tournament and 'Bowels' in the vernacular became all the rage up and down the line. Mr Walker had begun with the E&M in 1883 as a junior clerk at the TMO.

The Traffic Manager's Office itself had an interesting, not to say mysterious origin. King's Lynn was a market town and port which developed beside the estuary of the Great Ouse. The estuary was embanked and channelled in 1852, and subsequent development demanded construction of docks; the Alexandra in 1869 and the Bentinck in 1883, and the King's Lynn Dock Railway (KLDR) to connect them to the GER station. The principal home of Lynn's fishermen was the Fisher Fleet, a creek to the north of the town connecting the River Gay to the Ouse. Beside the Fleet was an area known as Austin Fields, by which prosperous merchants made their homes. One such house was known as 'The Priory', of which more later. Although originally navigable, the Fisher Fleet was culverted on construction of the Bentinck Dock, which cut off its access to the sea. The KLDR followed the course of the Fleet, passing to the north of Austin Fields.

In the 1870s all traffic for King's Lynn and the Docks was effectively controlled by the GER, whether it came from the west over the B&LJt or from the east over the L&F. No doubt separate access to the KLDR and even a station was an attractive idea which must have been mooted very early to be included in the Y&NN Bill of 1878, and again in the L&F Extensions Bill of 1879, becom-

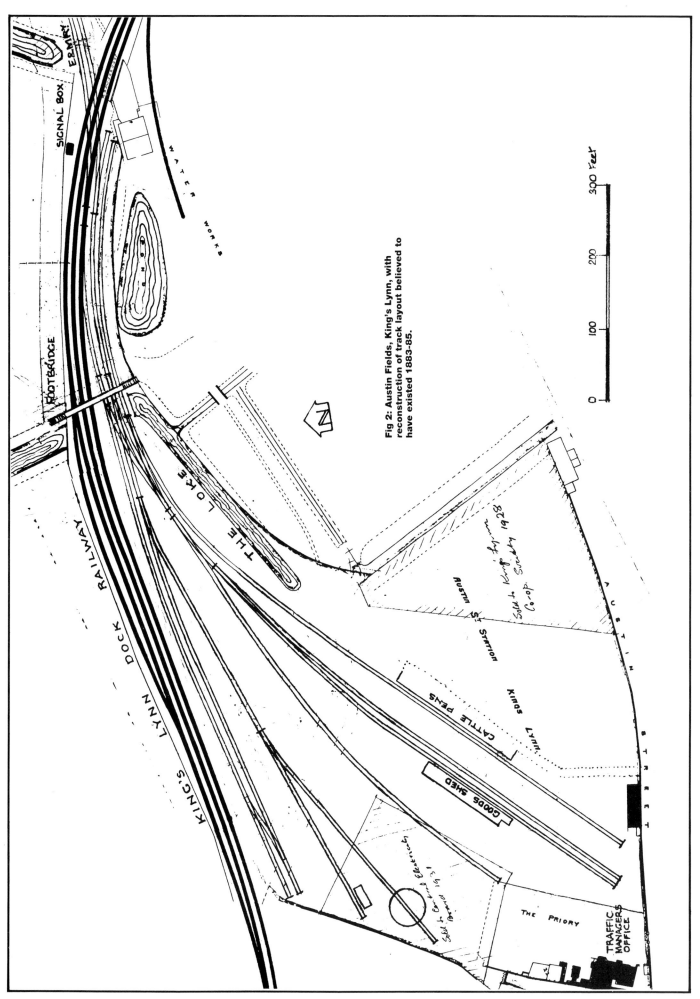

Fig 2: Austin Fields, King's Lynn, with reconstruction of track layout believed to have existed 1883-85.

300 Feet

SIGNAL BOX

EMBKT

WATER WORKS

FOOTBRIDGE

THE LORE

KING'S LYNN DOCK RAILWAY

N

Austin St Station

Sold to Kings Lynn Co-op Society 1928

Kings Lynn

CATTLE PENS

GOODS SHED

A U S T I N   S T R E E T

Sold to Eastern Electricity 19__

THE PRIORY

TRAFFIC MANAGERS OFFICE

ing law in August 1880. For many years it has been generally known that the L&F and the E&M planned to have their own station in King's Lynn but despite much conjecture it came to be accepted that no station was ever built. All that was known was that a large area of land was fenced and a large goods shed erected. However, new research has shown that a goods station and branch were indeed completed, but mysteriously never opened. The L&F apparently purchased Austin Fields north of Austin Street and all buildings thereon including 'The Priory' during 1881. Rather than demolish the house it was decided to establish offices there, later inherited by the E&M and the M&GN, and these became the TMO. (Fig 2.)

The Austin Street branch was a simple one, double track, leaving the GE Hunstanton line at Salters Road, a few chains south of Gaywood Junction where the L&F line branched off. It crossed on the level the meadows adjacent to the River Gay (or Gaywood River) and reached a crossing and junction with the KLDR near the Long Pond. After crossing The Loke it turned south into Austin Fields. The Long Pond and The Loke were water-filled earthworks dating from the Civil War period. There were several structures erected; gatehouse No 0, a goods shed, cattle pens, two signalboxes, a loco coal stage and even a turntable, although the position of the latter is uncertain. A footbridge (later No 52A) was constructed in January 1884. It is supposed that the major proportion of the works were completed by early 1883 and yet there was no official opening, and during 1885 the rails were all removed. It is not known why the station was abandoned, but one suspects that the imminent opening of the Lynn Loop to South Lynn must have been a major deciding factor. The TMO was thus left at the corner of a large field, empty except for the goods shed which was used as storage for stationery and other documents.

The TMO was an attractive building set in well-kept gardens and secluded from Austin Street by a high brick wall. The offices were pleasant to work in, with large and airy rooms overlooking the garden. The exception was the telegraph office which was at the rear of the building and had a glass roof; stifling in summer and freezing in winter. In the main part of the building were various departments: Passenger, Goods Commercial and Operating Departments. The Accountancy and Staff Departments were housed in offices overlooking Austin Street, built in 1895. The main building was entered through a spacious hall complete with marble fireplace. Originally the Traffic Manager

had his office upstairs in a large room with panelled walls, but during the tenure of Mr Walker this became the Board Room and he made his office downstairs.

The TMO closed on 1 October 1936 when the LNER assumed control. Mr Walker reassured the staff (about 80 in number) that with their excellent background and training on the M&GN they would have no difficulty in their new positions within the LNER organisation, and he was correct. In fact it must be said that their promotion prospects immediately improved; due to its limited size the M&GN could be a rather static organisation as far as TMO clerks were concerned.

If Austin Street could be considered the 'head' of the M&GN, then Melton Constable was undoubtedly the heart. This community set in deepest North Norfolk could be said to be unique in being a railway village as opposed to railway towns like Crewe or Swindon. As recounted in Chapter 6, the junctions and works were sited here due to the patronage of Lord Hastings, a director of the L&F who set aside land to the northeast of his Melton Hall estate. The estate had been held by the Astley family since 1236 and the Park was of considerable extent, but the communities of Melton Constable and Burgh Parva adjacent to it were essentially lost villages. The original Burgh Parva church was ruined (replaced by a corrugated iron church) and all that remained was Burgh Hall. The two parishes were united under the one church near Melton Hall. Lord Hastings made available a large tract of land across the road from Burgh Hall, straddling the boundary of nearby Briston, on condition that he be given in return a private station. It was not an easy site, sloping from west to east and being at a high level, but the station and works were begun in 1881. As there was no habitation in the area, a street of houses was constructed along with a 'Railway Hall' and a small gasworks. Lord Hastings contributed the Hastings Arms Inn. Marriott and his wife moved into No 1 Melton Street, one of the large houses at the beginning of the terraces, but about 1896 removed to Brinton Grange. The family also had another house, 'Roquebrune' in Sheringham.

The original railway facilities included the island platform station, goods shed, loco shed, turntable, water tower and coaling stage. Also built was the core of the locomotive and carriage works: an erecting shop, carriage shop, paint shop, foundry, drawing office and so on. Two L&F type signalboxes controlled the junctions at each end of the platform. Lord Hastings was provided with a small platform and waiting room on the Up side of

the station near the overbridge, with its own carriage drive from the Hindolvestone road. Over the ensuing years the works were gradually extended and improved, most of the work being carried out in the 1895-1912 period. There were extensions to the stores, signal shop, paint shop and carriage shop, and new boiler and erecting shops. The Melton 'buzzer' summoning the men to work became a familiar sound for miles around. By 1913 a concrete shop had been laid out along the south of the works. The whole site was served by a narrow gauge railway on which heavy items were shifted on trolleys, and on which certain young apprentices had been known to ride in a reckless manner! The domestic gasworks was extended in 1899 to include an oil gas plant for charging the gas cylinders of passenger rolling stock, and again in 1902 to cater for the large influx of gas-fitted stock from the GN and MR. Prior to this, most native M&GN stock remained oil-lit.

During the same period the village was also expanded to about 100 dwellings, with a school, Railway Institute and recreation ground. The Company was responsible for maintenance and decoration of the houses and the streets, which were tree-lined. To the north, across the Briston Road, speculative builders added several more streets of terraced dwellings, but these were not as well-appointed as the M&GN houses.

In 1901 the layout of the station was improved by the doubling of all but the Norwich line, and new M&GN signalboxes were provided. A further benefit was the improvement of the Down goods road into a relief line in 1915/16 with consequent replacement of the overbridge. A similar Up relief line could not be constructed because of Lord Hastings' private waiting room, even though the span of the new concrete bridge allowed for it.

The closure of the works in December 1936 was a sad blow to the whole district. Henceforth only small repairs were undertaken. The buildings were used for a time around 1939 for storage of WD materials and from about 1942 a wagon sheet factory and later a wagon and carriage repair works were established, but the village suffered a decline in its fortunes from which it has never fully recovered, although recently an industrial estate has been founded there, using some of the old buildings.

Below:
The carriage & wagon and paint shops in 1947, with the drawing office in the background.
H. C. Casserley

2. Station Architecture

The text of the following sections will refer to all architecture and other structures or fitments in the past tense, whether or not they still exist, thus avoiding confusion of meaning. Brief notes of the surviving remains are given with the station plans in Chapter 6. Dates where given are initially the official opening date (not necessarily the date of actual construction) followed by the known or suspected rebuilding dates. Dimensions are given in Imperial and abbreviations or initials are used widely and can be referred to in the Glossary.

M&GN architecture can be perceived as rather confusing but once the sequence of construction is known then the story becomes quite simple. The western section is relatively straightforward, but eastern section construction occupied the years 1877-1906 which can be broken down into three phases: contractor's period 1877-1883, 'arts & crafts' period 1884-1899, late period 1900-1906. The final phase from 1913-1936 could be called the 'concrete period' but this is covered in Chapter 5.

Contractor's period 1877-1883

The key to understanding the initial development of eastern section architecture is to cast aside the artificial distinction between the L&F and Y&NN railways and to consider them as one, since it was the contractors Wilkinson & Jarvis of Victoria Street, Westminster, who controlled the design of all L&F and GY&S/Y&NN buildings. As the lines progressed towards each other from opposite ends

of the county the designs changed, leaving a confusing picture for later observers.

The first construction by Wilkinson & Jarvis (henceforth W&J) was the line from Yarmouth to Ormesby. The two intermediate stations at Caister-on-Sea and Ormesby (Great Ormesby from 1884) were very attractively designed: two single-storey pitched-roof pavilions with gables toward the line, linked by a glazed booking hall under a pitched roof parallel to the railway. (Fig 3.) This layout was repeated later and for the sake of brevity will be termed the 'pavilion' design. The stations became asymmetrical when extensions for lavatory accommodation were added in 1898. The construction was pioneering and probably cheap in that it was of concrete blocks. Other early W&J buildings were similarly constructed but while the blocks used in the Yarmouth workshops (later the running sheds) were left rough, those for the stations were rendered smooth and fine joint lines scored on to give an 'ashlar' appearance, the only visible brickwork being the gothic arches over the window openings. The young William Marriott, who joined the contractor's staff in 1881 obviously learnt from W&J's use of concrete as he was to enthuse about it throughout his career and actually put it to practical use.

Yarmouth Beach station was originally of timber devoid of canopy, goods shed or yard wall. The timber office was re-erected at Holt in 1884 and gravitated to Melton Constable in 1886 as a reading room. When Yarmouth was rebuilt in 1879 at a

cost of £4,000, the plan form was again of the pavilion type but massively extended so that the building lost the fine proportions of the small stations. Unlike Ormesby and Caister the windows were normal flat-arched sashes, but the walls were again concrete 'ashlar'. Stationmaster's accommodation was included but this was disused by 1906 when part of it became a tea room. The canopy, goods shed and yard wall were not built until 1882 under Marriott's supervision.

Between 1878 and 1880, the majority of W&J stations were of a simple 'office' style with a pitched slate roof. (Fig 4.) The two sides were identical having four windows arranged symmetrically on either side of a central door. The stations built before 1880 (Hemsby and Martham in 1878; Grimston Road and Massingham in 1879) were concrete 'ashlar' as before but the rest (East Rudham, Raynham Park, Potter Heigham, Catfield and Stalham in 1880) were in plain brick. The barge-boards on the L&F stations were the concave curve so typical of most W&J construction, but Martham, Potter, Catfield and Stalham had a scalloped design. Finials were simply a carved batten. East Rudham was later refaced (c1916) in concrete block.

Hillington (1879) and Fakenham Town (1880) stations represent a turnabout in W&J design. Here we have a return to the pavilion type, but of larger proportions and simpler detailing. In future only two more W&J stations were to be built to the 'office' style: Honing (1882) and Felmingham

Fig 3: The first Wilkinson & Jarvis pavilion design as built at Great Ormesby, including tariff shed.

PLATFORM ELEVATION

ROADSIDE ELEVATION

0   10   20 Feet

Fig 4: Standard Wilkinson & Jarvis 'office' station building.

(1883) and these were probably planned at the same time as Stalham, Catfield and Potter, to which they were identical.

The new pavilion design occurred in two forms, the most common being the 'small pavilion' (Hillington in 1879; Thursford, Hindolvestone, Guestwick, Lenwade, Attlebridge and Drayton in 1882). Hindolvestone and Guestwick varied in having arched openings, Guestwick with keystones. The 'large pavilion' (Fig 5) was usually retained for more important stations (Fakenham in 1880, North Walsham in 1881, and Whitwell & Reepham in 1882). However, Hellesdon (1882) also had one despite being only a village at the time. Perhaps it was thought that Hellesdon would grow into a large suburb of Norwich. Most examples of the large and small pavilion were in red brick, many with yellow brick decorative quoins, but Hillington had the colours reversed. Bargeboards were the simple curved design with decorated pendant ends.

The last W&J construction was the link line between Melton and North Walsham, completed after the formation of the E&M, but the remaining stations were still constructed using the W&J designs. Corpusty and Bluestone were small pavilions, Aylsham was a large pavilion and Felmingham an office.

The two major L&F stations were unique buildings. By designing Melton Constable (1882) as an island site, W&J set themselves a new problem, as neither office nor pavilion was suitable (except for Lord Hastings' private station which was supplied with a tiny pavilion). Their solution was to provide simple single-storey accommodation in yellow brick with red brick detailing and semi-circular arched openings, the whole covered by an enormous gabled canopy. (Fig 6.) Access was from the adjacent overbridge through a covered stairway with brickwork and detailing to match the main building. Originally the accommodation provided was not very extensive, but by 1887 a waiting room block had been added outside the area of the canopy utilising the new 'arts & crafts' style with tiled roof. These waiting rooms were later refaced (c1916) with a concrete block skin. A free-standing timber structure enclosed the gentlemen's urinals. This was later rebuilt in brick to incorporate a lamp room.

Norwich City (1882) has been described as 'imposing' and 'well-balanced' and it was certainly the largest station building on the entire line. Italianate in influence, the design very cleverly divided the red brick facade into bays by using yellow brick pilasters detailed at the top to give the impression of Tuscan capitals without the expense of a single piece of stone. The main entrance was through a pedimented portico, consisting of a large elliptical carriage arch flanked by two smaller semicircular arches. The main mass was balanced by two squat end towers bearing pedimented triple windows on the upper floors. The frontage was not entirely symmetrical in that the right hand flanking arch of the portico was open and the far right tower had an open ground floor for vehicular access, whereas the left hand tower incorporated the stationmaster's dwelling. All lintels, arches, friezes and other details were executed in yellow brick. The same

Above left:
The second design, in concrete block: Martham seen c1958. The slope up to the loading dock is to the left.
Denis Seabrook

Left:
Corpusty & Saxthorpe was an example of the small pavilion design. This view, c1914, is full of detail: the timber nameboard with alloy letters; the original E&M paled fencing; the oil lamps and other platform furniture; the enamel 'Gentlemen' sign; and the name laid out in whitewashed pebbles.
Jarrold/M&GN Circle

Fig 5: Standard Wilkinson & Jarvis 'large pavilion' station building at Whitwell & Reepham.

ROADSIDE (EAST) ELEVATION

PLATFORM (WEST) ELEVATION

detailing was applied to the rear of the building, which did not have a portico and was dominated by twin gabled canopies.

Although giving the impression of a two-storey building, it was in fact three-storey as inspection of the side elevations reveals. This third storey was lit at the front by the delightful circular windows at the top centre of each bay. The design does have its faults, but it holds a valuable lesson for modern architects in the treatment of large brick buildings.

The platform canopies at Norwich were duplicates of those at Melton and Yarmouth, being substantial slated pitched roofs with tongue-and-groove boarded ceilings. Finely proportioned cast-iron columns of a simple Tuscan order supported each canopy through spandrels incorporating a circular design of interlocked letters: E&MR at Norwich and Yarmouth but CNR at Melton. The canopy edges were valanced with simple sawn battens and the bargeboards were scalloped in a 'bite and tongue' design later copied in the M&GN signalbox bargeboards.

Arts and Crafts Period

The Eastern & Midlands Railway undertook its first major task in the construction of the 'Lynn Loop', a new double track line which joined the western and eastern sections of the railway avoiding the GER at King's Lynn. There were two new stations on this line: Gayton Road and South Lynn (both of 1886). The latter was perhaps always meant to be temporary, being a timber structure. Not a great deal is recorded about it except that the main building was on the northern platform and was large and single-storey. A flat-roofed canopy was simply supported on timber posts. The southern platform had a long, narrow building in the same style, the canopy forming the roof. A portion of this building survived after the rebuilding of South Lynn, transposed to the west side of Saddlebow Road bridge. Both 1886 platforms were timber.

Gayton Road was a substantial brick and slate roofed station to a new design, incorporating the L-shaped two-storey stationmaster's house with the single-storey booking offices. The later Paston & Knapton station was similar in many respects. Gayton Road also introduced a design of window which was favoured throughout the subsequent period. This consisted of a one or two-pane lower sash, with an upper sash divided into eight or 10 square panes. Casement windows were given similar treatment, but of course applications were not universal.

The Cromer branch was extended from its temporary terminus at Holt, where the timber Yarmouth station had been reused for the opening in 1884. Marriott's assistant Mr Parkinson was in overall charge and Marriott's pupil Mr Aslett looked after the Cromer end. As there was no company architect at that time, Marriott designed most of the structures himself.

Holt and Sheringham (1887) were the two original passing stations on the branch, and they were provided with a new style of pavilion building. There was a recessed circulation area on the platform and street elevations, protected by a small valanced canopy. Bargeboards were plain, but they had enormous cut-out finials supported by a cross-

Left:
Aylsham was an example of the large pavilion, decorated with yellow brick dressings.
Denis Seabrook

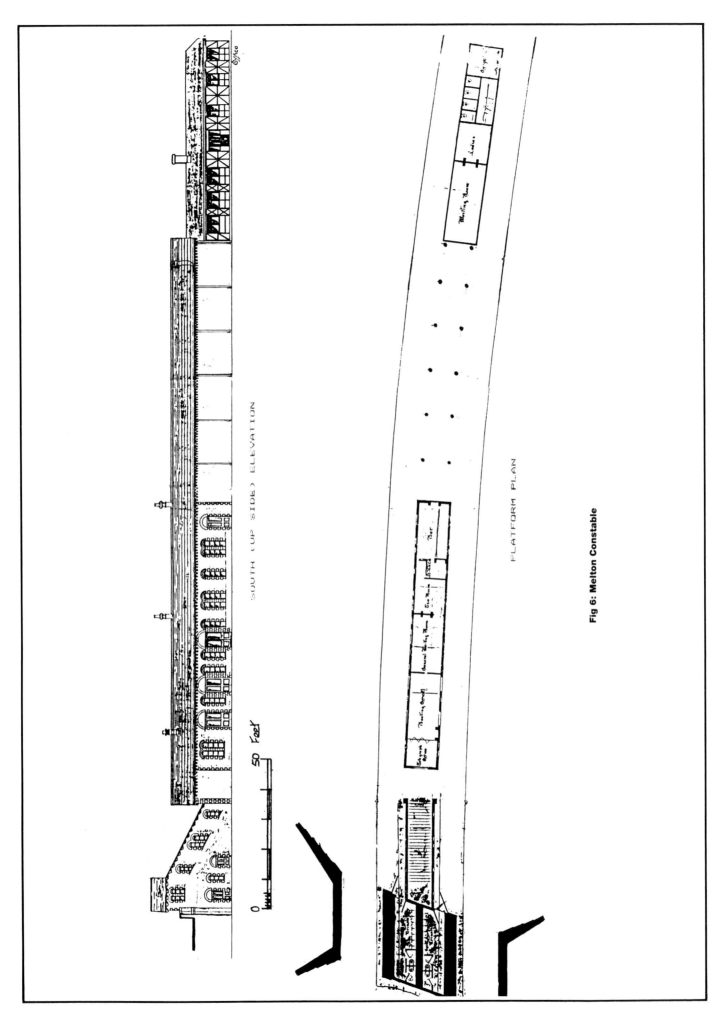

SOUTH (UP SIDE) ELEVATION

50 Feet

PLATFORM PLAN

Fig 6: Melton Constable

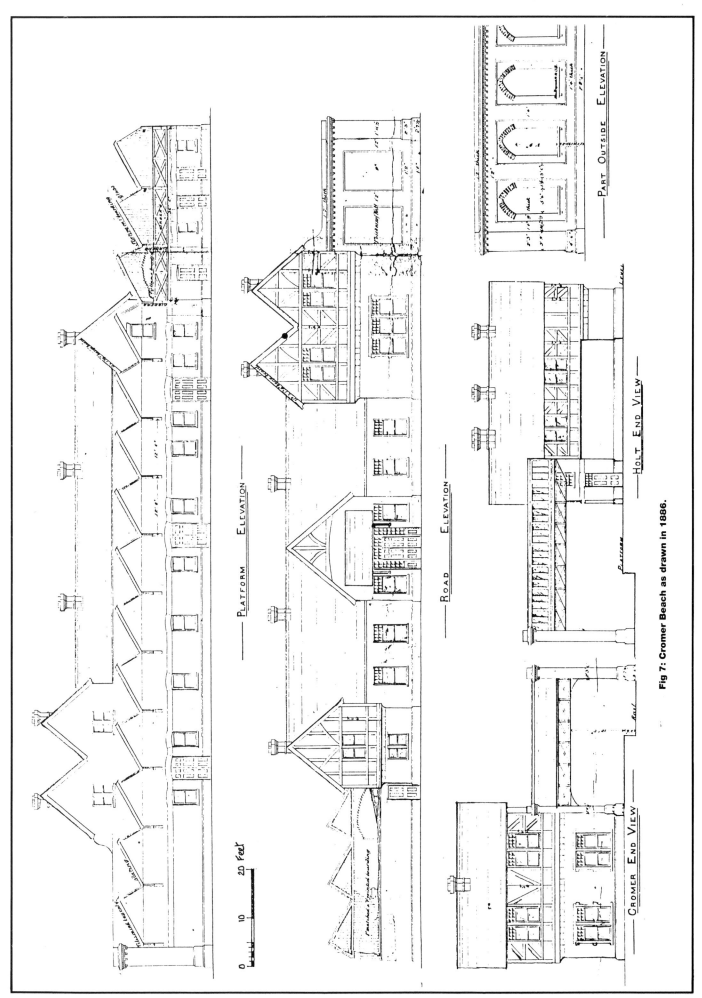

Fig 7: Cromer Beach as drawn in 1886.

— Platform Elevation —

— Road Elevation —

— Part Outside Elevation —

— Holt End View —

— Cromer End View —

20 Feet

10

0

timber. Openings were decorated with yellow brick quoins and lintels.

West Runton, opened later in 1887, was not a passing place and had only a single platform. The wooden building was meant to be temporary, but a more substantial station was never built. In design it could be said to be a wooden version of the Wilkinson & Jarvis 'office'. The planned building was a combination of the single-storey Sheringham design and the two-storey Cromer style. A passing station was planned for the opening of the 1906 N&SJt extension, but once more nothing materialised.

Cromer Beach was a new departure in station design and presaged nearly all subsequent eastern section architecture. The structure itself combined the usual offices with the stationmaster's house and a refreshment room. The main train arrival area was covered by a saw-tooth or 'north light' canopy supported on the outside by a screen wall pierced with 'gothic' windows. Cast iron E&MR spandrels supported the lattice cross-girders. However, it was the treatment of the exterior that was most significant. The steeply gabled roofs were tiled instead of slated, and timbering and herringbone brickwork were applied to the ground and upper floors in a version of the contemporary 'Arts and Crafts' architecture. (Fig 7.) Almost all subsequent new buildings and rebuilds were given this 'crafts' treatment. Cromer was unusual in that its window mullions and dressings were of stone, a rare material on the Joint. As a rule anything resembling stone was usually concrete.

Western section constituents

The first thing that strikes the observer is how different the western section stations are from the eastern section. Most of them are in brick and two-storey, resembling dwellings rather than stations. The picture is also blurred by the number of additional bedrooms and so on added over the years.

The Norwich & Spalding Railway, from Spalding to Sutton Bridge, opened four stations in 1858 and four in 1862, divided into three types of decreasing size. All incorporated the railway offices with a stationmaster's house. The large stations, Moulton, Holbeach (1858) and Long Sutton (1862) were all similar. The main building was L-shaped and two-storey with a prominent gable on the platform elevation. The railway offices were single-storey and appended along the platform. At platform level the gable end had three arched recesses, and Moulton and Holbeach had a distinctive chimney stack set at the diagonal supported by corbelled brickwork below. Moulton had a dormer on the platform elevation and was striped dark on light brick. Long Sutton was striped light on dark brick and with its differences of detail represents the later version of the large design.

The remaining four stations all originally seem to have been intended as the 'small' design.

Weston and Whaplode (1858) were nothing more than larger versions of the standard Norwich & Spalding crossing gatehouse having slated pitched roofs with a dentil course at eaves level and the same pair of blank windows on the first floor. A small lean-to canopy was fixed to the platform elevation. Weston was extended in 1895 with a new two-storey block forming an L-plan, and the canopy was also extended. Fleet and Gedney (1862) apparently represent the later form of the small design, having hipped roofs with no dentil course, decorative quoins in yellow brick and a more substantial hipped roof platform shelter flanked by two rooms with round-topped windows. Both stations were extended into what may be called the 'medium' size by single-storey buildings at both ends, the larger one at the Spalding end being hipped. This may have occurred in 1880.

Sutton Bridge (1862), the first station at that location and known later as the 'low level' station, was a large two-storey hipped roof building in the dark brick of most of the other N&S stations. However, this design featured 9in string courses in yellow brick linking each segmental brick arch over the window and door openings, also in yellow brick. There were an additional pair of string courses at first floor level. This style seems a common one in the area, possibly from the same local builder. The north end was built on a curve, or apsed.

The three intermediate stations on the Lynn & Sutton Bridge Railway (opened in 1864 for goods and 1866 for passenger services) were all very similar being once again in dark brick and slate. (Fig 8.) Openings had flat rubbed-brick arches. The two-storey gabled stationmaster's house had light brick quoins and was adjacent to the single-storey waiting rooms and lavatories. The booking hall was roofed parallel to the platform but the waiting room had a cross-gable. Originally all three stations had a small open area beneath the roof leading from the booking hall, but over the years two were filled in; Walpole with a pointed 'Tudor' arch plus door and window, Terrington with a normal door and pair of windows. Clenchwarton was a mirror image of the others. West Lynn station is very obscure, probably only having a timber platform with the nearby crossing house (No 54) doubling as a booking office. This house does seem to have been larger than normal and in addition was supplied with a bay window very similar to that on the platform elevations of the Spalding & Bourne stations.

Sutton Bridge L&SB station, known as 'high level', was quite unlike the other stations and strongly resembled the earlier N&S building. It was again two-storey and hip-roofed with yellow brick segmentally-arched openings, but string courses were restricted to one at first floor sill level. The platform was not very wide and there

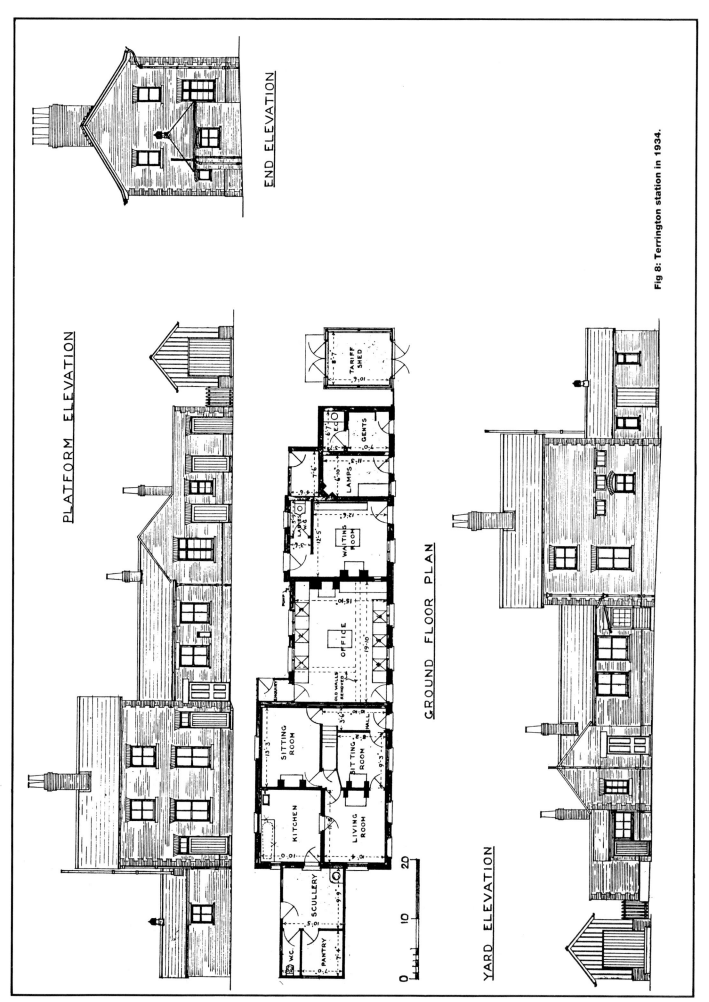

END ELEVATION

PLATFORM ELEVATION

GROUND FLOOR PLAN

TARIFF SHED

GENTS

LAMPS

WAITING ROOM

LADIES W.C.

OFFICE

OLD WALLS REMOVED

HALL

SITTING ROOM

SITTING ROOM

KITCHEN

LIVING ROOM

SCULLERY

W.C.

PANTRY

YARD ELEVATION

Fig 8: Terrington station in 1934.

0   10   20

17

was a narrow canopy extending the whole length of the elevation with a hipped leaded roof.

The three intermediate stations on the Spalding & Bourne Railway (1866) were originally small, again seeming to be larger versions of the crossing houses. North Drove had to be rebuilt less than a year after opening, due to subsidence. The buildings were simple, two-storey with gabled roofs and all originally featured a small bay window on the platform elevation; this was removed later at Twenty. Counter Drain had to have steps up to the platform, probably as a result of it being raised. Apart from one or two detail changes Twenty was the only one to be substantially enlarged in 1920/21.

The well-known station at Bourne was built in 1894 and little is known other than track plans of the earlier stations. The Elizabethan Red Hall was used for the railway offices and so the platform facilities were of limited size and probably in timber. It is known that there was a gabled canopy with valancing.

The Peterborough, Wisbech & Sutton Railway (1866) was the longest western constituent and opened with eight stations. It did not have a separate station at Sutton Bridge but joined the N&S at

Midland Junction (later Sutton Bridge Junction) and ran into the low level station. Apart from the unique timber station at Wisbech, two designs are apparent. Eye Green, Thorney and Wisbech St Mary (Fig 9) were the largest buildings and of the same basic design; a sort of gothic cottage approach with stone parapeted gables and dormer windows. All three had a bay window on to the platform and each had a single-storey open waiting area. Eye Green was a mirror image of the other two. Extra bedrooms were added to the stationmaster's houses at Thorney, Wisbech St Mary and Eye Green in 1897, 1898 and 1913 respectively.

Wryde, Murrow and Tydd were essentially the same design, but with detail differences. The main block of the house was a T-shaped plan with single-storey passenger accommodation (if any) along the platform. Murrow and Tydd houses had overhanging eaves and Tydd was a mirror image. Wryde was in light brick with dark brick string courses and had a distinctive timber waiting room and booking office adjacent to the house, possibly added in 1890 and of Midland parentage. Murrow had one brick waiting room attached to the house (possibly original although the canopy valancing was the later design) and one timber waiting room on the Up platform built in 1901.

The station house at Ferry was separate from the platform. The passenger accommodation was a timber waiting room erected in 1892 on the brick platform on the opposite, Down, side of the line. The house was originally smaller, but was enlarged to resemble the others in 1919.

Unlike the rest of the stations, Wisbech M&GN was a large single-storey timber building in the pavilion style, vertically boarded. Unusually the gables were valanced rather than having plain bargeboards. (Fig 10.) Originally the accommodation extended along the platform only to the west, the main building being on the Up or south platform, and the central waiting area was open-fronted, but in 1892 a stationmaster's office was added to the east and in 1903 the front of the waiting area was filled in with double doors and a pair of windows. Similarly the Down waiting shelter, also timber, was open-fronted until 1903.

The M&GN period

At the formation of the Joint Committee, work was proceeding on the new Bourne station. This station was a strong, plain brick building on an island platform, with generous accommodation divided into several blocks by through passages. Window and door openings were large with segmental brick arches. A huge flat-roofed canopy fringed the entire building, carried on steel through girders supported by decorative spandrels. The slate roofs of each block protruded above. As it was agreed that Bourne would remain a GNR station, the design is not likely to have been a Melton product.

There seems to have been a differing approach to station design on eastern and western sections, even by 1897, exemplified by Sutton Bridge and Sheringham, both of that year. The situation at Sutton Bridge had been simplified after 1867 by all passenger traffic being concentrated at the 'high level' station. However, it had become obvious that a new bridge was required across the Nene. This could only be built considerably to the south of the existing bridge and so a new island platform station had to be built. Completed in 1897, the new building was of timber with an outside frame on a low brick podium, resembling GNR timber stations. To window sill level the boarding was horizontal, but above was vertical. Because the station was on a 1 in 110 gradient which the platform had to follow, the large flat roofed canopy had to be stepped to keep it horizontal and the brick plinth was also higher at the Peterborough end for the same reason. The canopy acted as the roof and only several skylights and two brick chimneys pierced it. A Midland footbridge gave access from

—SOUTH ELEVATION—

0   10   20 Feet

—WEST ELEVATION—

PLATFORM

—NORTH ELEVATION—

—EAST ELEVATION—

Fig 9: Wisbech St Mary in 1921.

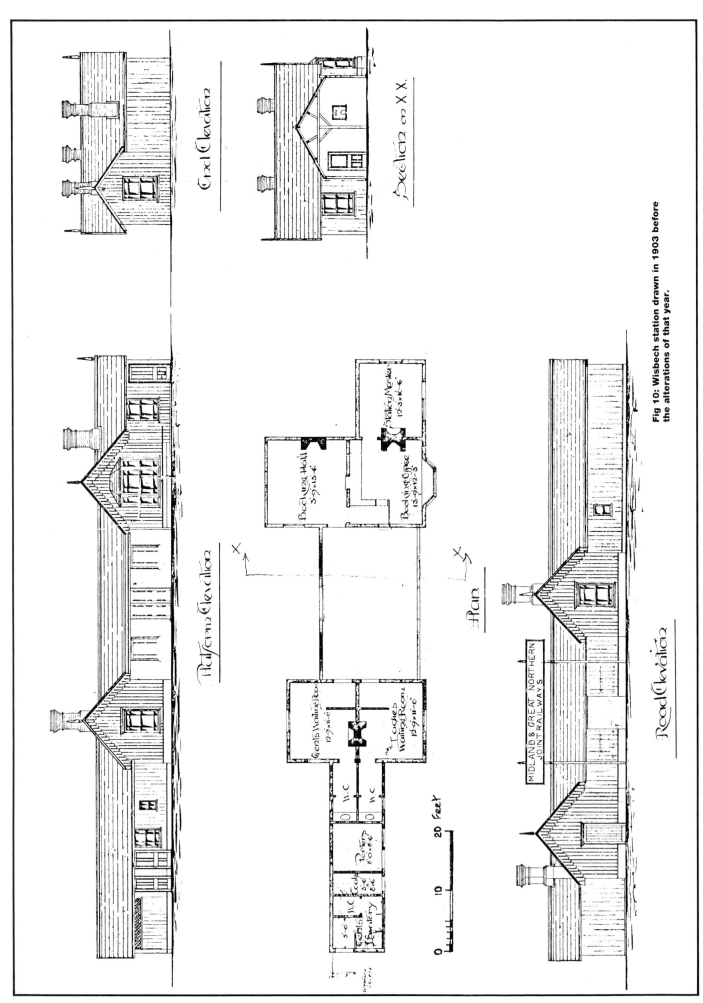

Fig 10: Wisbech station drawn in 1903 before the alterations of that year.

East Elevation

Section on X X.

Platform Elevation

Plan

Road Elevation

Booking Hall 3'9" x 13'6"

Booking Office 13'9" x 12'-3"

Station Master 12'3" x 6'-6"

Gents Waiting Room 12'-7" x 11'-0"

Ladies Waiting Room 12'9" x 11'-0"

W.C.

W.C.

Porters Room

W.C. Coals 3'-6" x 6'6"

Gents Lavatory 5'-0"

MIDLAND & GREAT NORTHERN JOINT RAILWAYS

0   10   20 Feet

the older buildings now used as offices. The bridge had originally been installed at the 'high level' station in 1892.

In contrast to the plainness of Sutton Bridge, the rebuilding of Sheringham (1897) and North Walsham (1898) followed the 'arts & crafts' style which had made its debut at Cromer Beach. Although the original slate roofs were kept, half-timbering and stucco were introduced into the gables. Sheringham's main building was considerably remodelled, the Up platform shelter removed to Eye Green and a new waiting room built to match the Down side. Beautiful ridge-and-furrow canopies replaced the old short awnings. At North Walsham, which had no canopy originally, the new canopy was flat-roofed except at the north end where there were three glazed ridges. The Up platform shelter was replaced by a substantial building with a matching canopy. The rear elevation, very tall due to the station's position on an embankment, was plain brick but the platform elevations were treated with half-timbering and stucco. The roof was tiled and half-hipped. Further examples of this style were new South Lynn (1901) and Hillington where two large 'Royal' waiting rooms were added in the 1896 alterations to make the station a crossing place.

New South Lynn was an island platform station with access from the adjacent bridge No 49. The accommodation was quite generous, under a continuous canopy. However, this was not of the recent ridge-and-furrow type but flat-roofed along each side of the buildings, supported by long rolled steel joists with ornate cast-iron spandrels. Over the circulation spaces and the entrance stairs the pitched roof was glazed, supported on special cast-iron arches. The treatment of the buildings was brick and stone to window sill level and half-timbering and stucco above. The timbering divided the elevations into equal bays, the lower part decorated to leave a diagonal cross of stucco. Tall windows occupied many of the bays, the top casement being a square divided into 25 square panes of green and purple glass.

In contrast, Weybourne (in 1901 but dated 1900 on the building) was a plain brick station, a development of the pavilion but with the steeply-pitched tiled roofs of the 'arts & crafts' style. Other features, particularly the windows, point to this being a design transitional with the late period discussed below.

North Walsham was rebuilt to meet the opening of the Norfolk & Suffolk Joint Railway, which originally had two stations: Paston & Knapton and Mundesley (1898). These were beautiful buildings erected by celebrated local builders and church restorers Cornish & Gaymer. Steep roofs and tiling were present but the half-timbering was again

Top right:
Murrow (pronounced 'Murrer') is an example of the smaller design of PW&S station, without the gable walls. The furthest part of the building appears to have been added or altered in the M&GN period. Note the oil lamps and the fire buckets.
M&GN Circle

Above right:
The 1897 timber station at Sutton Bridge. Note how the canopy steps down the 1 in 110 gradient.
R. E. G. Read

Right:
Sheringham after its 1897 rebuilding. Compared to the earlier photograph one can see that as well as the addition of further accommodation and the ridge-and-furrow canopy, the window openings have been enlarged. Also a good view of an E&M lifting type water crane. Note the E&M seat behind.
Author's collection

restricted to the gables. The woodwork inside the booking halls was excellent and gave the impression of a baronial hall. Mundesley had a ridge-and-furrow canopy, but Paston only had a small area covered by an extension of the roof. This period also saw a change in canopy valancing, of which Mundesley may have been the first example. Originally each board of the valance was finished in what may be called a 'heart', with a hole pierced above at each board joint, often with another hole and slot above that. Henceforth, alternating with each heart was a 'bell'; a board finished flat rather than pointed. Two holes were pierced at each joint, the upper one enlarged into a slot tapering down to the lower.

The other branch of the Norfolk & Suffolk Joint to Lowestoft (opened in 1903) had buildings and bridges all designed by the GER. The stations were apparently the standard GE architecture of the period and reminiscent of their Cromer line stations, particularly North Walsham. The buildings were plain but attractive, all with minor differences but basically in two sizes. Gorleston North, Hopton and Corton were the smaller size (but still remarkably generous), Lowestoft North was larger and Gorleston-on-Sea a special size. All buildings were in plain red brick, the openings with flat arches of splayed rubbed brick. (Fig 11.) The tiled roofs were at quite a steep angle with plain bargeboards and tall chimneys. Most stations had hipped roofs on two levels and small half-timbered dormers over the entrances on the main buildings, but the subsidiary waiting rooms, which were hardly smaller than the main buildings, had plain pitched roofs. Gorleston was unusual in having this plain type of building on both platforms, the booking hall being at street level with access via a footbridge and walkways. All buildings featured large lantern ventilators over the gentlemen's facilities. The canopies were supported by columns from the platform and spandrels from the rear and were much longer than the buildings, and so a backing wall extended on each side, nicely finished off with a 'Dutch gable' effect. The valancing was decorated with large saw-teeth of alternating size.

When the Lowestoft line was built, Yarmouth Beach station was extended by supplying another platform alongside the 1882 boundary wall, which was raised to support a flat canopy. Further support was given by a new design of column bearing M&GN spandrels. The same design was used for the new porch at Cromer Beach (1906) and the same columns with other spandrels at new South Lynn (1901). At Yarmouth a new circulation area was added to the original building with a gable on the roadside elevation. The 'crafts' style was dropped and a new style in red brick with terracotta and concrete quoins, lintels and other details was adopted. This final style was carried through to the N&SJ stations at Trimingham and Overstrand (1906), which were both island platforms. Astonishingly, their integral roof/canopies were clad in corrugated iron. (Fig 12.)

The very last station construction was the rebuild of Holt in 1926 after a fire gutted the old E&M building. Constructed in concrete brick with block quoins and dressings and reinforced concrete window frames, the new station was a development of the old pavilion design. Both public and

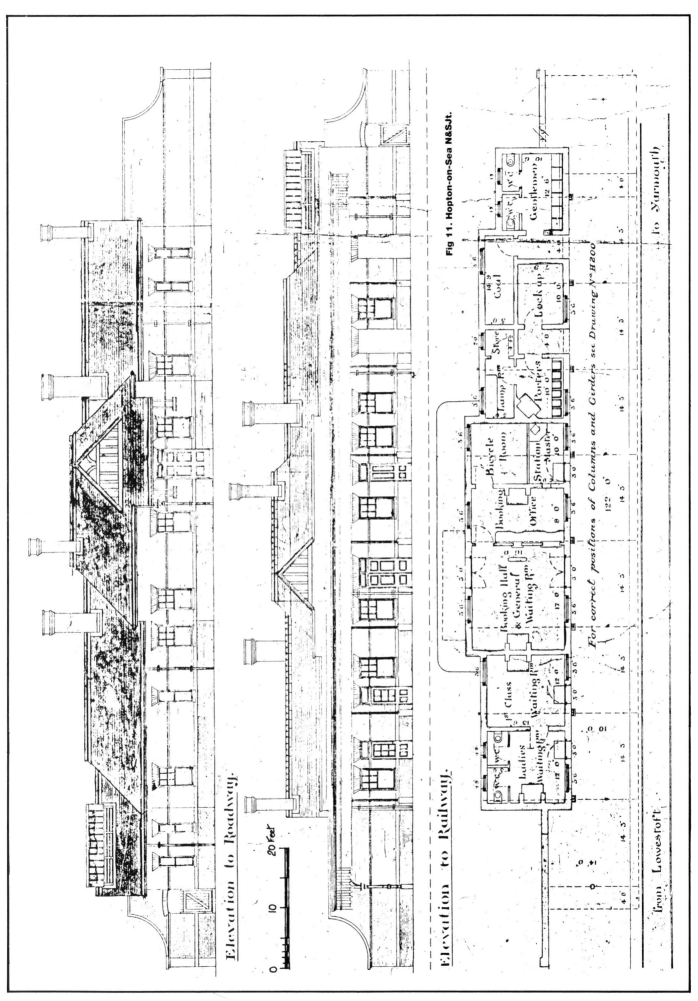

Elevation to Roadway.

Elevation to Railway.

Fig 11. Hopton-on-Sea N&SJt.

20 Feet

10

0

From Lowestoft

to Yarmouth

For correct positions of Columns and Girders see Drawing Nº H200

Gentlemen

Coal

Lock up

Store

Lamp Rm

Porters

Bicycle Room

Station Master

Booking Office

Booking Hall & General Waiting Rm

1st Class Waiting Rm

Ladies Waiting Rm

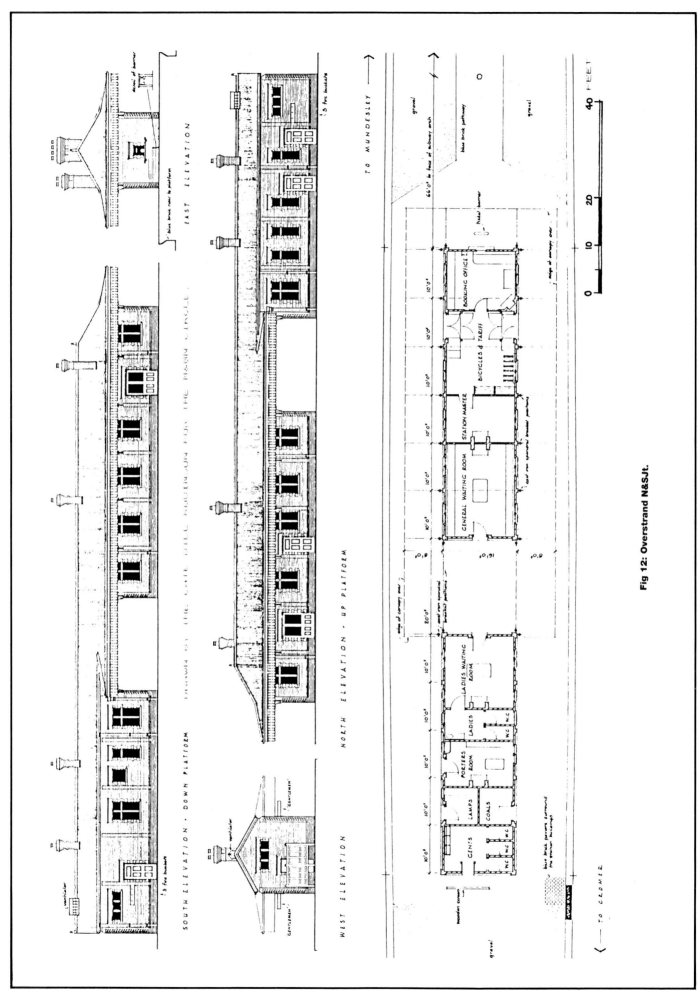

Fig 12: Overstrand N&SJt.

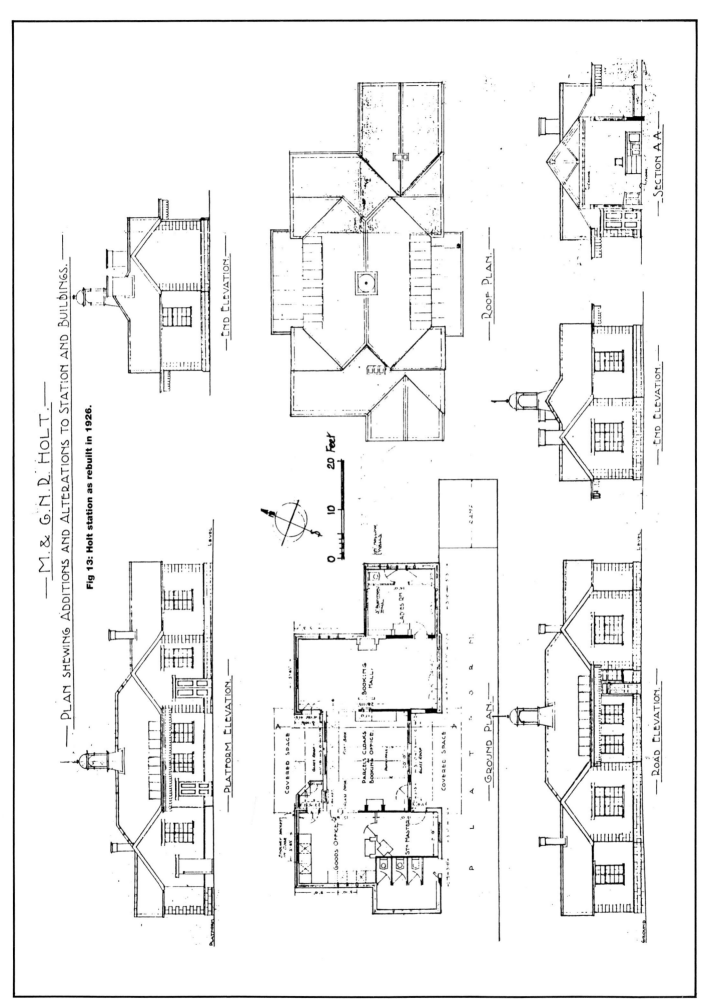

— M. & G. N. R. HOLT. —

— PLAN SHEWING ADDITIONS AND ALTERATIONS TO STATION AND BUILDINGS. —

Fig 13: Holt station as rebuilt in 1926.

— END ELEVATION. —

— ROOF PLAN. —

— SECTION A.A. —

— END ELEVATION. —

— PLATFORM ELEVATION. —

— GROUND PLAN. —

— ROAD ELEVATION. —

20 Feet

10

0

platform elevations had deeply recessed circulation areas under M&GN valanced canopies. (Fig 13.) The roof was half-hipped and had a leaded cupola surmounted by a weathervane stamped 'M&GN 1926'.

Platform Shelters

During the Wilkinson & Jarvis period, platform shelters on the eastern section appear to have followed the same basic design of a sort of greenhouse with a large number of windows at the front and sides, a rear sloping canopy/roof and decorated valance. The principal difference between the shelters on the L&F and the GY&S/Y&NN lines apparently was that the bases of the latter were of timber rather than brick as on the L&F. The size of canopy overhang varied between large or small, perhaps depending on lines of sight from an adjacent signal box. The exceptions were Corpusty, which had valancing but no overhang, and Stalham which had neither. Gayton Road (1886) was completely open-fronted, otherwise most others had double doors. Some had fireplaces and chimneys.

A new all-brick design was introduced at Holt and Sheringham (1887) with normal windows but no doors. The sloping canopy was retained. Sheringham was 'moved' to Eye Green in 1897, shortened by at least two feet and fitted with doors. Probably only the woodwork was transferred.

On the western section many shelters were timber of no standard design; Wisbech, Ferry and Murrow have already been mentioned. Twenty and North Drove had a neat design having a rear sloping roof but no canopy, erected in 1893. Both originally had a brick chimney, but only Twenty's survived. Holbeach had a large example of a shelter dating from 1890, with a canopy supported by crude timber columns. The original shelters at Thorney and Eye Green were an outside frame timber design with diagonal boarding, possibly Midland. Terrington also had a timber shelter erected in 1890.

The 1890s, when many stations all over the E&M/M&GN system were widened, saw the introduction of a system-wide standard design. A development of the E&M brick design, this shelter was all brick with a plinth, standard windows and double leaf doors, and retained the rear sloping canopy/roof generally with large overhang and valancing. It occurred at Eye Green (1897), Thorney, Wryde (1906), Wisbech St Mary, Moulton, Gedney, Walpole (1899), Clenchwarton (1899), Raynham Park (1900), Honing (1900), Potter Heigham (1898) and Weybourne (1901). Tydd (1896) had to have a narrow timber example for site reasons. Ormesby (1894) also had a timber example. Window toplights were attractively glazed in purple, yellow and green squares.

Sheringham, North Walsham, Mundesley and Hillington all had special waiting rooms rather than shelters. North Walsham and Hillington had the full 'arts & crafts' effect with tiled roofs, but the others were more simply decorated.

Goods Sheds

By no means all M&GN stations were provided with goods sheds, the proportion being greater on the western section. Here it seems that most of the original goods sheds were built in panelled brick with pitched slate roofs and one through siding, but there were of course detail differences. The PW&S featured sheds with arched panelling, but the GN-controlled N&S had flat-topped panelling. The exceptions were the Spalding & Bourne stations where large timber sheds were provided; Twenty, North Drove and Bourne with through sidings. All but Bourne were demolished in 1925, and North Drove was replaced with a small timber structure on a concrete block base.

Above:
An example of the 'small' goods shed at Massingham, seen from the railside. The roadside had one large full-height door, and there were a door and a window at the far end.
M&GN Circle

During the 1890-93 period timber grain sheds to a standard pattern, but varying sizes, were erected on several western section stations, for example Wryde and Tydd (both of 1890). South Lynn (1886) also had a large timber 'tranship shed' approximately 50ft x 45ft with two through sidings, but usually only one was used for goods. This shed was demolished and replaced by one in concrete brick in 1930. Some of the earlier brick sheds were extended and the newer brickwork can be seen on photographs: Eye Green and Wisbech (1889) and Sutton Bridge (1897).

The eastern section had a more complex situation. The intermediate GY&S/Y&NN stations apparently had no goods sheds, but most were provided with a rough timber coal shed about 60ft x 12ft with a monopitch roof. The only proper sheds were at Yarmouth (see later) and North Walsham. The latter was a timber shed 45ft x 18ft with a pitched slate roof on a timber frame clad in vertical boarding, each board joint being covered with 1 inch square beading. This type was repeated at Aylsham (1883).

On the L&F lines and generally from 1882 the majority of goods sheds were in brick and slate to three sizes: small, medium and large. The small sheds were confined to the earliest L&F stations. These were simple brick structures, about 24ft x 16ft at Grimston Road and Massingham, with low-pitched roofs, plain bargeboards and finials. Hillington was much smaller, being about 15ft x 10ft. The medium shed (approximately 40ft x 20ft) was a plain gabled structure with two or three large sliding doors (East Rudham, Thursford, Lenwade, Cromer). Cromer was slightly larger being 53ft x 24ft (Fig 14.). East Rudham was later refaced in concrete blocks c1916.

The large shed was very distinctive, having one end of the long, narrow structure raised to accommodate an internal crane. (Fig 15.) Roofs were pitched and provided with the standard curved bargeboards. Average dimensions were 92ft 6in x 22ft 3in (Fakenham, Melton Constable, Whitwell & Reepham, Drayton). An office was appended to the

raised end. Yarmouth Beach and Austin Street sheds (1882) were large double-ended versions 128ft long with two raised sections.

A common feature of many M&GN goods sheds were the timber weather screens protecting the trackside loading doors. These were very simply built on a sturdy timber frame, the horizontal boarding only being carried down to platform height.

Norwich City had the largest goods shed on the system, being a brick structure 250ft x 55ft with twin through-sidings sharing the same entrance front and rear. These sidings were shortened within the shed in 1922. From 1915 protection of the staff was given by two signals operated from inside the shed (Melton Constable had a similar arrangement). Originally Norwich had one full-length loading area canopy but another was added in 1896. Each loading platform communicated with the outside world via several segmentally-arched doorways similar to those of the standard sheds and at the rear was a range of offices. Norwich and South Lynn were the only through line goods sheds which engines were permitted to enter.

In addition to goods sheds, many stations were provided with tariff sheds for smaller consignments. That at Sheringham was built in brick with the station, and elsewhere there was apparently a programme of brick tariff shed building around 1900 resulting in large sheds being added at Grimston Road, Massingham, Raynham Park and Hillington. But the majority of original tariff sheds were of timber with small double sliding doors and the standard bargeboards and finials. They were apparently built with outside framing but later some, Ormesby for example, were reboarded outside the frames. Stalham, Thursford and Lenwade had rather crude monopitch sheds, and Felmingham's was apparently the redundant signalbox, later fitted with a sliding door. Some were rebuilt in concrete block (East Rudham, Lenwade).

Grain stores were also common, many of them very large; Drayton was about 110ft x 40ft and Norwich a vast 245ft x 32ft. On the western section, as we have seen, granaries were mostly of timber, but those on the eastern section were mostly in brick, plainly detailed and often with loading canopies. Some stations had a granary but no goods shed, although on later documents and maps they were sometimes referred to as such. Yarmouth also boasted a 'Fish Shelter' about 100ft long, with a

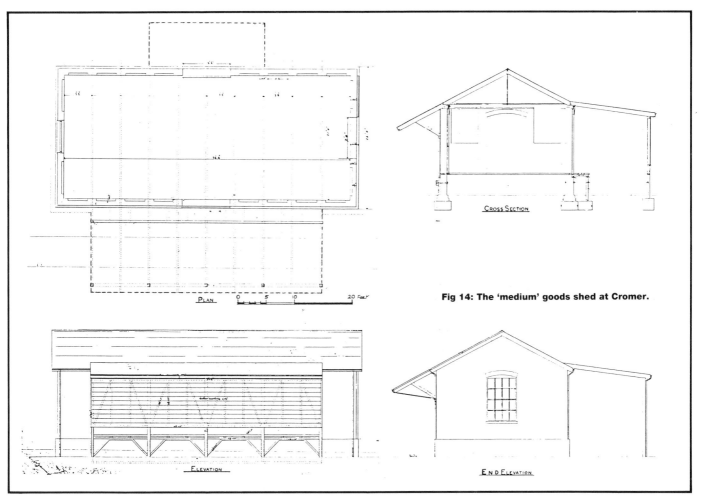

PLAN

CROSS SECTION

ELEVATION

END ELEVATION

Fig 14: The 'medium' goods shed at Cromer.

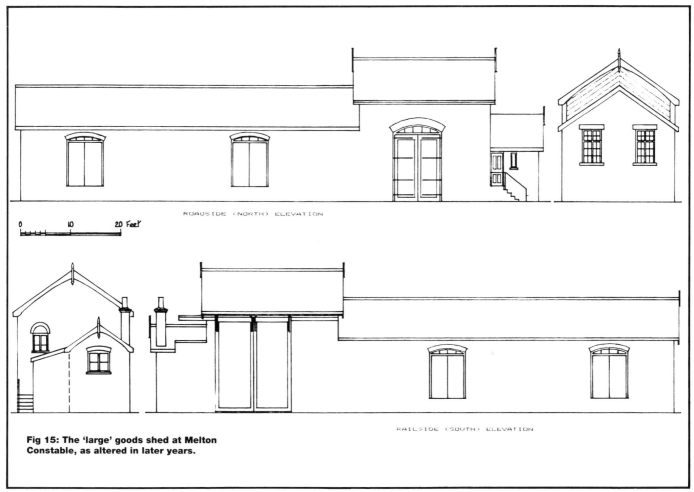

ROADSIDE (NORTH) ELEVATION

RAILSIDE (SOUTH) ELEVATION

Fig 15: The 'large' goods shed at Melton Constable, as altered in later years.

through-siding or siding under a canopy. This was probably in timber but no details have yet come to hand. It was demolished by 1926.

Engine Sheds

Compared to most other structures which can be seen to be standardised in various ways, M&GN engine sheds are of diverse pattern. However, there was a family resemblance between those at Melton Constable (1881), Norwich (1882) and Cromer (1887), with a variation on the theme at South Lynn (1886). Melton and Norwich both had large three-road sheds with deeply-panelled brick walls and pitched slate roofs. The gables were originally filled with vertical boarding, but by 1912 Norwich had had this replaced by glazing in vertical glazing bars. In addition, Norwich had a pair of ridge ventilators equipped with the standard bargeboards and finials as were the main gables. The other ventilator stacks looked rather flimsy in contrast to Melton's sturdy chimneys.

Cromer can be seen as the small version of these E&M sheds, having only one road, and the panelling in the brickwork was shallower, not having to support such a large roof. There was a continuous ridge ventilator, later supplemented by a single chimney vent, and the gable was filled with brick at the front and glass at the rear. (Fig 16.)

Fakenham had a two-road shed, but little is known about it. It was the original loco depot and workshops of the L&F in 1880 and appears to have resembled the original Yarmouth Beach shed (see later). It was used for engine storage in the winter months.

South Lynn was the largest shed on the M&GN and followed the general outline of the E&M sheds but was unique in being constructed entirely in timber. The first shed was only two-road holding four engines, with doors front and back and shear-legs at the rear for loco lifting. In 1895 the shed was more than doubled in size by the addition of another two-road portion holding six engines, copying the construction of the first. The whole building was based on a timber frame with the exterior weatherboarded in panels having one large window per panel. The pair of slate roofs had two large ridge vents and a number of smoke stacks on each, and as usual were finished with the standard bargeboard and finial throughout. A lean-to fitters' shop and stores were at the rear and in 1901 the shear-legs were enclosed with a taller structure having a cross-gable.

Of the larger eastern section sheds, Yarmouth was the odd one out. This is because an 1870s building was taken over by the loco department in the yard changes of 1903/04, before which time the building was a workshop and sheet factory. The 'new' shed was a temporary-looking building con-

sisting of two large arc roofs in corrugated iron over concrete block walls regularly pierced with large windows. The roof ends were infilled with more corrugated iron although the north end of the running shed was glazed. The main shed had two through-roads for four engines but the other side remained a sheet manufactory and workshop, divided from the running shed by a wooden screen. The original engine shed was a small two-road version of the above, having a ridge ventilator also arc-roofed in corrugated iron as well as smoke chimneys. It was demolished about 1905.

Mundesley also had an unusual shed, clad entirely in corrugated iron. It was authorised in November 1898 as a temporary structure. There were two roads holding one engine each, under one pitched roof with ridge vent. It was demolished in 1929 and the materials sold by auction on 1 January 1930.

On the western section there were only two M&GN-owned engine sheds: at Spalding and Bourne. Spalding shed was built for the Spalding & Bourne Railway, but was used jointly with the MR and GN until the GN withdrew in 1895. The

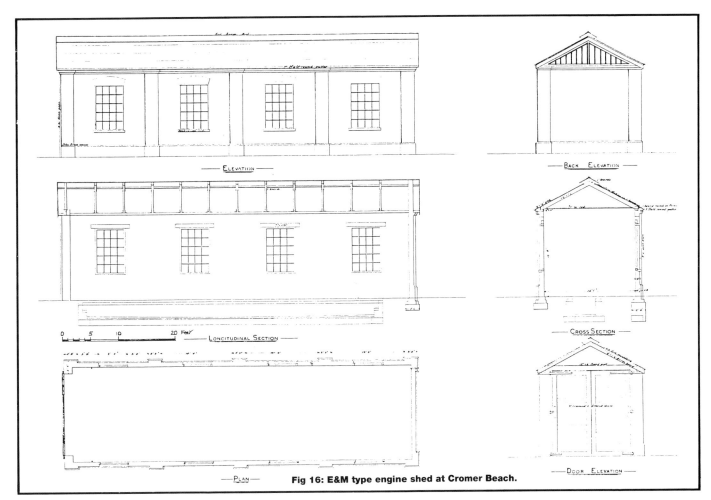

ELEVATION

BACK ELEVATION

LONGITUDINAL SECTION

CROSS SECTION

PLAN

DOOR ELEVATION

Fig 16: E&M type engine shed at Cromer Beach.

building was a sturdy brick affair in panelled brickwork with round-headed windows. The two through-roads for one loco each had semicircular-arched doorways; however, it was not possible to shut the doors on tender engines. The roof was pitched and slated with a ridge ventilator and additional circular vents in each gable.

The original sheds at Bourne were swept away in 1893 and replaced by a two-loco shed which was extended in 1898 to house four more locos, on two roads. The building was large and distinctive with a 'saw-tooth' or northlight roof over panelled brick walls. In this case there were no skylights, the roofs merely being slated. The shed was originally GN but built on M&GN land, and in 1897 it was transferred to the Committee.

Signalboxes

In the following section, the nomenclature referring to the various designs of Midland, Great Northern and Great Eastern signalboxes is taken from The Signal Box by the Signalling Study Group.

The origin of most types of western section signalboxes arose from the division of responsibilities of the old B&LJt. Thus, on the lines between Sutton Bridge and Bourne the GN box and signal specification were supplied, but on the Peterborough-Lynn lines the MR specifications were used. A survey of M&GN signal types is given in Appendix B.

Originally the only interlocked box was at Midland (later Sutton Bridge) Junction, supplied with

an MR type 1 box about 1880, but a GN type 1 brick box was opened at Sutton Bridge Dock Junction in 1879. A similar box was erected near Spalding at Water Lane (later Welland Bank) when block working was introduced in 1883. Interlocking of stations on the Bourne-Sutton Bridge section was introduced in 1891, the boxes being to a GN type 1 design with bargeboards betraying their construction by the Railway Signal Company (RSCo). Holbeach East and West were brick-based but the majority were timber with brick chimneys. In 1892/93 similar GN/RSCo boxes were erected at Bourne East and West, and at Welland Bank Junction, the latter replacing the 1883 box.

All these GN boxes were handsome, the timber examples having vertical close-boarding between external framing and the brick examples having panelled bases, the brickwork extending upwards to form the rear wall of the operating floor. Operating floor windows were arranged in a typical 'three up two across' narrow sash. The roofs were pitched in slate and bargeboards on the RSCo examples were their standard 'crescent and tooth' design.

The Peterborough-Lynn line was much improved in the 1889-92 period and supplied with MR type 2a boxes. The well-known MR design was based on prefabricated sections or 'flakes' mounted between tapering corner posts. At this time the lower storey was weatherboarded and the upper storey close-boarded with 6in wide boards between frame members. The windows were very distinctive with triangular fillets in the top corners of each sash. The hipped slate roof had prominent finials.

Left:
Yarmouth Beach engine shed showing the crude concrete block construction and corrugated iron roof. Class C No 39 was rebuilt with Class H boiler in 1908.
Real Photos/IAL

Right:
Four Cross Roads signalbox, an example of the GN/RSCo construction. The brick lower storey is not original.
P. H. Wells

Later boxes were of the MR type 2b, distinguishable from the type 2a by the omission of a frame member between the front two windows at the door end. The 6in boarding was also superseded by 3.5in.

The original signalboxes of the eastern section are rather more obscure. All necessary locations were interlocked from the start, for example the few crossing stations that then existed. The signals and the signalbox frames all appear to have been supplied by Saxby & Farmer. The signals were typical S&F slotted-post semaphores. It seems that W&J built the signalboxes to their own simple designs. Most Y&NN stations appear to have had platform-mounted boxes in timber, with weatherboarding between outside frames. Bargeboards were plain and windows small. Larger boxes at Yarmouth, Martham and Stalham apparently were reminiscent of later brick E&M boxes.

On the L&F a new design appeared which was sturdy enough to last into modern times. This box was pitched-roofed with plain bargeboards and a tall brick base. The operating floor windows generally had vertical glazing bars only. Small platform boxes were still of weatherboarded timber. Although the design first appeared in L&F days built by W&J, it was used subsequently and I prefer to call it the E&M-type box. The Central Norfolk link line was equipped with these boxes, as was the Lynn Loop, and even Austerby crossing in Bourne had a small gate box of this type.

The Cromer branch was equipped with a variant of the E&M type using weatherboarded timber. Holt and Sheringham were perched on narrow brick bases, oversailing front and rear, but Cromer Beach was all timber and very tall to see over an adjacent overbridge.

On the formation of the Joint Committee an M&GN box design was formulated, having certain aspects in common with both GN and E&M boxes. Of timber and with pitched slate roof the M&GN type 1a box had an outside frame, the panels filled with vertical close-boarding. The bargeboards were of a new and distinctive 'bite and tongue' design.

The operating floor window sashes were of a 'four up three across' pane arrangement, although some smaller boxes had narrow sashes of two panes across. The locking room windows were usually at the sides but earlier examples and larger boxes also had them at the front and rear. Heating was usually by stove, but some had brick chimneys. (Fig 17.)

After 1903 the design was altered; type 1b dispensed with the outside framing and the boarding

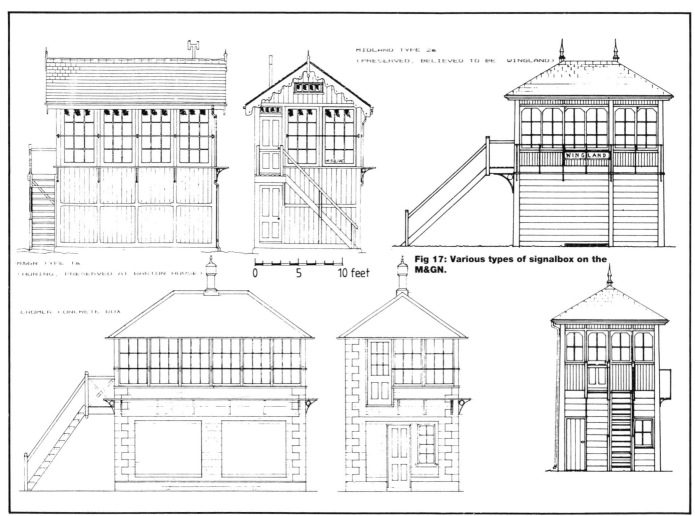

MIDLAND TYPE 2a
(PRESERVED, BELIEVED TO BE WINGLAND)

WINGLAND

0   5   10 feet

M&GN TYPE 1a
(THURNING, PRESERVED AT BARTON HOUSE)

CROMER CONCRETE BOX

Fig 17: Various types of signalbox on the M&GN.

Above:
A rare view of the rear of an M&GN type 1a box, taken at Dogsthorpe, near Peterborough. Other views of M&GN boxes are to be found throughout Chapter 6. Note the survival of the Midland paled fencing.
M&GN Circle

became horizontal lapped. The small gable vents also changed, becoming one square pane rather than a narrow band of four panes. Other details remained the same.

New and replacement boxes were now mostly of the M&GN design but this was not universally so. On the western section the boxes at Sutton Bridge (1897), Walpole (1899) and of course on the MR Saxby line were of MR type 2b, and Clay Lake (1896) was a GN type 1 box. On the eastern section also, Grimston Road, Massingham, North Walsham and Stalham all had Midland boxes, probably made up of components displaced from the western section, all of them apparently being parts from MR type 2a boxes. North Walsham (1898) later had M&GN type front windows as replacements, Grimston Road had an M&GN type base, and Stalham had large windows at the Catfield end giving the erroneous impression of a MR type 3a.

The Norfolk & Suffolk Joint line between North Walsham and Mundesley was equipped with M&GN type 1a boxes at Antingham Road Junction and Mundesley South, but the later line between Mundesley and Cromer featured a new variant on the M&GN design. Type 1c, probably erected by the line's contractor William Moseley, had coarser detailing around the operating floor windows and had a new GN-style pierced scallop bargeboard, but otherwise resembled type 1b. Overstrand and Trimingham had platform-mounted examples, and Roughton Road Junction was brick-based with a special ornate half-hipped tile roof, probably to please the trustees of the Bond-Cabbell estate based at Cromer Hall.

The 1903 Norfolk & Suffolk Joint line between Yarmouth and Lowestoft was equipped by the GER with a variant of the GE type 7, mostly brick-based with steeply pitched roofs to match the station buildings. The windows were a simple '3 up, 3 across' sash, the box usually being five bays long. The brickwork extended to eaves level at the rear and took up a third of the window end, leaving only two windows. Gables were weather-boarded and most boxes had rear closets.

The Lowestoft Junction line from Yarmouth Beach featured M&GN type 1a boxes, among them the largest on the whole M&GN: Yarmouth Yard, which replaced the original W&J box on the other side of Kitchener Road.

As well as full-sized signalboxes, there were many crossing cabins on the system. These were generally small and narrow, having pitched slate roofs with the gable facing the track. Windows were large and boarding was generally vertical. These cabins could also be used for ground frames. Some gate boxes were also used, these being small versions of the standard M&GN type.

Telegraph fault boards were retained even after communication by single needle instrument or telephone had been installed. The usual board was a 12in square hung from one corner, painted white on the 'normal' side and black on the 'fault' side. Midland boxes in many cases retained their elliptical boards, often reused even when the box had been replaced by an M&GN signalbox. Similarly, the GN types often retained their bell-shaped boards.

In common with many features after 1913, concrete was also applied to signalling architecture. Several small gate boxes were erected in concrete blocks and the new M&GN type 1b box at East Rudham (1916) had a concrete block base. The new box at Cromer Beach (c1922) replacing the tall timber E&M type box was the only application entirely in concrete. The construction was of concrete bricks between block quoins and dressings up to eaves level, with a hipped slate roof.

Building Colours

Over the years from construction to the LNER regime the painting scheme remained stable as a 'stone' colour, a pinkish cream, contrasted with a brown and complemented by black and white. The brown changed according to period; in E&M days it was quite a dark chocolate, but the M&GN lightened it to a biscuit or pale tan. From c1918 it darkened to a medium tan.

Buildings were all treated more or less the same way. Exterior framing, window and door frames, doors, bargeboards, facias, soffits, gutters and down-pipes were brown. Boarding between frames, finials and door panels were 'stone'. Window sashes and casements, fixed or moving, were white, but very large windows as at Norwich station or on engine and goods sheds were brown. Black was used for various iron details, walkway brackets and so on.

The striping of the canopy valances by painting alternate boards brown and stone appears to have been an E&M tradition and apparently only applied to the eastern section. The large pitched-roof canopies at Melton, Norwich and Yarmouth were not painted this way during the M&GN period, and neither were the newer canopies at Yarmouth and South Lynn and the N&SJt stations. Most other locations featured it, except for the period between c1900-c1914 when some stations had the stripes omitted on repainting, but during the immediate postwar period the striped style was resumed.

Treatment of columns and spandrels also varied over the years. The E&M painting appears to have been all-brown, with an exception at Cromer in 1887 which had 'stone' spandrels. These were repainted brown. The all-brown style survived into the early M&GN period, but by 1900 some stations had a brown and stone treatment. Norwich had its E&M columns painted brown from floor to ceiling, with 'stone' spandrels; Yarmouth's were brown only to waist height and all stone above. The newer columns at South Lynn were similarly treated. Cromer was the most elaborate; the columns were brown, as were the main members of the roof girders, but the spandrels and the lattice of the girders were 'stone'. The front porch columns and spandrels were brown with the 'M&GN' picked out in stone. After World War 1, painting was apparently standardised as brown columns to the capitals, all above being stone. Sheringham was treated more elaborately, with the raised surrounds to the spandrels picked out in brown.

Interiors appear to have been typical of the period; brown to dado level and stone or white above, with white ceilings. Workshops, engine sheds and similar buildings were also brown to dado height, and whitewashed above. Signalbox interiors featured most of the single and double line instruments in polished wood, with a highly polished brown linoleum floor, and black lever frame and stove. Levers were apparently red for stop signals, black for points, blue for facing point locks, brown for gate locks and white for spares. Distant signal levers were originally green but later (c1930) were yellow.

Below:
The typical GE/N&SJt signalbox at Gorleston-on-Sea. Note the door to the closet underneath the rear roof extension. The steps are a replacement. Hopton, Gorleston North and North Gorleston Junction were probably timber examples, being on embankments.
Ken Burton/M&GN Circle

3. Domestic Architecture

Houses and Cottages

Although there were no railwaymen's cottages (other than crossing houses) on the western section, the situation regarding stationmaster's accommodation was very straightforward. Almost every station had a house annexed to it, if not actually part of the structure. At Sutton Bridge part of the second (L&SB) station was used. Only at Wisbech did the stationmaster have to seek accommodation outside railway property. The rest of the staff lived or lodged in private dwellings as near their station as possible. The architecture of the station houses has thus already been dealt with in Chapter 2. An exception was at Whaplode where a new stationmaster's house was built in 1914.

On the eastern section the converse was true; quite a number of cottages and houses were built, particularly at Melton, but many stationmasters had to seek private lodgings as did their men. Of the original construction, Yarmouth Beach, Norwich City and Cromer Beach all had houses incorporated into the station building as did the later Gayton Road and Paston & Knapton. The only other stations where the stationmaster's house was provided in the original construction phase were Hillington, Massingham and East Rudham. These all had a distinctive tall and narrow house in red brick with yellow brick dressings. The roofs were slate with the typical curved bargeboards and cut-out finials. A single-storey wash-house was built on to the rear.

At some locations non-railway buildings were pressed into service as stationmaster's accommodation. At Grimston Road a small cottage in the local brown carstone opposite the goods yard was bought in 1920, and another was bought near Whitwell & Reepham in 1919. Other properties acquired were the handsome half-timbered house adjacent to Raynham Park, leased from the Marquis Townshend, and the rambling farmhouse known as 'The Grove' at Hempton purchased with the parcel of land for Fakenham Town station. This was used as Mr Curson's 'Outdoor Superintendent's Office'. Presumably he also resided there. Similarly, a pair of cottages was included in the land purchased for Overstrand station and these were retained for staff use. Two properties were also acquired at Hemsby; the stationmaster's house being a magnificent double-fronted villa.

Of course the premier site of M&GN domestic architecture was Melton Constable. The first dwellings erected in 1881/82 were those on Melton Street. The design of these terraced cottages was very pleasant, being in red-brown brick with yellow brick dressings and string courses. The roofs were slate with fire-break walls between each pair. Windows were large and square. Larger dwellings finished the terraces at the Briston Road end. At the rear were neat outhouses, and all gables had the curved 'L&F' bargeboards. Contemporary with Melton Street a Railway Hall was erected, also in red brick with yellow brick dressings, its windows round-headed to match the station. A gasworks was also established.

In about 1886 another 12 cottages were built up the hill and nearer the goods yard, which became Astley Terrace. The cottages were built in a plain style by an outside contractor and leased to the E&M with an option to buy — which they later did. It was about this time that the timber station was moved from Holt to become at first a reading room and then the technical workshop, opposite the Hastings Arms. In some correspondence dated November 1896 Marriott wrote that he paid for the greater part of this building from his own purse, which suggests very little of the original Yarmouth building survived.

The next development was in 1892 when a Mr Colman asked leave to lease a portion of company land near the Railway Hall and erect a grocery shop; this was finished in 1893. The E&M/M&GN got into a little trouble about this as Lord Hastings had not been consulted, and his Lordship had made an arrangement with Wilkinson & Jarvis that no shop would be put up without his consent. Nobody had thought to tell Marriott about it, however. The drawings for the shop are signed by Mr George Ratcliffe who became Company Architect from about this time, and it is his hand that guided the next period of architectural design.

The year 1895 saw the Railway Hall much enlarged into the Railway Institute, and the erection of Nos 1-16 Colville Street. The latter cottages were a new departure for the village and followed the half-timber and tile 'arts & crafts' style of the contemporary stations. The gable timbering was in an attractive herringbone design. Between 1896 and 1899 the rest of the site was filled with dwellings in the 'crafts' style. The terraces descending Briston Road, Nos 1-22, incorporated two shops at the corners of Colville Street, and the large end house was for a doctor's practice. Nos 1-6 were grander, having terracotta pediments over the doors. A school was also built jointly with Lord Hastings.

Regarding the naming of the streets, Marriott wrote: 'I have a very pleasant recollection of Lord Colville. I had called one of the new streets after him, as he was such a fine specimen of the English gentleman. . . One of the Directors caught sight once of the name and stopped, saying "Look there, Colville". He saw his own name on the terrace. The old gentleman (for this was shortly before he gave up the Chairmanship of the Great Northern) was so pleased at the compliment, and at the recreation ground we had made, also the houses and the school, that I cannot repeat the very complimentary remarks he made to me.'

Below:
The Outdoor Superintendent's office — 'The Grove' in Hempton. Described in 1872 as 'A very pleasantly-situated family residence with an entrance hall, breakfast and dining roms, drawing room (with bow window), kitchen, back kitchen, seven bedrooms, dressing room, two attics and a laundry'. Before it became Mr Curson's office, the L&F engineer Mr Millett lived here.
R. F. Bonny/M&GN Circle

Below right:
Looking over the gasworks towards Melton Street after closure. Note the neat detailing of the rear buildings. Astley Terrace is to the left.
M&GN Circle

The Railway Institute was again extended in 1912 to have a frontage on the Briston Road, and Mr Colman's shop front was also enlarged; a plan to build another shop next door fell through.

Outside the environs of Melton Constable, the building of railwaymen's accommodation was more limited. Cromer Beach featured a short terrace of eight cottages overlooking the station yard. From the arrangement of the chimneys and differences in the brickwork, it seems that there were originally only six dwellings almost immediately extended by a further pair. The design was plain but elegantly executed in local red brick and pantile. A string course in yellow brick relieved the front elevation and No 1 had a bay window, added later. The rear accommodation was roofed by bringing down the slope of the main roof, quite a usual Norfolk feature.

The turn of the century saw a phase of house building at various locations. The handsome terrace of cottages at Mundesley (1899) had the steep, tiled roofs and timbering of the 'crafts' style. Ten cottages were stepped in pairs down the slight gradient, each pair sharing a gabled dormer on the front elevation. The stationmaster's house finished the terrace, being taller and having a cross gable. A similar style was used for a pair of cottages at Hindolvestone (1899).

The pair of cottages at Guestwick (1902) appear to represent a change of heart for the Architect's Department. These were plainly built in brick and pantile and had no woodwork at all. Each front door was protected by a small tiled canopy supported on the open side by a timber strut. The station house at Weybourne (1903) and the station house and cottages at Trimingham (1906) continued the plain design. The simple two-storey houses, L-shaped at Trimingham and T-shaped at Weybourne, were in brick and pantile. The cottages were semi-detached with half-hipped roof and front dormers. The side elevation was very deep with the main entrance in the middle.

The pair of cottages at Langor Bridge (1898) were built by an outside contractor when the line was doubled and gatehouse No 13 demolished. They had no features in common with M&GN houses of the period, being a utilitarian design in brick and pantile.

The next phase of house building occurred just before World War 1. At Felmingham (1913), Whaplode and Catfield (1914) stationmaster's houses were provided in a new style, probably coinciding with the arrival of Mr Arthur Roy as Company Architect. Based on red brick, the houses were L-shaped and slate roofed with overhanging eaves. The upper storey was rendered with a pronounced rainwater throw-off at the lower edge. The front door was protected by a small canopy. The outer corner at Felmingham featured a castellated cast-iron rainwater hopper which was lettered 'M&GN

1913'. Four cottages in the same style were provided at Hillington (1914) adjacent to crossing No 5 and fronting on to the main Lynn road. These were arranged as two semi-detached dwellings set in a generous amount of land. The centre of each front elevation was dominated by a large pair of gables, and at the gulley between the two gables a castellated half-octagonal rainwater hopper was positioned, the one to the east being cast 'M&GN

and the other '1914'. The front doors were placed at each end and canopied by sweeping the roof down from the side gables.

The cottages at Hillington represent the end of M&GN domestic architectural development and the story is now taken up by the concrete crossing houses covered in the next section. However, two gatehouses Nos 104A and 105A were built in 1930 following the last domestic style outlined above.

Top right:
Looking east along Briston Road with the M&GN housing to the right. Colville Road begins between the two taller houses, which incorporate corner shops.
M&GN Circle

Above right:
The Railway Institute after its extension in 1912. The 'Country Club' as it is now known is still the social centre of the village.
M&GN Circle

Right:
The timber gatehouse No 12 near Fakenham pictured in c1900. This has the typical plan form, copied when construction changed to brick. The timber gatehouses at the Yarmouth end were weatherboarded. Note the exposed lever frame. This building was replaced by a concrete chalet in 1915.
R. F. Bonny/M&GN Circle

Level Crossing Gatehouses

On the eastern section almost all gatehouses built by W&J and the E&M had the same basic design: that of a small bungalow usually gable-on to the railway. The main part consisted of a living room and bedroom under a slate roof of medium pitch finished with the usual curved bargeboards, with a subsidiary structure containing the kitchen/scullery under an extension of the roof at a lower pitch. However, not all examples had this last feature.

It seems clear that those gatehouses built before some time in 1880 (Lynn-Fakenham, Yarmouth-Catfield) were of lapped timber boarding, but the remainder were of brick (Fig 18). Most had a central chimney but some had chimneys at each end. Front windows were variable, the timber examples tending to have small square ones, others being quite tall. For the later E&M work a longer plan was used, the brickwork having decorative yellow quoins and arches. This could be seen on Nos 1A and 53.

Gatehouse No 50 by the White Swan in Yarmouth was unique in that it was not built by the railway but an adoption of an existing dwelling.

The first phase of refurbishment appears to have been the cement rendering of some older brick examples and the addition of second bedrooms. These were positioned at the rear alongside the kitchen under an extension of the low-pitched roof. In some cases a third bedroom was added at the front to form a T-plan. Some also received small porches. The majority of this work was carried out from 1901.

A major rebuilding scheme began in 1915 with the replacement of the timber gatehouses Nos 6, 7, 9, 10, 12, 40 and 43 with a new design executed in rock-faced concrete block. This was a two-storey 'chalet', the upper room being incorporated into the steep, tiled roof with a small dormer window. A cast concrete number block was let into the gable wall nearest the railway. This picturesque design was probably a product of Mr Arthur Roy, using Marriott's block as the design module. The last new example was No 44 of 1922, replacing a small gate box. This was an entirely new design, being a plain two-storey house with hipped roof, constructed in smooth-faced concrete blocks complete with quoins, string course and number block.

Most postwar gatehouse work consisted of the addition of a third bedroom in concrete block construction with a cavity. This new room was built on to the front elevation forming a T-plan. The rest of the building was faced with 2in thick concrete blocks in an 'ashlar' treatment having quoin blocks at the corners and a cast number block.

On the western section the gatehouses looked less railwaylike than their eastern section counterparts, having sash windows and being detailed like ordinary dwellings. The Norwich & Spalding line (Nos 81-102) featured a narrow two-storey design in red-brown brick with pitched slate roof. There was no overhang; at eaves level was a cornice and dentil course. The rooms were arranged as a 'two up two down' sharing a central chimney. The main entrance was on the narrow front gable elevation and had a small flat canopy supported on two timber brackets. Each side elevation had a pair of blind windows at first floor level, a feature shared by other N&S buildings. Two later gatehouses Nos 97 (1892) and 88A (1899) were to individual designs, No 97 being a terrace of two dwellings. No 102 (Cowbit Road) was unusual in that it was gabled the other way to fit on to the adjacent terrace.

The Spalding & Bourne gatehouses (Nos 103-108) were very similar but had more conventional overhanging eaves. Nos 103, 105 and 108 were single storey; No 108 was enlarged by a building alongside in 1906 and No 105 similarly in 1914. No 103 was refaced in concrete block. Nos 104A and 105A were built in 1930 in the domestic style with rendered first storey introduced in 1913.

The Peterborough, Wisbech and Sutton line (Nos 66-80) featured a picturesque style of gatehouse. Single-storey and in red brick with yellow brick quoins and detailing (also vice versa), they had hipped slate roofs and a small entrance porch.

Between 1913 and 1923 several were enlarged by the addition of a third bedroom at the rear.

The Lynn-Sutton Bridge gatehouses (Nos 54-65) are more elusive as all but No 65 have been demolished. Most of them originally seem to have been single-storey gabled buildings, and between 1907 and 1914 several of them were enlarged by raising the walls and building two new rooms above. However, No 65 at Sutton Bridge seems to have been two-storey originally and was hip-roofed; it may have been an adoption of an existing house. No 54 at West Lynn resembled S&B stations in that it had a small bay window, which tends to confirm that the building was used as the booking office for West Lynn station until its closure in 1886.

Gatehouse numbering was built up from an origin in L&F days; Nos 1-22 were on the L&F line from Lynn to Norwich (No 0 was on the unopened Austin Street branch), and once the Melton-North Walsham link was completed the numbering was carried through to Yarmouth and on to the Union line up to No 50. The Cromer line saw the addition of Nos 51-53, and the Lynn Loop the duplicate No 1A.

On the formation of the full Joint Committee in 1893 the numbering was extended to the western section when all crossing houses, even if their function had been replaced by subsequent signalboxes, were given a number. Prior to this date the old numbering of the constituent railways was used, as shown by a drawing dated 1892 of new gatehouse No 7 near Spalding which later became M&GN No 97. Prior to the extension of L&F numbering to the Y&NN, gatehouses were probably known by name, for example 'Briggate' gatehouse, later the stationmaster's house at Honing where Marriott had his construction office for a time.

Numbers were painted on to a wooden diamond of the signalbox type which could be reversed to show a black face if there was an equipment fault. Some of the Midland elliptical boards survived on the PW&S line.

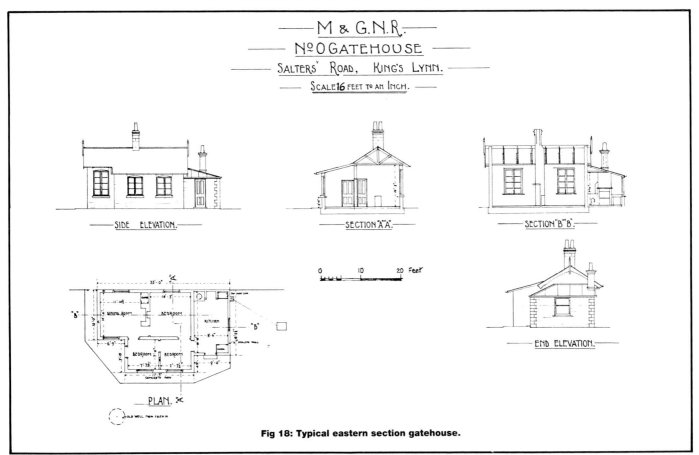

Crossings & Gatehouses

No	Name	Type	Built	Extended/Rebuilt	Signalbox	Demolished
Eastern Section						
0	Salters Rd	B	1882	1917		
1A	Hardwick Narrows	B	1886	*		
1	Wootton Rd	T	1879			*
2	Bawsey	T	1879			*
3	Common Rd	T	1879	modern		
4	Roydon Rd	T	1879			*
–	GRIMSTON ROAD					
–	HILLINGTON					
5	Flitcham Rd	T	1879	modern		
6	Hillington Rd	T	1879	1915 C		
7	Peddars Way	T	1879	1915 C		
–	MASSINGHAM					
8	Massingham Rd	T	1880	modern		
9	Kipton Heath	T	1880	1915 C		
10	Weasenham Rd	T	1880	1915 C		
–	EAST RUDHAM					
–	RAYNHAM PARK					
11	Dunton Rd No. 1	T	1880	modern		
12	Dunton Rd No. 2	T	1880	1915 C		
–	Hempton Rd					
–	FAKENHAM					
13	Langor Bridge	B	1881		1898	1898
14	Holbrigg Lane	B		*		
–	THURSFORD					
15	Thursford Rd	B	1881	*		
16	Gunthorpe Rd	B	1881	*		
17	Hindolvestone Rd	B	1881	*		
18	Freshgap Lane	B	1881	1923 C		
19	Skitfield Rd	B	1881	1923 C		
–	GUESTWICK					
20	Foulsham Rd	B	1882	1923 C		
21	Themelthorpe	B	1882	1923 C		
22	Heath Lane	B	1882	1923 C		
–	LENWADE					
–	ATTLEBRIDGE					
23	Reepham Rd	B	1883	*		
23A	Oulton Rd			1916 converted from Bluestone stn.		
24	Bluestone Rd	B	1883	*		
25	Codling Lane	B	1883	modern		
26	Green Lane	B	1883	1923 C		
27	Banningham	B	1883	1923		
28	Skeyton Rd	B	1883	*		
29	North Walsham	B	1883	*		*
30	Worstead Rd	B	1881	modern	1901	
–	HONING		1881	stationmaster's house	1882	
31	East Ruston	B	1881	*		
32	Stepping Stone Ln	B	1881	1923 C		
33	Stalham	B	1880			*
34	Catfield Rd	B	1880			*
35	Sutton Staithe	B	1880			*
–	CATFIELD					
36	New Rd	T	1880			*
37	Potter Heigham Rd	T	1880			*
38	Reynolds Lane	T	1880			
39	Ludham Rd	T	1880	modern		
–	POTTER HEIGHAM					
40	Common Rd	T	1880	1915 C		
41	Martham & Repps	T	1880			
42	Repps Rd	T	1880	1897		*
–	MARTHAM					
–	HEMSBY					
43	Thoroughfare Lane	T	1878	1915 C		
44	Mill Lane	C	1922			
45	Mill House	T	1877			*
–	CAISTER					
–	Salisbury Rd				1901	
46A	Beaconsfield Rd	B	c1890			1902
–	Kitchener Rd					
46	Nelson Rd	B	1882			1902
47	Churchill Rd	B	1882			1902
48	Caister Rd	B	1882			1902
49	Ormond Rd	B	1882			*
50	White Swan					*
51	Briningham Rd	B	1884			*
52	Thornage Rd	B	1884		1900	
–	HOLT					
53	Kelling Heath	B	1887			
–	SHERINGHAM					

Western Section

No.	Name	Type	Date			
54	West Lynn	B	1864		1898	1960
–	CLENCHWARTON					
55	White Cross Lane	B	1864			*
56	Greens Lane	B	1864			*
57	Terrington	B	1864		1891	*
58	Bates	B2	1864	1907		*
59	Buntings Well	B2	1864	1911		*
60	Market Lane	B	1864			*
61	Fencebank	B2	1864	1914		*
–	WALPOLE					
62	Pingle Lane	B2	1864	1911		*
63	Walpole Bank	B2	1864	1914		*
64	King John Bank	B	1864			*
65	Sutton Bridge	B2	1864	1900		*
–	SUTTON BRIDGE					
–	TYDD					
66	Foul Anchor	B	1866			
67	The Chase	B	1866			*
68	Catlings Lane	B	1866			*
–	FERRY					*
69	Gipsy Lane	B	1866	1923		
70	Bludwick Drove	B	1866	*		
71	Horseshoe Lane	B	1866		1892	*
–	Leverington Rd					
–	WISBECH					
72	Barton Lane	B	1866	1913	1891	
73	Panswell	B	1866	1909		*
74	Sandbank	B	1866	1923		
75	Murrow Lane	B	1866			
–	MURROW					
76	Murrow Rd	B	1866	1923		
77	Turf Fen Lane	B	1866	1920	1891	*
–	WRYDE					
–	THORNEY					
78	Mill Hill Rd	B	1866			*
79	Dogsthorpe Rd	B	1866		1900	*
80	Paston Rd	B	1866	1923		*
81	Silt Lane	B2	1862	1904	1879	*
82	Hospital Drove	B2	1862			*
83	Hundred Lane	B2	1862			
84	Seagate Rd	B2	1862			
–	LONG SUTTON					
85	Garnsgate Rd	B2	1862			
86	Carters Lane	B2	1862			
–	GEDNEY					
87	Stonegate Yard	B2	1862			
88	Pinstock Lane	B2	1862			
–	FLEET					
88A	Hockles Gate Rd	B2	1899			
89	Fleet Hall Rd	B2	1862			
90	Branches Lane	B2	1862			*
91	Dam Gate	B2	1862	1899		
–	HOLBEACH					
92	Cranmore Lane	B2	1858			
93	Crane's Lane	B2	1858			
–	WHAPLODE	B2	1858			
94	Hog's Gate	B2	1858			
–	MOULTON					
95	Long Lane	B2	1858			*
96	Delgate Rd	B2	1858			*
–	WESTON					
97	Whyles Bank	B2	1892			
98	Kellet Gate Rd	B2	1858			*
99	Low Rd	B2	1858			
100	Cunningham's Drv	B2	1858		1891	
101	Clay Lake	B2			1896	*
102	Cowbit Rd	B2				
–	London Rd					
–	Winsover Rd					
103	Hawthorn Bank	B	1866	* C		*
104	Cuckoo Junction	B2	1866		1893	
104A	South Drove East	D	1929			
–	NORTH DROVE					
105	Iron Bar Drove	B	1866	1914		*
105A	Counter Drain Drv	D	1929			
–	TWENTY					
106	Four Cross Rds	B2	1866			
107	Austerby Rd	B2	1866			
108	London Rd	B	1866	1899/1906	1893	*

Key:		B	= brick	D	= domestic
—	= crossing controlled by station or box	B2	= brick (two-storey)	*	= date uncertain
T	= timber	C	= concrete		

4. Miscellaneous Fittings

Station Nameboards

These seem to have occurred in three categories which are chronologically separated: type N1 (a standard timber board), type N2 (an enamelled metal board) or type N3 (the well-known concrete nameboard). (Fig 19.)

Of all M&GN station nameboards type N1 once predominated and seems to have been the earliest style adopted. It could be mounted on rear posts, sometimes with turned finials (eg Holbeach) or on a wall, particularly on the western section, or between posts. Commonly, these posts were plainly capped, but on the more important stations, for example North Walsham and Fakenham, ball-and-spike signal finials were used. Other types of finial arose from the old MR design (Eye Green) or a freelance E&M or M&GN design (Cromer, Sheringham and South Lynn new). Melton Constable and South Lynn were the only known examples of the Midland layout where four boards were mounted on three posts in a diamond arrangement to show a face to all four directions of running. Signal finials were fitted.

The enamelled nameboards seem to have been a mid-period design, probably coincident with the opening of the N&S lines at Yarmouth (1903) and Cromer, Overstrand and Trimingham (1906).

Cromer's new board was certainly in place by 1914. Other type N2 boards occurred at Hillington, Grimston Road and Clenchwarton. The lettering was generally sanserif, but Overstrand and Trimingham were seriffed.

From the early 1920s, replacements were of the famous concrete boards, the earlier design having additional moulded post beading abandoned later in favour of plain posts. The early board at West Runton was dated 1922. By the mid-1930s almost all nameboards were in concrete.

Timber types were simply planks mounted in multiples to the required dimensions with the edges built up to a raised surround by various beadings. The sanserif letters were of an alloy 10in high overall, tapered to 9¾in on the reading face, screwed on to the background. The screw heads were countersunk and then plugged with putty. The thickness was ½in.

Concrete types had the 14in letters moulded in the construction process itself. The existing board at West Runton, often a source of puzzlement, has been rendered blank by the simple expedient of cementing over the letters to the depth of the surrounding moulding, possibly in the last war. Early examples actually used letters separately moulded in a brown-coloured concrete, which were then

incorporated into the main moulding. The posts were separately moulded, and hollow, the concrete thickness being one inch. The ball finials were also separate.

The earliest colour scheme appears to have been white letters on black, but from c1910 the colours were reversed. Supporting posts and surrounds generally seem to have been brown to match the stations. Beading could be white or black.

The mid-period enamelled nameboards were a pale red/orange (one source refers to it as 'salmon') on a white background. Posts and surrounds appear to have been brown. There is also a suggestion that some of the earlier timber boards had their letters repainted in red to match.

On the introduction of concrete replacements, black letters on a white background once again became usual but in the LNER period colours were reversed, although the rest of the concrete was left white. West Runton and Holt, both early examples, appear to have been left unpainted at first, to show the coloured concrete lettering.

Signalbox Nameboards

These were miniature versions of the timber station nameboards, with 6in cut-out letters usually

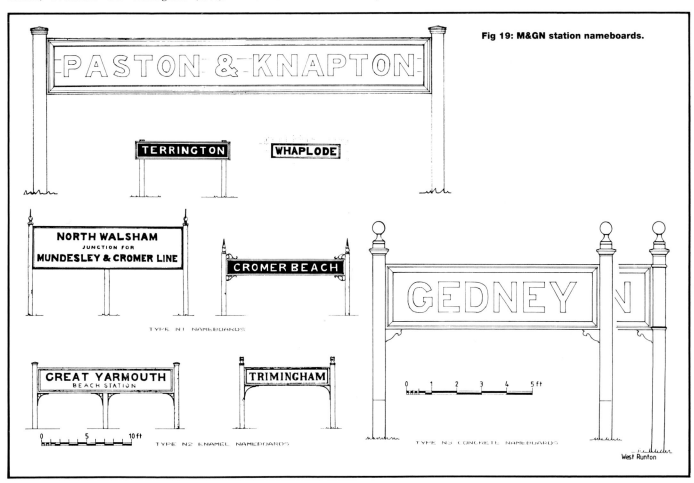

Fig 19: M&GN station nameboards.

PASTON & KNAPTON

TERRINGTON   WHAPLODE

NORTH WALSHAM
JUNCTION FOR
MUNDESLEY & CROMER LINE

CROMER BEACH

GEDNEY

TYPE N1 NAMEBOARDS

GREAT YARMOUTH
BEACH STATION

TRIMINGHAM

TYPE N2 ENAMEL NAMEBOARDS

TYPE N3 CONCRETE NAMEBOARDS

West Runton

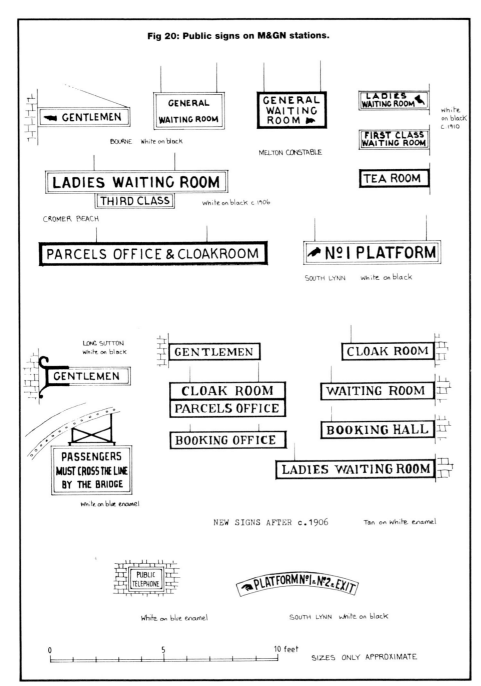

Fig 20: Public signs on M&GN stations.

← GENTLEMEN

GENERAL WAITING ROOM

GENERAL WAITING ROOM →

LADIES WAITING ROOM →

white on black c.1910

FIRST CLASS WAITING ROOM

TEA ROOM

BOURNE   White on black

MELTON CONSTABLE

LADIES WAITING ROOM

THIRD CLASS   white on black c 1906

CROMER BEACH

PARCELS OFFICE & CLOAKROOM

← No I PLATFORM

SOUTH LYNN   white on black

LONG SUTTON   white on black

GENTLEMEN

GENTLEMEN

CLOAK ROOM

CLOAK ROOM PARCELS OFFICE

WAITING ROOM

BOOKING OFFICE

BOOKING HALL

PASSENGERS MUST CROSS THE LINE BY THE BRIDGE

LADIES WAITING ROOM

white on blue enamel

NEW SIGNS AFTER c.1906   Tan on white enamel

PUBLIC TELEPHONE

← PLATFORM No I & No 2 & EXIT

White on blue enamel

SOUTH LYNN   white on black

0   5   10 feet   SIZES ONLY APPROXIMATE

Above:
One of the first examples of the famous concrete nameboards, with the additional post beading. The board has been repainted by the LNER.
L. Ward/M&GN Circle

on one line. Their normal position was in the middle of the gable end, above the window framing, except on the ex-Midland boxes where they were generally on the front above the walkway. During the period around 1906 enamelled metal nameboards in wooden frames appeared, matching the contemporary station nameboard and coinciding with the arrival of the type 1b signalbox design. Some of the longer names (eg Runton West Junction) were on two lines. These enamel boards used the red lettering but the frames, where present, were black. Lettering was seriffed on the M&GN and sanserif on the N&SJt. The usual position of the boards changed to the front of the box, although there were exceptions. Later boxes once more resumed the use of timber nameboards. The timber and cut-out letter boards followed the example of the station nameboards by being painted white on black until after c1910 when black on white was adopted.

Public Signs

On M&GN stations these at first appear to have been entirely of cut-out metal sanserif letters on wooden finger boards. The size and method of fixing (suspended or cantilevered) appeared to depend on situation and ease of viewing. All painting followed the usual scheme of white on black until c1910 and then black on white, with black framing.

At Bourne the signs probably represented GN practice as did perhaps the decorative cast iron brackets supporting the 'GENTLEMEN' signs on some of the Norwich & Spalding stations. Midland

Left:
The original nameboard at Melton seen here in c1930. The only other example of the Midland-type arrangement of four boards in a diamond formation was at South Lynn. Note the signal finials. Class A No 32 is in the final livery with Deeley smokebox, and was withdrawn in 1933.
H. C. Casserley

Above:
Mrs Field and Miss Morgan outside the Tea Room at Melton Constable, this view (of c1910) showing well the assembled gas lamps, poster boards and enamelled notices on the M&GN during this period.
Mrs S. Kirk/M&GN Circle

influence may have extended to the signs on the PW&S line. Certainly at Sutton Bridge there was a typical MR white and blue enamel footbridge sign, but information on this line is inconclusive.

From about the time of the opening of the Norfolk & Suffolk lines a new enamelled design was introduced and began to replace older signs where appropriate. The lettering was seriffed and of the same light red or salmon colour as described above, on a white ground to match the contemporary station nameboards. Wooden frames appear to have been black. (Fig 20.)

Poster & Timetable Boards

These appeared in a variety of styles. On the western section, which had been part of a joint committee for some years, dual use of Great Northern and Midland boards seems to have been widespread from early in the line's history. The E&M had its own poster board design, and a surviving example has a varnished hardwood frame. The only clear contemporary photo of one in situ seems to show a similar treatment. The E&M boards appeared in conjunction with GN and MR boards at Lynn and probably on the rest of the eastern section and this tradition was continued in M&GN days. The M&GN poster boards had enamelled name strips with a variety of wording, probably in red on white. Midland colours were white letters on black; GN boards were black but the name was in white on a red strip. M&GN frames may have been brown at first but with the appearance of a simplified design by about 1926 the colour was black. After 1936 the background to the white letters is reported to have become red. With the advent of the N&SJt, Great Eastern boards appeared on

Right:
The cattle pens at Melton Constable; although some posts are in concrete, and the platform has been extended in concrete block, they remain typical of most M&GN pens.
D. A. Digby

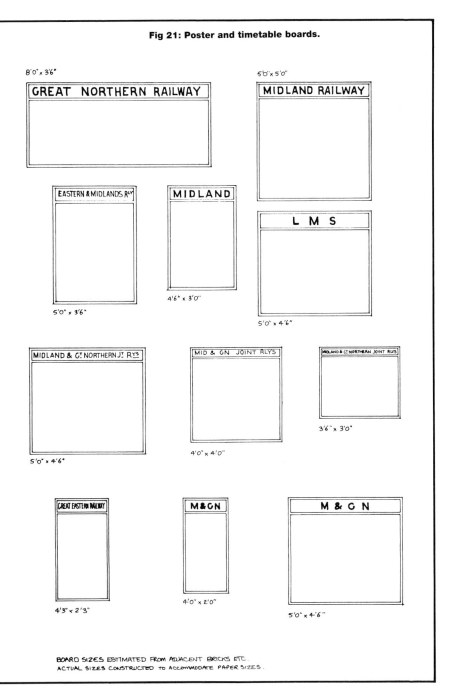

Fig 21: Poster and timetable boards.

8'0" x 3'6"
GREAT NORTHERN RAILWAY

5'0" x 5'0"
MIDLAND RAILWAY

EASTERN & MIDLANDS Rl.y
5'0" x 3'6"

MIDLAND
4'6" x 3'0"

L M S
5'0" x 4'6"

MIDLAND & G! NORTHERN J! RYS
5'0" x 4'6"

MID & GN JOINT RLYS
4'0" x 4'0"

MIDLAND & G! NORTHERN JOINT RLYS
3'6" x 3'0"

GREAT EASTERN RAILWAY
4'3" x 2'3"

M & G N
4'0" x 2'0"

M & G N
5'0" x 4'6"

BOARD SIZES ESTIMATED FROM ADJACENT BRICKS ETC.
ACTUAL SIZES CONSTRUCTED TO ACCOMMODATE PAPER SIZES.

related stations which now could have boards for MR, GN, M&GN and GE information. (Fig 21.)

Platform Seats

These appear to have been of two main types. The earliest style was apparently the attractively curved and slatted seat with three 'rustic' cast iron supports. Judging by photographs this type of seat was present at first only on the L&F and Y&NN lines. This suggests that they may be survivors of an order placed by Wilkinson & Jarvis. That they were an 'off the peg' item is demonstrated by an identical seat seen in Mid-Wales. They were certainly pre-M&GN as one was present at North Walsham c1890. they were later moved around the system, shown by one example which did not arrive at Cromer until about 1910.

The standard seat from E&M times appears to have been the plain 'barred' design consisting of a large plank seat and two back rails all on plain cast-iron supports. Originally the supports incorporated E&MR in the central aperture but it seems that many of these were knocked out later. However, this type without lettering was proliferated all over the system, so it seems likely that the M&GN ordered or manufactured more of this standard design.

Some Midland 'rustic' seats survived on the western section but GN examples were no different from the standard barred seat except they were usually much longer, with three supports.

Seat colouring was variable. It seems that some examples, possibly the earliest ones, were merely grained and varnished and remained in that state until painted green by the LNER. However, it is known that the majority were painted the standard brown then in use. The ironwork became standardised as black after c1918 but before then the colour had been variable. By examination of an E&M example which apparently had stood at Cromer since 1887, it seems the first painting was chocolate with the 'E&M' picked out in vermilion. Before the standard black the M&GN colours were 'stone' followed by brown. The LNER colour was green.

Lamps

On most stations the lighting was by oil lamp inserted into various lamp cases. The most common, type L1, appeared all over the system, mounted from the back on posts (latterly concrete) along the platform fence or on the station walls. An equivalent was type L2, distinguishable by the arched cover. This appeared at only a few stations and may have been fabricated at Melton. Some stations, mainly the larger ones, had free-standing lamps on plain timber posts, type L3. This case had a simple pyramidal cover with chimney and in most cases a small finial. This type was also used for gas lighting (see below). All station foot crossings featured these lamps nearby. Many stations also had one suspended over the main doors on an iron bracket. The station name appeared on all these types as blue letters on a white ground or vice versa. Most cases could be bodily removed from the mountings. (Fig 22)

Some stations were lit by town gas: Thorney (from 1892), South Lynn (1896), Bourne, Holbeach, Sutton Bridge, Melton Constable, Sheringham, Cromer (1899), Mundesley, Norwich, Yarmouth, the N&SJt stations to Lowestoft, and possibly several more. However, even some gas-lit stations still used oil lamps at various locations. Those gas-lit stations with canopies had elegant octagonal lamps suspended beneath them, and these could also be seen as yard lighting suspended from tall, swan-necked iron posts, particularly at Melton and South Lynn. The more ordinary lamps, similar to oil type L3, were supported on iron or

Above:
The water tank at Mundesley was supplied in 1899 and assembled from 4x4 standard M&GN panels.
Denis Seabrook

wooden posts, mounted diagonally at Cromer (iron posts) and Sheringham (wooden posts). Another type of glass pot lamp was used on the open platforms of Yarmouth and Norwich, being used again when those stations were converted to electricity in 1929.

As might be expected, some GN and MR lamps survived on the western section. The Peterborough-Lynn line retained Midland lamps of the later standard (without decorative petticoats) very similar to type L3 which may actually have been of Midland origin. However, no MR hexagonal iron posts appear to have been used, except at Sutton Bridge and also North Walsham. Some of these lamps were replaced by the flat-top case of type L1. A few of these on the Bourne-Spalding line had

slightly arched tops, possibly of GN origin. Freestanding GN lamps were again similar to type L3, but the chimney was much smaller, with no decoration. Gedney had attractive 'barley sugar' twisted iron posts.

Painting of lamp cases seems to have been brown throughout, with pyramidal copper tops left as the polished metal, but painting of the posts varied. It seems that eastern section posts were mainly brown, but on the western section many of the posts were 'stone' with brown bases. Cromer's lamp posts were thus painted c1906 and fitted with wooden boards pointing helpfully to the 'REFRESHMENT ROOM' in white on blue or black.

Huts

From early land plans it seems that few platelayer's huts were provided by the original eastern section companies, possibly because of the high proportion of gatehouses. Where provided, these huts

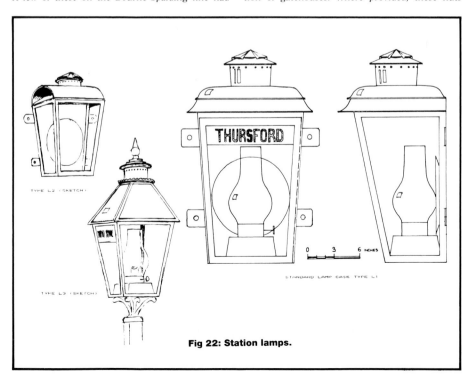

Fig 22: Station lamps.

seem to have been of timber, often reclaimed sleepers assembled vertically with a beading strip over each joint. Roofs were pitched, and the whole building was tarred or creosoted. Huts in station precincts on the western section and later along the eastern section lines were usually brick and of a similar type. The basic design was simple, commonly about 11 x 9 ft, with a pitched slate roof, one door in the gable end and one window overlooking the track; in general they were parallel to the line but a few examples had their gables facing it. There was usually a brick chimney opposite the door and one or two bench lockers along the walls inside, flanking the fireplace.

From the 1920s, huts appeared in concrete block with timber or metal window frames. Dimensions were more or less as before, but bitumen felt was now used as much as slate for roofing. Quite a few gate and ground-frame huts were also built or replaced in concrete block.

Cattle Pens

At one time cattle formed one of the most important traffics on the railway, as evidenced by the Joint's 136 cattle wagons, and most stations had cattle loading facilities, although several did not. The majority of stations had only one or two pens, but the larger market centres (Stalham, Melton, South Lynn, Whitwell & Reepham, Fakenham and Wisbech) had three or four. Norwich was the largest centre with over a dozen pens. Such was the volume of traffic that special trains were often required on the various market days: Tuesday (Lynn, Spalding), Wednesday (Yarmouth), Thursday (North Walsham, Fakenham, Wisbech) and Saturday (Norwich).

The usual design was of a plain brick platform wall with steep ramps, often having steps. Each pen was bounded by five- or six-rail fencing, narrowing to one pair of gates, usually set back from the edge of the dock. The lowered flap and open doors of a wagon and the dock formed a droveway inside. The approaches were also fenced and gated and used as lairage for cattle waiting to be loaded. Flooring for the whole area was usually blue brick 'cobbles' and all pens were washed down and limewashed after use to prevent disease.

Moulded concrete gates were tried on several pens, the concrete gate imitating the wooden one, having five bars and a diagonal brace.

Water Tanks & Other Loco Facilities

Although not strictly architectural, these items were major features of several stations. Possibly the earliest watering facilities were those at Wisbech where there was a standard MR tank assembled from bolted iron sections (6x4x2 units) on a brick base.

On the eastern section the earliest facilities favoured were a swing arm direct from an iron tank on a brick base, which housed a pumping engine. This occurred at Grimston Road, where the tank was assembled from square sections (4x3 units) having a moulded raised beading with incurved corners.

It seems a standard design of tank was introduced about 1881. A cast iron panel 4ft 6in x 3ft 6in was used, bolted together by internal flanges. Corners and undercurves were castings with 12in radius. A raised beading with incurved corners was moulded on each panel. At both Melton and Norwich these panels were used in a vertical aspect to fabricate identical tanks to a size of 6x6 units. Bases were in brick with semi-circular arched openings. Starting at Aylsham (1883 2x2) the panels were assembled in the more normal horizontal aspect, and Cromer followed in 1887 (4x2), both brick bases being similar to those above.

Bourne (1893) was a large GN design of tank on a very tall brick base, but all subsequent tanks were the standard panels, now with a small central area containing 'M&GN'. Yarmouth Beach (c1893 5x4) was apparently the last brick-based tank, the remainder using wooden, and later iron posts: South Lynn (1895 10x4), Mundesley (1898 4x4), Melton Constable (1898 16x8x2), Yarmouth (1903 5x4), Fakenham (3x3) and Spalding M&GN loco (4x3 units). Several were roofed: Aylsham, Cromer, Yarmouth and Fakenham with single pitched; Melton and Mundesley with twin pitched; and the enormous 1898 tank at Melton with three pitched roofs. Spalding had an arched roof but it, and the Yarmouth roofs, were removed by 1936. Bourne had a very low-pitched leaded roof. Stalham had a tank from c1894. In the 1950s this was a Ransomes & Rapier tank of 4x4 castings, but I suspect it to be a replacement. Painting of water tanks was standardised as brown with stone panelling.

Apart from the tank-mounted water cranes mentioned above, there were several other designs.

Their positions are noted on the station plans in Chapter 6. The earliest on the eastern section were standpipes probably erected by Wilkinson & Jarvis. They were plain columns incorporating a valve wheel, and the leather bags hung unsupported. They occurred at Fakenham (one) and Melton (one). The next type formed the major class and was used extensively by the E&M, consisting of a fluted column with valve wheel and knob finial. The bag was free-hanging but could be lifted by a system of folded arms operated by a handle with a balance weight, although some were not thus fitted. They occurred at South Lynn (four), Fakenham (one), Melton (one), Aylsham (one), Stalham (two), Yarmouth (one) and Sheringham (two). Originally there was another on the Down platform at Melton but by 1913 this had been changed to the M&GN type. The M&GN design was of a long swing arm balanced by a large water-filled ball. The arm was mounted to move in a vertical arc and then pivoted to swing by an elbow tube into the top of the column. The valve wheel was adjacent to the base. This type occurred on the platforms at South Lynn (two), Melton (two) and Mundesley (one). What appears to be a later design occurred at South Lynn (one) and Spalding M&GN loco shed (one). In appearance it resembled a combination of E&M and MR features.

There were also M&GN examples of the owning companies' designs, as well as those on their lines at Peterborough (MR/GN) and Spalding (GN). The well-known Midland swing water column with 'MRCo' on the casting occurred at Wisbech (two) and Bourne (one), and the GN swing type incorporating a Tuscan column occurred at Bourne (two), Four Cross Roads (two) and Yarmouth (two). All M&GN water cranes appear to have been painted brown throughout their lives.

During frosty weather, lit fires were necessary near water columns. Various braziers and tall-chimneyed stoves were used and can be seen on photographs. The locomotive department was responsible for maintenance and also for lighting the fires except at Wisbech, Grimston Road, Fakenham, Sheringham and Aylsham, where a porter or signalman was responsible.

Drivers were also asked not to damage the paint on tenders by allowing the chain, used for pulling round the jib, to swing back on to the sides, especially when using the GN pattern column.

Coaling stages were to no particular standard, usually being brick or timber platforms with a crane; at first this would have a timber jib, but later a steel one. South Lynn's coal stage was covered by a large weatherboarded timber shed until 1929 when an electric coaling plant was installed and the wood shed replaced by an arched-roof corrugated iron cover on a steel frame. Yarmouth also had an electric coaling plant installed in 1929/30.

Turntables were all hand-operated and to similar designs, probably best exemplified by the one at Cromer. Originally the sizes were small; 42ft (Sutton Bridge), 45ft (Bourne, Fakenham, Norwich), 46ft (Yarmouth), 47ft (South Lynn, Melton, Cromer). Bourne, South Lynn, Norwich and Yarmouth were given 60ft turntables in 1930/31. Melton Constable had a 70ft example by the 1950s, and Cromer received a 65ft turntable (from Cromer GE) as late as 1954.

Left:
A standard M&GN type water column seen in action at South Lynn in 1936. Note the post on the platform to which the jib was attached when out of use. Class C No 46 received a G7 boiler in 1915, and is seen here in final livery with restored splasher cut-outs, hauling an express passenger train. The first vehicle is an ex-LNWR brake-third, M&GN No 181.
H. C. Casserley

5. Civil Engineering

Bridges

There were over 350 numbered 'bridges' on the M&GN including the largest viaduct and the smallest culvert; many still exist and some are still in railway use. There were 366 numbers allocated but a total of 372 number positions including the duplicates 52A, 181A, 162A, 247A, 247B and 248A but due to demolition over the years the actual total never reached that figure. Before 1900 the total was 323, in 1906 it was 368, reaching a peak of 370 in 1913 and dropping to 367 by 1936.

There is no documented reference to the date of the M&GN numbering scheme. However, limits can be set by two facts: the 1903 Lowestoft line bridges are in the middle of the series; and the earliest available drawing featuring a numbered bridge is dated 1906. An anomaly is encountered in the Yarmouth area where the Barnard Avenue bridge (1913) has the number 162 without the duplicate usually assigned to later bridges, but this number was transferred from a small rolled joist underbridge near California, which was demolished at about the same time.

Bridge number plates were the well-known ellipses fastened either to the end pillars of underbridges or abutments of overbridges. Where no masonry was convenient a post or the wooden fence often nearby was used. The Lowestoft N&S line was numbered in the GER series Nos 2419-2449 with GER lozenge plates. During the LNER period similar plates were fitted to M&GN bridges at road level for easier identification.

The actual numbering was quite straightforward:

Nos 1-163 Peterborough-Yarmouth.
Nos 164-180 Yarmouth-North Gorleston Junction
Nos 182-245 Sutton Bridge Junction-Little Bytham Junction
Nos 246-289 Norwich-Melton East Junction
Nos 290-315 Melton West Junction-Cromer
Nos 317-366 Runton West Junction-North Walsham Junction

Nos 181 and 181A are missing because they were not railway bridges at all; they were road bridges built c1885 over the old and new courses of the Wensum at Lenwade on the estate of Viscount Canterbury. Bridge No 316, an elliptical brick arch, was across the approach to Cromer Beach, necessitating the tall signal box. It was demolished in 1920.

Other gaps in the numbering occurred at Nos 47, 159, 160 and 323. No 47 was a brick arch occupation bridge directly beneath South Lynn single line junction, probably demolished in the 1930 alterations. Nos 159 & 160 were timber occupation overbridges near Hemsby, dealt with later. No 323 was a lattice girder footbridge over the N&S in Felbrigg Wood which was removed to Whitwell & Reepham in 1930. Its nearby twin No 325 was demolished c1938 and its number transferred to a new concrete underline bridge at Holt ballast sidings.

Some duplicate numbers reflected the late construction of their bridges: Nos 162A (1938), 247A (1908), 247B (1922) and 248A (1932), but No 52A

which was the footbridge over the King's Lynn Dock branch at The Loke near Austin Street can only be a result of its distance from the main line, being in position from January 1884.

In addition to the numbered bridges and culverts, there were many anonymous streams and drains which crossed the line in pipes and even some small masonry and timber culverts present on the land plan which remained unnumbered, possibly because they were later filled in.

The number of examples and drawings needed for a gazetteer of M&GN bridge types is considerable, and so the information is split into sections in descending order of numerical examples: Culverts, Rolled Iron Joist Bridges, Plain Girder Bridges, Arched Masonry Bridges, Lattice Girder Bridges, Footbridges and Timber Bridges. By referring to the tables the reader can see at a glance the types to which each bridge belongs and their relative proportions, and the overall trends on each portion of the line.

Culverts

The largest class of bridge on the M&GN was the humble culvert (30% overall) but with a higher proportion on the western section; 56% as opposed to 23% of total bridges on the eastern section. Most examples are in the 3-5ft span range and over

Above:
River Glen bridge No 225 near Counter Drain. The girders of No 27 near Tydd were very similar, but on iron legs rather than masonry. The masonry of No 225 was rebuilt in concrete block in 1921. Crossing house No 105a can be seen in the distance.
Author

half listed in the bridge book (some have no note) are circular. The remainder are equally split between semicircular and rolled joist, most of the latter arising from 1912 flood repairs. Semicircular culverts can be the minimum of two or three rings of brickwork arched over a concrete invert or be miniature versions of a full semicircular bridge with vertical sides and a small parapet. Materials used could be Staffordshire blue class A engineering brick or the cheaper local red varieties; the latter particularly on the older lines.

In earlier years there were several examples of timber culverts, large beams typically 15 x 15in supported on timber piling, but the majority of these had been rebuilt by the 1930s. Indeed a number of culverts were rebuilt either using the rolled iron joist and concrete jackarch method or entirely reinforced concrete even as early as 1906, although the latter seems to be more common on the western section where there seems to have been a sweeping programme of renewals.

Rolled Iron Joist Bridges

This is the major class of what might be called 'true' bridges, 23% of eastern section structures. Western section examples were mostly as culverts; bridges Nos 6 & 9 near Eye Green and No 49 at South Lynn were the only overbridges. Both they and No 146 near Honing (1895) were unusual in having cast-iron or mild steel screens instead of brick parapet walls. Both under and overbridges are represented, roughly half-and-half overall, but with differing proportions on different sections of the line. (Fig 23.)

The rolled iron joist (RIJ) bridge appears to be the favourite of later years, bridges wrecked in the 1912 floods being replaced by them as well as some early wrought iron girder bridges. It was on the RIJ bridge that William Marriott first tried his concrete experiments, although these were more by way of protecting the iron than for any development of reinforcing. However, in his 1905 address to the Institute of Civil Engineers he made it clear he was aware of innovations in that area. He says:

'Portland cement...is one of the best antidotes to rust and deterioration of iron and steel, and for this reason it would appear probable that some kind of reinforced concrete will take a prominent place among the construction materials of the future. The Author has constructed bridges of rolled joists filled in with concrete, and has been severely criticised because there could be no examination of the iron. After nearly 20 years however, he has had the concrete cut away, and the iron has been found the same as when erected. He now makes a practice of coating all...with a layer of concrete. In fact, wherever it is possible to place concrete so that is will not break up, it has been successfully used to prevent rust and to avoid painting.'

At that time the concrete was being applied *in situ*, and it wasn't until later (c1913) that each joist was entirely enclosed in concrete before erection. With the evolution of his concrete blocks, and later a pre-cast jackarch system, bridges could now be constructed entirely from that material. Several examples appeared; No 143 (Bengate) and

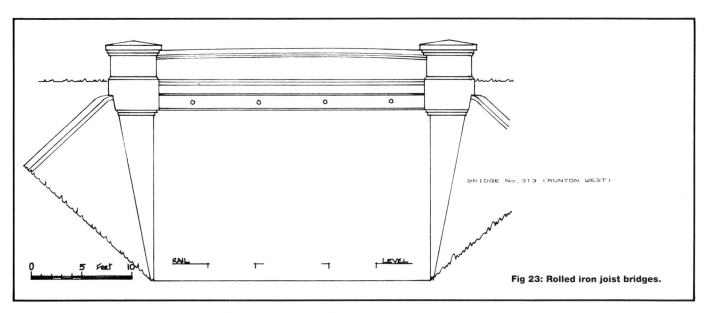

Fig 23: Rolled iron joist bridges.

No 104 (Melton Constable) being the most well known. Other bridges were built in concrete by or for Corporations: Nos 162 (1913) and 162A (1938) in Yarmouth; and Nos 247B (1922) and 248A (1932) in Norwich.

Concrete casing of the joists had been used for otherwise normal overbridges where the main concern was from the effect of sulphurous locomotive exhaust. Coats of tar and lime were applied to stave off the acid, but over many years such a hostile atmosphere must have some effect, and this can be seen at No 312 (West Runton station) where the concrete casing is falling away from the joists.

Occasionally, the joists of overbridges were given a curve or 'pre-stressed', examples of this being the bridges at Stalham and Hellesdon stations.

Most masonry of RIJ bridges was the standard blue engineering brick or for the later bridges plain or rockfaced blocks. Often parapet walls were provided, but some smaller underbridges had iron posts and rails. Spans ranged from 12 -26ft.

Girder Bridges

As a class this includes many major viaducts and large bridges on the line, but some of these are lattice girder and are dealt with later.

Ordinary 'main girder' bridges made up 18% of the eastern section total in 1899 but the new construction of 1903 and 1906, in which girder bridges featured strongly, brought the total up to 21%. Marriott was concerned about his steel bridges, observing in 1905 that they tended to rust more quickly than wrought iron, prompting his concrete coating experiments. However, after 1906 steel girders made up 60% of examples.

On the western section girder bridges were used widely to cross the many large watercourses, and made up nearly half of the total of true bridges (excluding culverts). On the eastern section girder overbridges were uncommon on the original lines except where crossed by the GER. Even No 89 where the Wells line crossed the M&GN at Fakenham was originally a brick arch, replaced in the 1898 widening. No 305 (Sheringham) was the result of the 1906 enlargements. However, there were three on the 1898 Mundesley line.

Although there were quite a few spans under 25ft, over half the examples are larger with peaks around 35, 50 and 70ft spans (Fig 24). Earlier

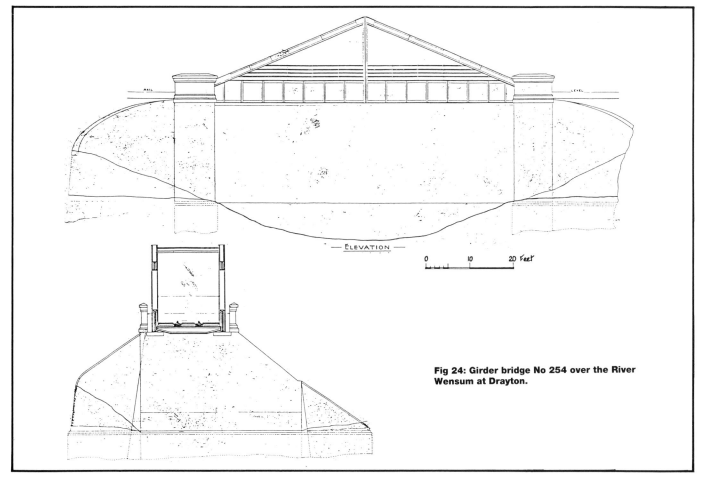

Fig 24: Girder bridge No 254 over the River Wensum at Drayton.

bridges tend to be of the 'main girder with cross-girder' construction, with either brick jackarches or longitudinal girders bearing the track. There were also some small-span examples of box girders, and trough girders with running timbers. Most of the later construction in steel featured floors made up of steel troughs filled with concrete. Masonry was mostly blue brick, although some of the earlier bridges used red brick, and probably the last girder bridge erected by the M&GN (No 158 at Hemsby in 1924) used Marriott plain faced concrete blocks, with a cast concrete number block.

Lattice girders aside, this class of bridges includes examples of what might be called viaducts. Principally these are No 1 (New England), No 170 (Vauxhall), No 225 (River Glen) and No 229 (Bourne Eau). We have a drawing for No 229 but unfortunately no dimensional information for No 225. Bridge No 170 over the approaches to the GER Yarmouth Vauxhall station

was of main girder and trough floor construction and had five skew spans; 60ft 7in, two of 34ft 8in, 66ft 4in and 37ft 2in. Bridge No 1 (also known as Rhubarb Bridge) was a steel plate girder bridge on brick abutments reconstructed in 1891/92 and widened in 1899/1900. It had four skew spans (west to east) of 65ft, 61ft, 58ft 2in and 40ft, at a skew angle of 56°, 52°, 50° and 49° respectively, being on a curve.

Masonry Bridges: Elliptical, Segmental & Semicircular Arches

One can deal with these bridges together because in a sense they are all subdivisions of the same phenomenon and are responses to certain site conditions. (Fig 25.)

The semicircular arch is ideal for a small span underbridge with no height limit. Cattle creeps or

Above left:
Toft Tunnel No 237 was the only tunnel on the M&GN proper, although there was a 'cut and cover' tunnel under the Cromer GER station on the N&SJt, coincidentally No 327.
M&GN Circle

Above:
Great Ouse bridge No 46 at South Lynn pictured after strengthening. Note the 10mph board and the fire buckets; the decking was timber. West Lynn box and gatehouse No 54 are just visible at the far end of the bridge.
Real Photos/IAL

occupation bridges of this type, although the total number is low (7%), are spread evenly throughout the eastern section except on the Y&NN and Lowestoft line. Spans are typically 9-10ft and are usually 'square'. The only example of an overbridge is the celebrated 'pop bottle' bridge (No 183) near

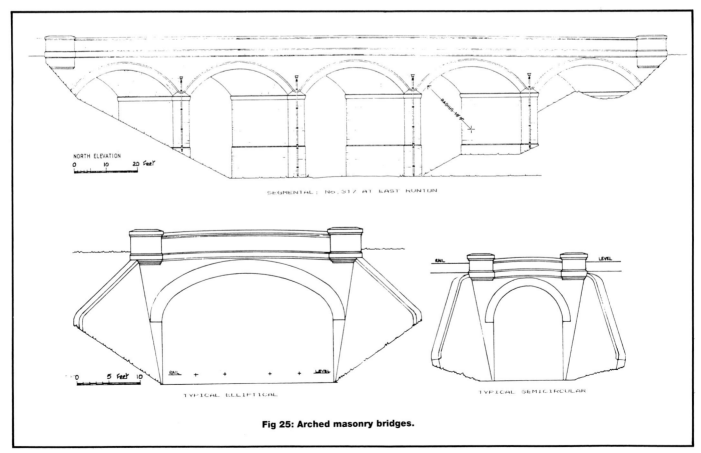

NORTH ELEVATION

0   10   20 feet

SEGMENTAL : No.317 AT EAST RUNTON

RADIUS 18' 9"

0   5 Feet   10

RAIL   LEVEL

TYPICAL ELLIPTICAL

RAIL   LEVEL

TYPICAL SEMICIRCULAR

Fig 25: Arched masonry bridges.

Long Sutton. This is an early structure in red brick with two arches and is unique on the line.

For an overbridge giving maximum loading gauge clearance for a minimum of masonry height the elliptical arch is ideal. Exactly one third of all overbridges on the eastern section are elliptical, but occur mostly on the lines built 1882-87. On the western section most of the overbridges between Little Bytham and Bourne are elliptical, but of three arches. Even Toft Tunnel is elliptical, but with a vertical major axis. Incidentally this line features nearly all the overbridges (other than footbridges) on the western section, there being only four others between Bourne, Peterborough and King's Lynn, reflecting the flatness of the landscape in that region.

The segmental type of design is useful for many applications and is particularly suited to multiple arch bridges and sites either where height is required when the arches can be raised on high piers, or where height is limited and the arch can be flattened. On the eastern section, segmental bridges make up 10% of examples, over half being overbridges. Their incidence is virtually confined to the Cromer Branch and the N&S Joint, with several three-arch examples as well as the Runton viaducts. On the western section, the PW&SB and L&SB lines have some examples, particularly the cattle creeps on the Wisbech line, and the original bridge at South Lynn. Otherwise the only other is Lound Viaduct (No 239) and here the arches are wide enough to become nearly semicircular. The structure was found to be settled over one arch (in the 1920s I believe), and the parapets were replaced with concrete bricks during the repair work. The crack has since reappeared. Interestingly the same thing occurred at No 350, a segmental bridge near Knapton on the N&S, and in 1926 the arch was replaced by joists in concrete and concrete jackarches. In its original state it is featured in Fig 103 of Ronald Clark's *Short History*.

Lattice Girder Bridges

The actual number of bridges in this class is tiny compared to the whole, but since they are physically large they require a separate treatment. The bridges concerned are: No 32 (Cross Keys), No 46 (West Lynn), No 155 (Potter Heigham), No 168 (Bure), No 172 (Breydon), No 201 (Welland), No 216 (South Drove) and Midland No 43 (Bytham). Although the latter is not strictly an M&GN bridge, it is a major feature of the line and worthy of inclusion.

Cross Keys bridge is so well known that little need be written about it. Completed in 1897, it is the third successive bridge at the site. The lattice swing span is 168ft 6in long, asymmetrically pivoted so that the longer half over the navigable channel is 99ft 3in. The bridge is approached from the east on two plain girder spans: 50ft from the abutment and 70ft to the east pier. The bridge has recently been rebuilt, having the overhead control room and end braces raised to allow heavy lorry traffic more headroom. (Fig 26.)

West Lynn bridge, the M&GN's '*bête-noir*', was completed in 1864 by Waring & Eckersley. The design was suspect from the first — the bridge had to be strengthened by order of the Board of Trade, and this work was always coming loose. Marriott remarks that the 15:1 ratio of its girders was one rarely adopted in modern practice. I suspect he was being diplomatic. By 1894 the thing was in an appalling state, so Marriott carried out his clever strengthening and replacement work, well documented elsewhere. The main girders had to be unbent as much as two inches from their buckled condition. Much is made of the probable £40,000 saved by this work, but in the light of the £80,000 the joint partners were willing to spend of Cross

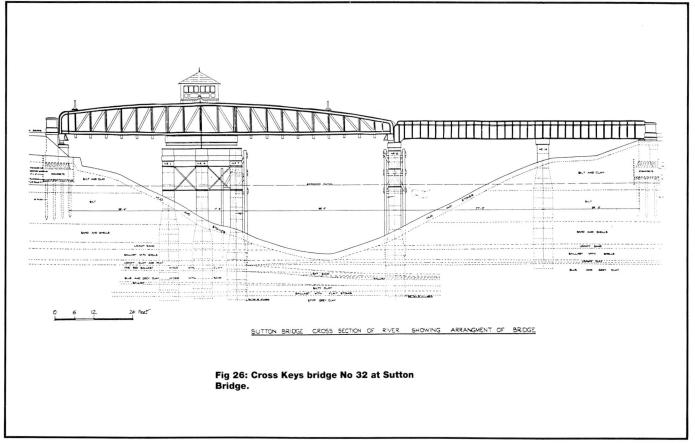

SUTTON BRIDGE   CROSS SECTION OF RIVER   SHOWING   ARRANGMENT OF   BRIDGE

Fig 26: Cross Keys bridge No 32 at Sutton Bridge.

Left:
Breydon Bridge No 172 viewed from the southwest bank in 1931.
LGRP

Keys bridge, I am surprised that they allowed bridge No 46 to remain. The bridge consisted of three central spans of 117ft and two end spans of 70ft each. Each pier was formed of two groups of five 18 screw piles, the heads being braced together by cast-iron distributing girders.

The Potter Heigham bridge was of three pairs of trussed girders each 79ft long 15ft 6in high (centre to centre), arranged as through girders with overhead bracing. It has been quoted that the bridge was bought second-hand but Marriott merely says it was built for the Y&NN by the Stockton Forge Co in 1879. This bridge also required strengthening work, all connections being deficient in rivet area, and the cross-girders being too shallow. This was carried out in 1894.

The Yarmouth Bure viaduct was really three bridges in one, having to cross two roads as well as the river. The main 117ft span was a pair of trussed girders arranged as a through girder accommodating the double line, braced with lattice girders overhead, concrete-filled troughs forming the floor. The east approach was over a 20ft plain girder and trough span, and from the west a 30ft span of the same type. The entire structure was skewed at an angle of 52°.

Breydon Viaduct could be considered the flagship of M&GN engineering. Designed by Marriott and his assistant Mr Gribble in 1899 under the nominal supervision of Mr Alexander Ross of the GN, the bridge was opened in 1903 at a cost of £65,131 6s 2d and became a local landmark. From the north, the swing span of 169ft 8in was approached over three spans of 169ft 10in, all 24ft high. The last span to the south shore of Breydon Water was 110ft 6in and 16ft high. Three inches expansion was allowed between adjacent girders. The line over the bridge was single and so North and South signalboxes were provided (M&GN type 1a) to control the change from double line, interlocked with the control turret atop the swing span. The swing span was pivoted on a central ball-bearing and rollers running on a circular path. An 11hp gas engine turned the span (habitually anticlockwise) via two vertical shafts with bevel gears engaging with a toothed circular rack fixed to the outside of the roller path. River traffic had the priority and the bridge was kept open except to pass a train. Closed to trains in 1953, it was demolished in 1962.

Unfortunately I have no dimensional information regarding No 201 over the River Welland at Spalding. This bridge was erected in 1893 to replace the earlier single line bridge.

The Little Bytham bridge, No 43 in the Midland series numbered from Saxby Junction, was also a magnificent structure, spanning 97ft 6in across the GNR main line. Although removed in 1964, its abutments are still visible and there is a pile of the hugh parapet stones a little way up the former line to Saxby.

Footbridges

On the eastern section, the footbridges fall into three categories which are apparently chronologically separated. The earliest type was the 'braced girder' footbridge: No 52A (Austin St), No 79 (Massingham), No 129 (Aylsham), No 139 (North Walsham), No 256 (Drayton) and No 275 (Whitwell & Reepham). This design could be L&F or E&M. Originally the entire bridge was wooden, but eventually (c1900) the main girders were replaced by thin section steel, leaving only the wooden stairways. Indeed at North Walsham there seems to have been a programme of gradual replacement of components. The wood palings along the walkway were replaced by an iron hoop-top fence and some of the wood cross-bracing was replaced by wire, before the whole girder was renewed in steel. This last item was probably for sighting the Up starter from the signalbox.

The span was generally 43ft 6in. No 275 was replaced in 1930 and No 256 was reused by BR alongside the main road bridge at Drayton until closure of the City goods line. One of these bridges survives as the footbridge over the Bure Valley line at Coltishall.

Above left:
Welland Bridge No 201 in Spalding pictured looking east from the footbridge. Gatehouse No 102 is just visible over the left hand girder. Note the concrete bracket signal, and the original pattern crossing gates (with LNER roundels added).
E. L. Back/M. Back

Left:
Little Bytham bridge, Midland No 43, crossed over the GN main line. Although carrying double track, only one was a running line.
Author's collection

The second design of footbridge appeared at Fakenham in 1894 (No 86) and subsequently at Sheringham (No 306, 1897), Mundesley (No 345, 1898) and South Lynn (No 48, 1901). This design consisted of a steel trellis girder with angled arch. The example at Sheringham was doubled in length, probably in 1907. Spans were: Fakenham 33ft 4in and Mundesley 43ft 3in. Sheringham had arched stanchions over the walkway, and South Lynn had an arched corrugated iron roof.

The third type again had a trellis girder, but this time with curved arch. It seems to have been based on the GER type of footbridge but the construction was different as the girders were supported by a simple lattice tower instead of cast-iron columns. Both were on the N&S Joint (Nos 323 & 325) near Felbrigg. No 323 was moved to Whitwell & Reepham in 1930 to replace the L&F/E&M bridge No 275. Their span was 38ft 4in.

The N&SJt Lowestoft line had standard GER lattice footbridges. All were supported on cast-iron columns except at Gorleston-on-Sea which was on brick abutments, and all were fitted with arched corrugated iron roofs which were connected to the platform canopies. These roofs were later removed. Today, an example of the GE footbridge can be seen at Weybourne (North Norfolk Railway).

On the western section the footbridges seem to resolve themselves into two general types: Midland and another trellis design based on the GNR type. No 25 at Wisbech (1892) and No 31 at Sutton Bridge were both standard Midland.

The other examples all appear to date from early M&GN times. In June 1893 Maj-Gen Hutchinson, for the Board of Trade, required footbridges at Bourne, Austerby Road, Twenty, Cuckoo Junction and Hawthorn Bank. In October 1894 a tender was accepted from Messrs Handyside & Co of Derby for the footbridges at Bourne, Austerby Road and Hawthorn Bank. The long bridge at Green Lane, Spalding (No 205) dates from 1896, and Welland Bank (No 202) also probably dates from then. All these examples had trellis girders on cast-iron columns, except for No 205 which had special trellis towers. As Bourne station was GNR property, the footbridge there was No 6 in their sequence. Footbridge No 233 just beyond Bourne West had tall brick piers.

Timber Bridges

As well as the original station footbridge, the eastern section at one time boasted four timber overbridges. Nos 159 & 160 were both occupation bridges erected by the Y&NN near Hemsby station. They were really composite bridges because although the piers, handrails and braces were timber, the main span was rolled iron joist. No 160 was demolished in 1922, and No 159 in 1924.

The other two timber bridges were footbridges near Melton. No 103 'Belle Vue' gave access to the plantation of that name owned by Lord Hastings, and No 295 at Hunworth on the Cromer line was for the convenience of Lord Rothermere's estate. Both still exist and are essentially the same simple beam and trestle construction.

Painting

Marriott advocated one or two coats of high quality iron oxide applied by brush over cleaned iron or steel, with all rust burned or sand blasted away, and a thick top coat of paint containing at least 90% white lead.

Bridges over waterways were left white. Other iron or steel bridges were brown, similar to the wagon colour. In the period before 1914, footbridges were painted the standard station brown with the latticework painted 'stone'. Underneath spans tar varnish was used, and concrete was treated with alternate coats of tar and lime.

M&GN BRIDGES

Builder	Culverts	Rolled Joist	Girder	Masonry Bridges Ellipitl.	Segmntl.	Semiclr.	Others
Eastern Section							
Y&NN	147	140o	138				159o d24
	148	141o	143r				160o d33
	149	142o	144				
	150 d36	145o	155xxx				
	152	146or	161				
	153	151or					
	154	157r					
	156	158or					
		162 d10					
L&F	75 77	76o	78	96o	89or	94	103
	83 87	80o	81	102o	255	98	
	90 91	85o	82	257o		100	
	92 93	104o	84	260o		263	
	95 97	250o	88	262o		264	
	99 246	251	101or	278o		266	
	248 252	253	247		288		
	259 268	258o	249				
	269 271	270o	254				
	272 273	274	261r				
	277 280	276r	265				
	282 285	279	267				
	286 287	281	283				
	289	284					
E&M	55	58	53	59o	133	110r	52Afb
	57	63	54	60o	301	122	79fb
	62	69o	56	71o	302o	124	129fb
	65	70o	61	72o	304o	293	139fb
	67	105o	64r	109o	311o	294	256fb
	74	107	66	111o	314		275fb
	106	108r	68r	112o			295
	113	114	73	115o			
	117	116	126	119o			
	118	135	132r	120o			
	125	136	137o	121o			
	127	181	303	123o			
	134	181A	307	128o			
	290	291	308	130o			
	300	292		131o			
	309	297o		296o			
		310		298o			
		312o		299o			
		313o		305or			
				315o			
				316od20			

Builder	Culverts	Rolled Joist	Girder	Masonry Bridges Elliptl.	Segmntl.	Semiclr.	Others
M&GN and **N&SJt**	169	163	165	355o	317	179	86fb
	173	164	166	361o	319	318	306fb
	175	329o	167		320o	333	323fbd30
	176	330	168xxx		321o	336	325fbd38
	178	331	170		322	357	345fb
	347	332o	171		326o	359	247fb
	363	334o	172xxx		327T		
		337o	174		328		
		341o	177		335		
		353o	180		338o		
		362o	324		339o		
		162o	344o		340		
		162Ao	349		342o		
		247Bo	352o		343o		
		248Ao	354o		346		
			356		348		
			358		350r		
			360		351		
			364				
			365				
			366				
M&GN Rebuilds	325	64	89o				323fb
		68	108				
		101o	157				
		110	158o				
		132	261				
		143	276				
		146o	305o				
		350					
		151o					

Western Section

Builder	Culverts	Rolled Joist	Girder	Masonry Bridges Elliptl.	Segmntl.	Semiclr.	Others
N&SR	182		201xxxr			183o	
	184		203r				
	185						
	186						
	187						
	188						
	189						
	190						
	191						
	192						
	193						
	194						
	195						
	196						
	197						
	198						
	199						
	200						
	204						
S&BR	215		216xxxr				
	218		217r				
	219		223r				
	220		225r				
	221		229r				
	222						
	224						
	226						
	227						
	228						
	230						
	231						
L&SB	33		32r		47 d30		
	34		46xxx		49or		
	35		51				
	36		52				
	37						
	38						
	39						
	40						
	41						
	42						

Builder	Culverts	Rolled Joist	Girder	Masonry Bridges Elliptl.	Segmntl.	Semiclr.	Others
	43						
	44						
	45						
	50						
PW&SR	4	6o	1		3		
	5	9o	2		7		
	11		13		8		
	12		15		10		
	14		16		29		
	17		27				
	18		28				
	19						
	20						
	21						
	22						
	23						
	24						
	26						
	30						
M&GN after 1889	206	49o	207	234o	239		25fb
	208		211	235o			31fb
	209		213	236o			48fb
	210		32xxx	237T			202fb
	212		201xxx	238o			205fb
	241		203	240o			214fb
			216xxx	242o			232fb
			217	243o			233fb
			223	244o			
			225	245o			
			229				

KEY TO SYMBOLS

o	overbridge	T	tunnel
fb	station footbridge	r	rebuilt
xxx	lattice girder	d10	demolished 19__

Fencing

Fencing is detailed in the contract between Wilkinson & Jarvis and the Great Yarmouth & Stalham Light Railway as follows: 'The posts of good sound wood shall be six feet apart, and if round four inches in diameter; if rectangular 4x3 inches and seven feet long. There shall be seven strands of strong bullock wire laid longitudinally as the Engineer may direct.' That this was the fencing erected is confirmed by Marriott who observed: 'The fencing was composed of pit-props and wire'. No tensioning method was mentioned but the wire was probably simply fixed on to diagonally-braced posts as seen in a photograph of a Y&NN train on Potter Heigham bridge.

During M&GN days the fence posts in common with most other railways became disused sleepers sawn to between 3 or 4.5 x 4in, and this remained the most common trackside fencing despite later developments. The standard number of wire strands had now become eight: 4in from top to first wire, two at 9in, one at 8in, 7in, 6in, 5in and 5in spacing. Sometimes the lower five were supported in between the main posts by small section stub posts, and from the later E&M period the top strand was often barbed wire. Tensioning was achieved by the use of special bent and bolted strip iron posts equipped with toothed spindles which could no doubt be turned with a handle or a spanner until the wire, secured by being passed through a hole in the spindle, was at the required tension. The spindle was then retained by a small spigot engaged in the teeth. Spacing of these posts seems to be roughly every 150yd. Terminal posts (where the wire fencing ends or has to turn a corner) were often these tension or 'strainer' posts with only the one required brace, but could also be whole sleepers with sawn tops and diagonal bracing, as shown in the accompanying drawing. (Fig 27.)

Whole sleepers sometimes appeared in the ordinary fencing runs, probably as stabilisers between the strainer posts, many of them the old contractor's half-round sleepers, still bearing the spikes in some cases. At one time they may have been more widespread; on the Up side of the line near Felmingham there are groups of these sleepers which may be the remains of a run of considerable length. The half-round sleepers were also used as close-boarded fencing where required; there are good stretches of this at Gatehouse No 53 on Kelling Heath and behind White Swan Yard on the Yarmouth Union Line. The sleepers are jammed side-by-side with the rounded surface, rail and spike marks on the public face, and linked by timber rails behind.

The more common type of close-boarded fence was of creosoted 7in x 1in boards on a 6in x 6in post and triangular rail frame with alternate boards 4in shorter than their neighbours. Total height was variable, commonly being over six feet to restrict public view and access. An alternative, seen at Cromer and Sheringham, was merely to 'dog-tooth' the top of each board, two teeth per board. The drawing illustrates both types.

Use of reinforced concrete for fence posts is said to have been introduced in 1909. The first design was round-topped and 4.5 x 4in with cham-

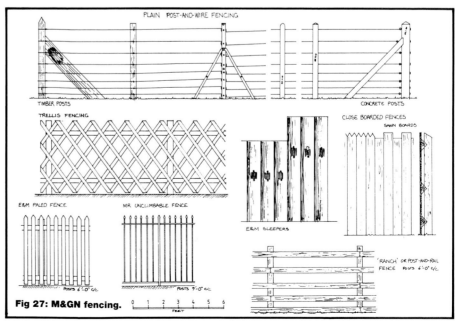

Fig 27: M&GN fencing.

Above:

Standard concrete loading gauge seen at Holt; the original timber examples were similar, and topped with a signal finial. Note the gauge plate on the post. This also provides a good view of Holt's complex layout.
M&GN Circle

Above:

An experimental installation of concrete products alongside the Yarmouth line at Melton: the bracket signal has the early 'plate' bracing and the telegraph pole is of triangular section.
M&GN Circle

Runs of concrete posts could last for anything up to a mile before reverting to timber posts, but there were longer stretches. The major installation period of all types appears to have been between 1921 and 1925.

Of all public fencing, the trellis, lattice or criss-cross sawn timber fence is perhaps the most famous M&GN feature. It can be shown to be present in E&M days at least at Cromer, but in general it appears from photos that a normal vertical paling fence similar to an MR design was mostly used in those days. However, its use must have increased quite swiftly as by c1900 most stations on the eastern section featured it. The angle of the lattice in general varied from 48° to 53° but the late Bill Robinson measured an example at Sutton Bridge with a 60° separation. As this example had concrete posts it may represent a later form or be an isolated phenomenon.

The trellis fencing, despite the use of sawn sleepers for its construction, must have been extravagant in the use of materials and so where public impressions mattered less a simple post-and-rail fence of 4sq in posts and five 4in x 1in boards was employed. This commonly occurred on the approaches to bridges and a great deal survives today. Some sites, for example the new Hemsby bridge No 158 approaches of 1924, have concrete posts slotted to receive each rail.

Before the advent of the trellis fence the 3in x 1in wrought vertical paling fence with sawn tops saw almost universal application, mostly with saw-tooth tops, but a round top could be seen at Long Sutton and perhaps elsewhere. This was the only timber fencing to be painted. It survived at several stations, eg Sheringham, for many years.

The Midland metal 'unclimbable' fence appeared at Eye Green and Wisbech and probably other stations on the Peterborough line. However, no MR diagonal fencing ever seemed to appear, except for some inexplicable reason in a home-grown form at West Runton.

Gates

General and occupation crossing gates were of a standard five-bar type. Each 12ft gate was divided into two bays by a central vertical member and each bay braced by a diagonal. Gateposts were of square section timber rounded at the top, main posts being 12sq in and closing posts 9in. Corners were chamfered and gates and posts were painted white. Gates on public road level crossings operated by hand were originally of this simple type in pairs, but in many cases they were replaced later by the larger gates described below.

Mechanically-operated level crossing gates were of a very attractive and distinctive design. The top and bottom rails were joined by vertical struts dividing the gate into a series of rectangles which were cross-braced, forming a series of triangles. The last triangle of each gate was occupied by the warning board, at first solid but at a later date the central portion was cut away leaving only the outer few inches. Closely-spaced vertical iron rods fenced the open spaces. Gateposts were large square section timber, chamfered and finished off with a low pyramidal cap. Tall posts and iron tie rods were not generally used except for unusually long gates, for example Dogsthorpe.

Public crossing gates were fitted with gate-lamps showing a red light to the front and green lights to each side, and lampcases were black. Woodwork was painted white with black ironwork and red 'target'.

In the 1920s almost all gateposts were replaced by cast concrete ones. General posts imitated the

fered corners, and pierced to accept the eight strands of wire. Some examples of this early type are to be seen at Aylsham and over Kelling Heath. All posts were dated; the Aylsham examples of 23.2.16 are still in good condition.

From personal observation it seems it was in January 1919 that a second design was introduced. Of the same dimensions as before but without the chamfers, these posts had pyramidal tops. However, it seems that it was produced simultaneously with the earlier type until at least 1925. Round-top posts cease to be dated by 1925, and all dating appears to have been abandoned after that year.

Concrete strainer posts were of thicker section (6in x 5in). The earliest examples were single-sided and used at the end of runs, with the iron posts in mid-run. They were diagonally braced with a socket to accept the 4in x 4in raking post which was slotted to allow the wire to pass through. It appears that about 1921 an experiment was made with free-standing strainer posts of thicker section (8in x 6in), with no raking posts. The toothed spindles were held in position by iron straps bolted to the sides of the posts. Mid-run posts had the spindles on alternating sides. All the strainer posts seem to have had pyramidal tops and bore the circular 'MRC' trademark.

Later replacements of concrete posts in LNER days appear to be wholly of tapering round-topped posts of inferior moulding. Although pierced to accept the wire, these later posts are usually added to the inside of the wire run with the holes at a right angle to it, and then a short piece of wire threaded through and twisted to secure each main strand.

Left:

Typical E&M buffer stops, fabricated from flat-bottom rail, seen here at Holt.
M&GN Circle

timber ones being round-topped and chamfered. Posts for the large crossing gates were at first an exact copy of the timber type, but this was soon changed to an elegant design featuring recessed panels on each face and a domed cap.

During the LNER/BR period damaged or broken gates were often replaced by gates of a different pattern giving rise to odd pairs. The old sidelight lamps were also discontinued and replaced by standard red-painted LNER lamps.

Lineside Posts

Mileposts were originally wooden, and at their bases featured an area of painted stones with a shape indicative of each quarter of the mile shown on the post. The mile was shown by a small cast-iron circular plate on a thin post with a circular area of stones, the quarter mile posts had two boards set in a 'vee' to show a face to each direction of running, with the relevant quarter painted on. The quarter had a triangle of stones at the base, the half had a diamond, the three-quarter had a square. From c1916 a start was made on replacing wooden posts with concrete ones, which were triangular in section with the mileage shown in a rectangular recess on two faces. 'M&GN' or 'N&S' or the quarters in Roman numerals were cast below the mileage. Contrary to the notes in the *Railway Year Book*, mileposts were generally sited on the Down side of the line. (Fig 28.)

Gradient posts were also originally wooden, round-topped with each finger board morticed into the post. The elegant concrete design from 1916 imitated them and at first added a knob finial, later omitted. Gradient posts were generally sited on the Up side of the line.

Speed limit signs were ellipses of enamelled iron on a wooden backing approx. 3ft x 2ft on a 4in post about 5ft off the ground. The border, large sanserif figures and small 'MILES AN HOUR' were enamelled the standard light red on white. The rest was black.

Boundary posts were used to denote ownership of lands outside the line of fencing. There were several variations but by far the most common were those pressed from a piece of reclaimed bullhead rail. The result was a round, flat area embossed with 'M&' 'GN' in two lines, merging into the old rail. Another common post was the Parish Boundary. This small item was specially cast with a cruciform stem, a flat inclined head cast with 'PB' and a small face at the rear cast 'M&GN'.

Telegraph poles were standard pitch pine with gabled metal rain caps, but at stations finials were often fitted. A simple arrangement of two or three crossbars with an insulator at each end was generally used and sufficient for the small number of wires needed for the Tyers system. At more complex locations with more wires very tall posts with many crossbars were used. Multiples of insulators on the same crossbar were rare. One of the experiments with Marriott's concrete system was to install reinforced concrete telegraph poles. Sheringham was equipped with rectangular section poles, the egg-shaped holes revealing their similarity to the signal posts.

Where overbridges crossed the line the telegraph wires were terminated at insulators bracketed to the abutments. The insulated wires were then stapled along the abutments under the span to a similar bracket on the far side. Telegraph poles were generally on the Up side of the line, except from Melton to Cromer and Yarmouth-Lowestoft, where, because of reversal of direction, they were on the Down side.

Loading gauges were present at most stations, being the usual 'gibbet' arrangement in timber with a signal-type finial. The gauge bar was suspended from an adjustable chain, the end ring

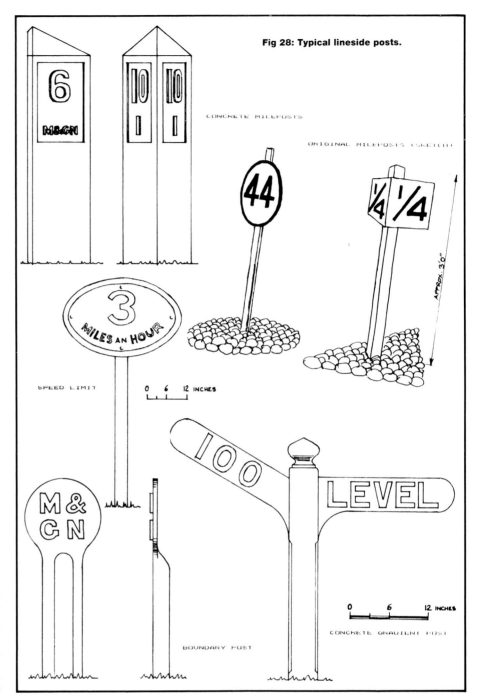

Fig 28: Typical lineside posts.

being placed over hooks on a cast iron gauge plate. Both M&GN and N&SJt dimensions were:

* Max width over 3ft 6in from rail   9ft 3in
* Max height in centre from rail   13ft 9in
* Max height at side from rail   10ft 9in

Most of the timber examples were replaced in concrete, the posts being pierced like the signal posts.

Permanent Way

The Western section, being built under the auspices of the Midland and the Great Northern railways, was supplied originally with bullhead rail and chairs, the PW&S and L&SB having Midland inside-keyed track which survived at some locations both as sidings and on the main line until the 1900s.

On the eastern section the original permanent way was 70lb flat-bottom wrought iron rails in 25ft lengths spiked on to 9in x 4.5in half-round sleepers, ballasted with sand. Although upgraded in E&M days with 70lb steel flat-bottom rail spiked on to rectangular sleepers ballasted with local gravel, the track remained relatively light at the formation of the M&GN.

A re-laying campaign was started immediately, and the GN being responsible for permanent way their design of 'four-bolt' chair and 85lb bullhead rail in 30ft lengths was used. Each chair was cast with the date and 'M&GN'. However, although all running lines and some heavily-used sidings were relaid, many ordinary sidings were left undisturbed and survived in their flat-bottom state until much later or in some cases until closure. The last line to be relaid was the Cromer branch in 1906. The N&SJt lines were laid from new in chaired track. After Grouping 'three-bolt' chairs were introduced.

Pointwork was laid according to GN standards and a Diagram Book was produced from GN drawings in 1914. In 1906 Marriott had developed a special joint-supporting chair and strengthened fishplate to reduce the weakness associated with rail joints. Presumably this saw widespread application but it is not known to what extent. An example was recovered from the Cromer branch in 1981.

Marriott also designed a reinforced concrete sleeper in c1916 with the chair actually part of the casting. By 1922 this part of the design had been dropped so that normal chairs could be fitted. It is not known to what extent these sleepers were used on the M&GN's permanent way.

Point hand levers generally seem to have been a simple weighted 'throw over' type, usually painted white. A variant seen at Melton combined the weighted arm with a vertical hand lever. Other types seen were a straight vertical lever, with and without guardrail, but these may have been later examples.

Point rodding was round section linked by bell cranks and carried by cast-iron rodding stools on rough timber stands. Compensators, restoring rod movement lost through long runs of rodding stools, were mounted vertically inside a timber box and sunk into the ground. All rodding was painted brown. Signal wires were carried on pulleys mounted on small stub posts. Corners were turned by the use of large pulleys, over which the wire was replaced by chain. Marriott brought his attention to all these small details and rodding stools, signal wire stubs and crank support beams were all produced in concrete at Melton in the 1920s.

Bufferstops on the western section were mainly made up of standard GN or MR rail-built types, although there were some earth-filled boarded examples. On the eastern section most stops were survivals from the E&M period and were made up from flat-bottomed rail. Free-standing stops were made up by cleverly cutting and bolting up to four lengths of rail side by side to form the verticals, braced from the front only. The buffer beam was two or more lengths of rail mounted with the heads forward. Most other examples were earth-filled enclosures boarded with old sleepers and braced internally and externally with flat-bottom rail. The buffer beams were again rail as described above. Later some standard GN types appeared but most of the older ones survived until closure.

As was standard with all railway formations, the slope of embankments and cuttings was 1.5:1 or approximately 33.7°. At no point did the M&GN pass through rock or other material that would allow steeper slopes, and at only one place were retaining walls needed: at Yarmouth on the Lowestoft Junction line from Nelson Road crossing to bridge No 165 over Caister Road. Single line earthworks at formation level were generally 15ft 6in and double line 31ft on embankments and 32ft in cuttings.

Drainage, although essential, was not an obvious item usually only being seen as a grating at the trackside. However, in cuttings in the Cromer area of the M&GN and on the N&SJt Mundesley line, brick manholes were built up above track level. Sometimes they were arranged opposite one another on each side of the line and sometimes alternately; spacing was approximately 50yd.

Cast-iron Signs

Most of the usual M&GN iron signs are well known, although the Joint's apparent willingness to cast one-offs probably means there are unique examples yet to be discovered. The drawing shows only a representative selection. (Fig 29.)

Five types of 'TRESPASSERS' board have been identified but only two designs were common, variations being mainly in the size of the 'By Order' signs.
* i) 'NOTICE' (illustrated) was the most common, but not found beyond Bourne.
* ii) 'BY ORDER' (illustrated) occurred on the ex-PW&S line.
* iii) 'BY ORDER', slightly smaller with condensed lettering, beyond Bourne.
* iv) 'BY ORDER', squarer (about 27in x 17in) seen near Fakenham and probably elsewhere on the eastern section.
* v) 'WARNING TO TRESPASSERS' a rarer type found on the western section and 27in x 15in.

A common notice associated with trespassers boards at almost every public or occupation crossing was 'BEWARE OF TRAINS'. This design was lifted straight from the Midland and may even have been supplied by them. The weighbridge and fire bucket signs were reproduced at stations all over the system, but the only known example of the anti-drink notice was at Trimingham.

Signs associated with bridges were the weight restriction notices and of course the bridge number plate. The weight restriction notices apparently were not very common but at least four locations with weights of 5, 8 and 10 tons are known. Some N&SJt bridges had GER diamond signs. The bridge number plates were an interesting design, there being individual ellipses for each increase in number size (1-9, 10-99, 100-199, 200-366). Note the slope to the 297 which seems to be typical of this series. Bolt holes vary between sides or top and bottom apparently according to the structure to which the plate was fixed. During the LNER period, small lozenge-shaped number plates were fixed to bridges at the roadside. Another plate associated with bridges was the 'STICK NO BILLS' whose favourite haunt was the abutments of road underbridges.

A feature of occupation crossings were the 'SHUT THIS GATE' plates, with 'ANY PERSON WHO OMITS TO SHUT AND FASTEN THIS GATE / IS LIABLE TO A PENALTY NOT EXCEEDING FORTY SHILLINGS' as an alternative. It appears that 70% of gate notices between Lynn and Melton were the latter type but beyond Melton there were, in February 1936, only three, all the other many hundreds of examples being 'SHUT THIS GATE'. A unique alternative at Beeston crossing near Sheringham was 'USERS OF THIS LEVEL CROSSING ARE EARNESTLY REQUESTED TO CLOSE THE GATES', possibly a survivor from the earlier period.

Associated with crossings were the 'WHISTLE' boards, but these were quite rare, there being only 10 crossings thus protected and, of these, two near Honing were so close together that perhaps only one pair of boards were provided. To be protected by whistle boards it seems a crossing had to be a frequently-used lane or footpath positioned on or near a curve. There may have been other applications but unfortunately none of the land plans or track surveys show them.

The positions of underline pipes were denoted by elliptical plates very similar to the bridge plates on which the size of the pipe(s) was shown in large figures with 'INCHES' below in smaller letters.

Colours in the early M&GN period were white on black, changing to black on white after c1910. Black on yellow was used for other restriction notices, and white on red for fire bucket and whistle boards.

Marriott Reinforced Concrete

Throughout the 19th century concrete was used increasingly in its simple massive form or in blocks, for example the walls of the Alexandra Docks (1869) in Lynn or Caister station (1876), but it was not until the 1880s that experiments were made with reinforcement in Britain using primitive rods. Reinforced concrete (RC) in its true form was developed in the 1890s in France. However, it seems from contemporary engineering reports from all over the world that the new material was still little understood and most of what was called 'reinforced concrete' was only strengthened massive concrete. The advantages of a welded cage of steel reinforcement were not generally grasped except by individuals like William Marriott and it seems it was his development and patenting of such methods of reinforcing that was his major contribution to the advancement of RC in this country.

As mentioned in the introduction, the young Marriott joined the staff of Wilkinson & Jarvis in 1881, constructing the Y&NN and L&F in Norfolk. Here he found buildings erected in concrete block and bridges constructed using massive concrete infilling, and became an enthusiast for the material. By 1885 he was experimenting with concrete coating as a method of rust prevention on iron and steel girders. He was also aware of developments on the continent and so he was in the right frame of mind to attempt his own RC when it became expedient. Factors influencing his decision were

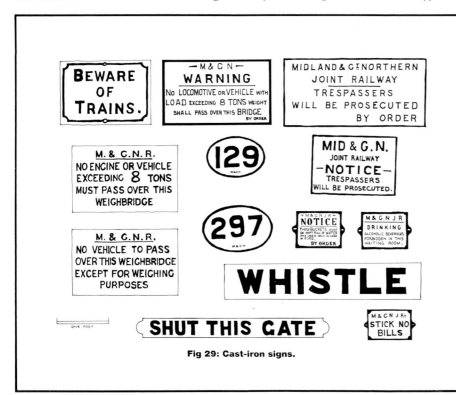

Fig 29: Cast-iron signs.

Above:
Bengate Bridge No 143, near Honing, was constructed from standard Marriott concrete components. Note the post and rail fence, typical of bridge approaches.
Author's collection

probably a combination of economy measures, availability of materials and the shortage of timber during World War 1. Certainly the knowledge that by using the large quantities of sand and gravel available on railway land at Kelling and Holt to make components which would save money by virtue of their cheapness, durability and maintenance-free life must have made RC a very attractive option.

Marriott's first foray into true reinforcing was the fencepost, an ideal subject for multiple prefabrication. The first type was round-topped and bevel-edged and pierced with holes to accept the wire. The reinforcing cage was of simple ^{3}/8in hooped mild steel rods joined by ^{1}/8in crosswires and gas-welded. The earliest the author has examined dates from February 1916, but they were apparently produced from 1909.

The pinnacle of achievement for Marriott Reinforced Concrete as it was registered and stamped, must be represented by the evolution of the RC signal post which was taken up by several other railways, in particular the GN and LNWR. Using the experience gained from the fenceposts the first RC signal post was erected in 1915, positioned on the Down Cromer line from Melton West Junction. The first design had pierced holes extending right to the top of the post, the holes being of squarer outline than that used later. A finial was provided, possibly also in concrete. Before the final form was evolved the design passed through an intermediate stage. The first bracketed signal post was probably the Melton East Down starter, incorporating GN-type ironwork in the bracket. Later a simple concrete beam was supported by two bolted brackets, apparently thin concrete plates. These earlier examples used thicker section posts and the squarer hole, but the final design had a slenderer section with egg-shaped holes. Strategic areas were left solid for metalwork, pivots and so on, and by alteration of these both Midland and GN signals could be accommodated. A simple pyramidal cap

was now standard. This final design of bracket signal was particularly clever and elegant, incorporating simple bolted half-joints to unite a main post, beam and doll post(s). The walkways were made up of a simple repeated component saddled and bolted over the beam. Thus a handful of components could be quickly assembled, be more durable than timber and would not require painting. Marriott co-operated with Ellis & Sons of Leicester to produce signal posts for other railways under licence; use of these timber-free items could be particularly attractive to railways in tropical countries.

In parallel with RC work ordinary concrete items were being developed. By 1913 a concrete block system had been evolved and was used thereafter for several new bridges and many culverts as well as most new M&GN architecture. The blocks evolved into a complex series; rock-faced and plain blocks of various thicknesses, corner blocks with raised quoins, cornice and bevelled string course blocks, parapets, number blocks and so on, all based on a module of 18in x 9in. A larger rock-faced block based on a 27in x 9in module could be used for platform walls, and quadrant blocks were used for circular or round-ended bridge piers. The module lines followed the centre of the mortar joints and so the actual dimensions were half an inch smaller. Concrete bricks of normal size were also produced.

From 1916 concrete activity at Melton increased significantly, rising to a peak in 1922. It was during this period that most of the familiar concrete items first appeared. Mileposts, unreinforced at first, began to replace the old timber ones, apparently starting at zero in 1916 and working up the numbers, reaching the 20s by 1920, the 30s by 1921 and the 40s in 1922. It appears that 'M&GN' was originally intended to be cast on all posts whether whole numbers or number and quarters, but this was quickly dropped from the quarter-mile posts to give a less cramped layout. The quarters were depicted by Roman numerals.

Also in 1916 the first type of gradient post with knob finial appeared. The arms imitated the timber posts they replaced. No doubt the same methodical replacement was instituted as with mileposts but because the gradient posts were much more numerous, a great many date from after 1925 and are thus not date-stamped. The finial was soon dropped.

By 1922 rodding stools, crank beams, various gateposts, platform fencing posts, sleepers, inspection pit sleepers, permanent way length markers, telegraph poles and window frames had all made their débuts. A new type of fencepost with pyramidal top and no bevelling was introduced in 1919, manufactured in parallel with the round-topped post. Gateposts also saw a change; the hingeposts were still 12in square, but the clapping posts now became a smaller 9in version of the same, replacing the octagonal section used formerly.

The famous concrete nameboards also appeared during this period. On these early examples the letters were actually moulded separately in a brown coloured concrete and then incorporated into the main board. The later design which was reproduced all over the system did not use this method; the letters were plainly moulded. A decorative beading on the posts was also dropped. These nameboards were adopted by the GN and LNER for several stations.

As mentioned above, many buildings were erected in concrete or refaced in blocks, including stations, crossing houses and ground-frame huts. Bridges used the blocks, plain or rock-faced, as the loadbearing masonry, but reinforced beams never seem to have been used. All examples appear to have been rolled iron joists coated in concrete.

Most items were dated at their manufacture, no doubt to assist in monitoring the weathering process and calculating rates of deterioration but in 1924 there were changes in dating format and position, and after 1925 it seems to have ceased completely. The near coincidence of dates with Marriott's retirement is interesting, but it may be more a case of the satisfactory end of a 10-year trial period. Of course production continued and even increased. The fact that apparently none of the second type of gradient post and nameboard and some of the mileposts (eg the N&SJt Mundesley line) were unstamped seems to indicate a post-1925 manufacture. Signal wire stub posts also seem to have been a later phenomenon.

Concrete activities ceased with the closure of the works and apparently the drawings were dispersed to the various LNER district offices and the Lowestoft concrete works. Concrete fenceposts did continue to appear on the M&GN but they were of a different, LNER/BR design; round-topped and tapered and of a rather inferior finish.

6. The Line and its Stations

On its way from Great Yarmouth to Saxby and Peterborough the M&GN crossed sand dunes and marshy Broadland, climbed to the central plateau of rolling claylands, dropped through chalk downland to the reclaimed levels of the Wash and finally climbed again to the green hills of Leicestershire. The branch to Cromer assaulted the sandy mass of the Cromer Ridge, and the Norwich line penetrated the rural heartland of central Norfolk, hugging the side of the Wensum valley and crossing the river with a series of distinctive bridges before arriving within sight of the spire of Norwich Cathedral.

The fact that most of the railways were laid as cheaply as possible meant that very often the gradients followed the contour of the land, keeping earthworks to a minimum, and when gradients were necessary they were often severe; Norfolk is not flat. Anyone who insists it is should be made to ride a bicycle across it! It has been stated by commentators that the line was 'easily graded' and in comparison to the S&DJt or the mountain roads of the Midland that could be said to be true, but when one considers the enormous trains (14 bogie vehicles were commonplace) hauled by venerable locomotives without any regular double-heading, the 'easy' gradients take on a new significance. The M&GN boasted many miles of 1 in 100 and 1 in 90, and banks of 1 in 80 on the Cromer line and N&SJt. Nevertheless, foreign engine crews were constantly amazed by a single M&GN 4-4-0 walking away with the enormous excursion that they had just double-headed with much fuss and bother into South Lynn.

Despite the differences of topography in the various sub-regions of Norfolk, a great deal of the line passed through flatly rolling fields divided by grassy banks and narrow meandering lanes lined with oaks and elms. There were also large areas of deciduous woodland. The whole region was quite densely populated and there were many villages, hamlets and farms within sight of the railway. Church towers were a common landmark; from some vantage points six or more could be seen at once. The local building style was pretty much standard all over east, north and central Norfolk. The indigenous materials were the round nodules of chert known as cobbles and the soft pink or orange local brick used as the quoin material. Generally the cobbles were laid in courses. Roofing would be thatch or pantiles, glazed black on some better houses. From Georgian times more dwellings were built entirely in brick but it was the arrival of the railways that gradually changed local construction into hard red brick and slate. In west Norfolk, although there were buildings of the brick and cobble type, the indigenous material was a red-brown sandstone called carstone. This could be easily cut and coursed and in general treated like a large brick. The M&GN passed examples of this construction, principally at Hillington. The building material of the fenlands was brick, mostly red or brown, but around Peterborough yellow brick was common.

Because of the rural areas traversed by the M&GN the goods traffic created was largely of a seasonal and agricultural nature. The year opened with the flower bulb season based on the western section. At first the bulbs were imported from Holland via Lynn Docks, but after World War 1 home production of daffodils, narcissi and so on was established. Small consignments of bulbs and cut flowers would go by passenger train but larger amounts by fast goods. The rest of the system was handling potatoes and, increasingly from 1916, sugar beet. As the year progressed new potatoes would supersede the old ones, and many other green vegetables were also carried. The summer saw vast amounts of soft fruit in ventilated vans on Class A trains. In late summer the western section carried the hard fruit produced by the many orchards there, particularly around Wisbech, while the eastern section was occupied by the grain harvest. A short season of blackcurrants followed from the Broads area. The rest of the year was taken up with potatoes and other late vegetables, and later sugar beet formed the main winter traffic.

Herring formed the other important seasonal traffic from late September until April. Three daily afternoon fish trains were run from Lowestoft and Yarmouth with specials as required for this heavy traffic to the Midlands, North and London. In return the fishing season created inwards traffic of salt and empty fish barrels as well as coal for the fishing fleet. The Cromer branch also had a fish season but this was mainly crabs, lobsters and other shellfish, largely handled by passenger train.

A major all-year-round traffic was livestock. Each large town on the system had its cattle market and on its market day often justified special trains. Apart from local stock, Irish cattle were also imported for fattening on the lush Norfolk grass before being sent to Birmingham or London for slaughter. Another regular traffic was grain from stores to local stations and to Burton on Trent for brewing, along with malt. Hay for the horses in the great conurbations of London, Manchester and Birmingham, and for the MR provender store at Oakham was also a common load.

The main inwards traffic was coal, either to station merchants and gasworks companies or in large quantities for the Yarmouth and Lowestoft fishing fleets. Major coal merchants represented at many M&GN stations were Moy, Co-op, Bessey & Palmer and J. O. Vinter, who apart from their own wagons, received deliveries direct from the main collieries in the Midlands and the North. Of the general inwards traffic suffice it to say that almost anything one could think of was carried at some time from sources as diverse as Taunton and Killiecrankie, in wagons of almost every railway company, but naturally concentrating on the parent companies and the large centres: Leeds, Nottingham, Leicester, Birmingham and London (Bishopsgate, Somers Town, King's Cross, Farringdon Street). Building materials made up a large proportion: bricks from the Peterborough area; lime from the Buxton area; and slates from Wales. Timber in baulks or deals was imported through Sutton Bridge, Wisbech, Lynn Docks and Yarmouth Quay.

Passenger services were as usual divided between local stopping trains, semi-fasts, and expresses to and from London, the Midlands and the North. Most eastern section trains were subjected to the complicated marshalling of portions at Melton Constable but more detailed references to this and the other services is made in the text in Appendix C.

To analyse the entire M&GN in its landscape is a large task, and to aid the reader the information is broken down into sections using the Midland Railway distance diagrams as the key. In addition these roughly conform to the various geographical sub-regions which affect the surrounding topography and the gradients. Each section is preceded by a summary which deals with these geographical areas and follows the line from the point of view of a passenger leaving Lowestoft, Yarmouth, Cromer and Norwich for the Midlands or Peterborough.

To follow the course of the railway today requires a mixture of walking and motorised transport and with each summary a brief catalogue of surviving remains is given, although not all details are supplied, so that the reader can make discoveries of his own. As it would be impossible in the space available and monotonous for the reader to give specific directions, an OS map is essential. Fortunately many miles of the former trackbed have been opened as footpaths, principally the 'Weaver's Way' and 'Marriott's Way'. Leaflets about these walks can be obtained from the Tourist Information offices.

Following the summaries are the details of each individual station. As well as stations, some goods-only sidings are included, but the smaller private or ballast sidings and some junctions have been omitted. Facilities such as cranes and cattle pens, and features such as bridges, mileposts and gradient posts are shown on the drawings.

Broadland

Of all the areas the M&GN passed through this is probably what outsiders think of as the most typically Norfolk. Actually this area is only a small fraction of the county but thanks to the popularity of the Broads (helped in no small way by the Joint) it assumes a disproportionate importance. Although the centre of Broadland on the M&GN was usually taken as Potter Heigham, this geographical sub-region is actually centred on Yarmouth. The typical scenery of Broadland is that of wide river valleys and plains of pasture between uplands of cornfields or woodlands. These valleys are the remains of the 'Great Estuary' of Roman times, and the later peat diggings in the upper reaches of these valleys created the Broads. Rising from the alluvial plain are uplands, principally Lothingland between Yarmouth and Lowestoft and the Flegg to the north of Yarmouth. Lothingland was crossed by the N&SJt and because the early life of David Copperfield was set here the M&GN ambitiously named the area 'Dickensland'. The Flegg was traversed by the M&GN proper, giving rise to the few earthworks required on this part of the old GY&S. The soils here are fertile supporting arable farming and woodland but Lothingland is composed of sand and gravel and at the time of the railway's construction was covered with extensive commons and heaths.

The N&SJt Lowestoft-Yarmouth line was double track throughout and well-engineered with many earthworks and bridges to keep the gradients relatively easy. The longest climb was the ascent from Lowestoft at mostly 1 in 100 starting immediately at Coke Ovens Junction, sweeping the line round northwards in a cutting and under several bridges, climbing out of the Waveney valley into Lothingland and reaching the summit of the line just beyond Lowestoft North station. From there the line kept within half a mile of the coast passing through the small villages of Hopton and Corton, where it was hoped new development would follow, to Gorleston, which was already a quiet holiday resort. The M&GN approach to Yarmouth Beach after leaving the N&SJt at North Gorleston Junction was entirely on an embankment, curving round to the north of the town and narrowing to a single line across Breydon water, then doubling once more to cross the GE Vauxhall line and the Bure.

At the point where the line crossed Caister Road on bridge No 165 it was joined by a goods-only branch, the Yarmouth Union, giving access to the fish wharves with a small coal yard behind the White Swan public house. This line, predating the Lowestoft Junction Railway, had originally crossed Caister Road on the level but on the upgrading of the route the M&GN was forced to install a bridge approached by plain embankment to the west but the descent to Yarmouth Beach at 1 in 106 was on high retaining walls. The Union Line was also raised on a 1 in 92 gradient to approach the new junction.

The M&GN also ran close to the sea; for the first five miles of its route the single line was virtually laid on sand dunes with gradients frequently changing as the formation followed the undulations of the land. So close to the sea did the line come that the railway actually owned the foreshore and concrete defences had to be built to protect the formation from erosion. It was along this stretch that several halts were constructed in the 1930s to serve the holidaying public. Beyond Caister the line left the seashore and took a short climb into the Flegg, where Ormesby and Hemsby stations were situated. The line skirted Ormesby Broad but it was beyond Martham that it descended into the more well-known areas as it encountered the wide pastures that skirt the River Thurne at Potter Heigham.

There are quite a lot of remains still to be found today. Starting on Denmark Road alongside Lowestoft Central station, by following the road and turning left on to Eastern Way (formerly Laundry Lane) brings one to the site of crossing No 1. Coke Ovens Junction was to the south but only a short length of single line remains and even the GE signalbox has gone. Beyond the crossing the land is fenced off but the line can be regained at the site of footbridge No 2419 by a footpath from Rotterdam Road. Several bridges survive over the trackbed along this stretch, but No 2424 carrying the Yarmouth Road has been removed and filled and to the north Lowestoft North has gone completely, covered by houses and chalets.

Backtracking to Corton Road one can follow the line up the coast past Pleasurewood Hills theme park to Corton, which is the only surviving station on this line. It can be reached by taking Station Road off Bridge Road. The main building and canopy still stand, together with the platforms, stationmaster's house and pair of GE-style cottages. The goods yard has been built upon. Further north part of bridge No 2430 can be seen but beyond a large part of the line has been ploughed into fields.

Bridge No 2433 and Hopton station have both gone, the site being occupied by a housing estate named 'The Embankment'. However, the yard gates, stationmaster's house and a pair of GE-type cottages survive. Beyond Hopton a single fence remains and only a wide grassy strip meeting Links Lane on the south side reveals the position of the embankment and Gorleston Links halt. To

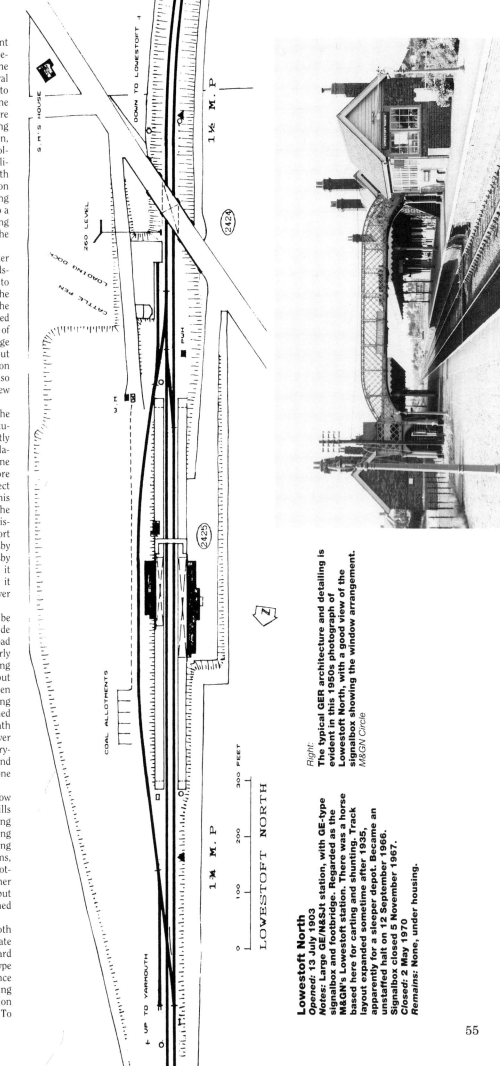

Lowestoft North
Opened: 13 July 1903
Notes: Large GE/N&SJt station, with GE-type signalbox and footbridge. Regarded as the M&GN's Lowestoft station. There was a horse based here for carting and shunting. Track layout expanded sometime after 1935, apparently for a sleeper depot. Became an unstaffed halt on 12 September 1966.
Signalbox closed 5 November 1967.
Closed: 2 May 1970
Remains: None, under housing.

Right:
The typical GER architecture and detailing is evident in this 1950s photograph of Lowestoft North, with a good view of the signalbox showing the window arrangement.
M&GN Circle

55

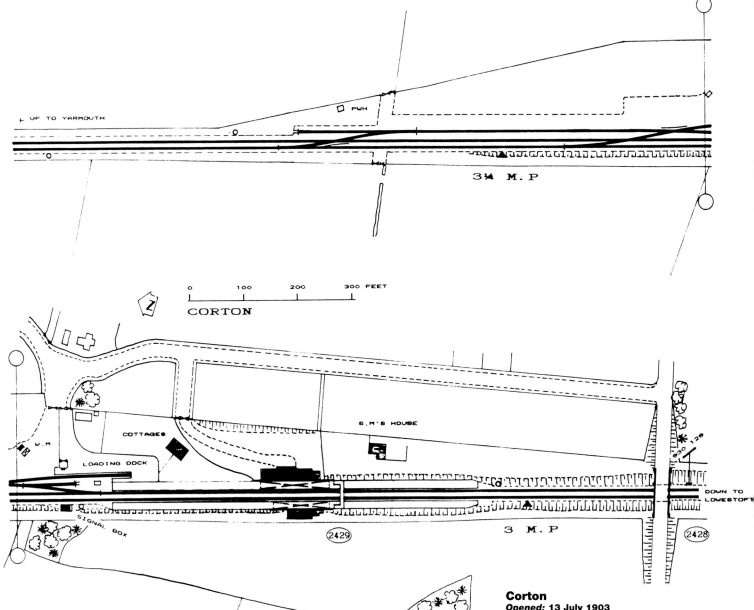

UP TO YARMOUTH

PWH

3¼ M.P

0   100   200   300 FEET

CORTON

S.M'S HOUSE

COTTAGES

LOADING DOCK

W.H

DOWN TO LOWESTOFT

SIGNAL BOX

2429   3 M.P   2428

the north houses occupy the trackbed but a single fence and footpath follow the alignment under bridge No 2436 (Bridge Road) where the line continues as a lighted bridleway in the cutting towards Gorleston-On-Sea station. From Gorleston the trackbed is at present being occupied by a new road, through the site of Gorleston North station until it joins the Yarmouth bypass, completed several years ago, that exactly follows the line of the M&GN over Breydon Water.

Crossing Vauxhall station and the river, the White Swan pub and the old mediaeval tower are prominent landmarks, revealing the position of the White Swan yard. There are some crossing gates and fencing on Garrison Road and gateposts on Ormond Road, but the crossing house has gone and only the curve of Alderson Road shows where the line climbed on embankment to Caister Road Junction. All the embankments have now been removed, but one retaining wall of the line along Beaconsfield Road towards Beach station still stands. The northern half of the station yard along Nelson Road is under housing and the actual station has been razed, with only two columns and a length of track left as a reminder. The M&GN trackbed continues north of Salisbury Road past the site of Newtown Halt and under concrete bridge No 162 but then is lost under grass alongside the Yarmouth race course. The best method of following the line over the dunes between here and California is to walk, as there is little or no vehicular access except at Caister or California. Caister

station has gone, replaced by housing but following the sandy trackbed past Caister Camp the platform of Caister Camp Halt and the fencing at its rear still exist, although not obvious unless viewed from behind. Further north are some of the concrete sea defences surviving from the early part of the century, with E&M flat-bottom rail ends visible in the surface. Curving inland through California the line heads for Ormesby. Fenceposts can be seen alongside the road, but gatehouse No 45 and the site of Scratby Halt have gone under the coast road improvements. Further towards Ormesby, concrete gatehouse No 44 still stands in excellent condition. Great Ormesby station is in private hands but still relatively complete, although the yard is under housing. Curving north as a private track the line passes concrete gatehouse No 43 and the site of Little Ormesby Halt, where some trellis fencing can still be seen. In Hemsby the coast road now follows the route, but a car park occupies the site of the station. The trackbed has been ploughed into fields all the way from Hemsby to Martham, but girder bridge No 158 still sits in solitary splendour on the Martham road. Martham station building survives, but the platforms have gone and the yard and site of gatehouse No 42 have all been covered with housing. On a by-road is the best surviving example of a timber gatehouse (No 41) and in the distance concrete gatehouse No 40 can be descried, but access to it is private. No trackbed remains between here and Potter Heigham.

Corton

Opened: 13 July 1903
Notes: Small version of GE/N&SJt station, with GE-type signalbox, footbridge, stationmaster's house and cottages. Not a very successful station. Two camping coaches were stationed here in LNER days. The signalbox was closed on 20 January 1965, and on 12 September 1966 the station became an unstaffed halt. The footbridge was cut up c1968.
Closed: 2 May 1970
Remains: Quite complete, but signalbox and waiting shelter demolished and housing on the goods yard.

Above:
Corton in June 1954. The main building is to the left, the half-timbered dormer of the GE/N&SJt small size can be seen, also the 'Dutch gable' finishing of the canopy backing wall. Footbridge No 2429 has lost its roof. Overbridge No 2428 is in the distance.
D. Thompson

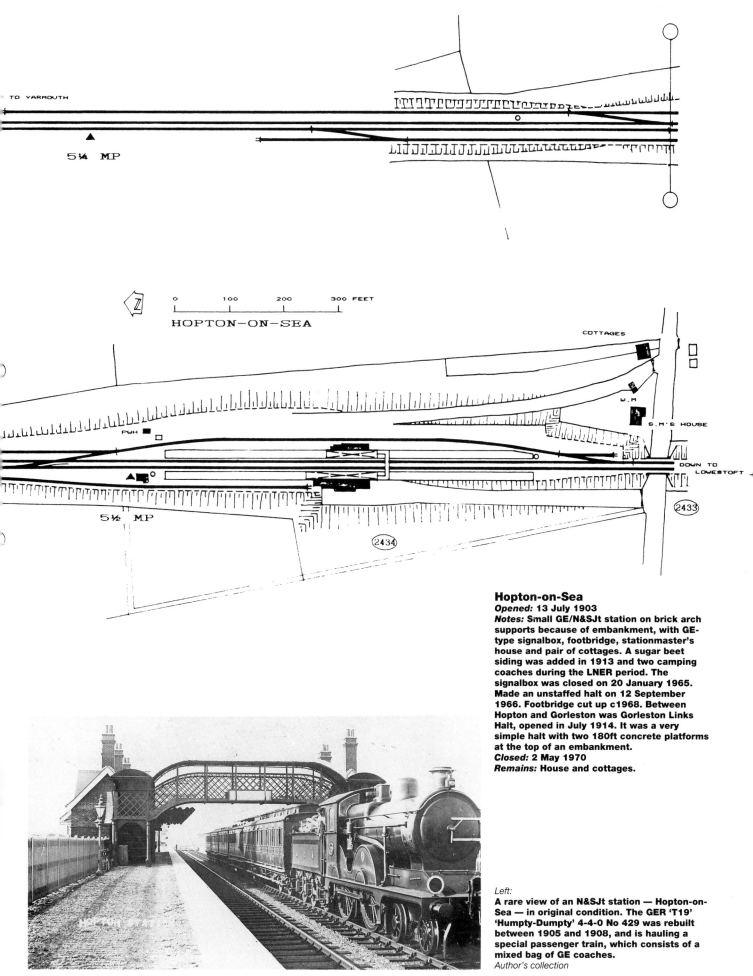

TO YARMOUTH

5¼ MP

N

0   100   200   300 FEET

HOPTON-ON-SEA

COTTAGES

W.M

S.M'S HOUSE

PWH

DOWN TO
LOWESTOFT →

5½ MP

(2434)

(2433)

Hopton-on-Sea
Opened: **13 July 1903**
Notes: **Small GE/N&SJt station on brick arch
supports because of embankment, with GE-
type signalbox, footbridge, stationmaster's
house and pair of cottages. A sugar beet
siding was added in 1913 and two camping
coaches during the LNER period. The
signalbox was closed on 20 January 1965.
Made an unstaffed halt on 12 September
1966. Footbridge cut up c1968. Between
Hopton and Gorleston was Gorleston Links
Halt, opened in July 1914. It was a very
simple halt with two 180ft concrete platforms
at the top of an embankment.**
Closed: **2 May 1970**
Remains: **House and cottages.**

Left:
**A rare view of an N&SJt station — Hopton-on-
Sea — in original condition. The GER 'T19'
'Humpty-Dumpty' 4-4-0 No 429 was rebuilt
between 1905 and 1908, and is hauling a
special passenger train, which consists of a
mixed bag of GE coaches.**
Author's collection

57

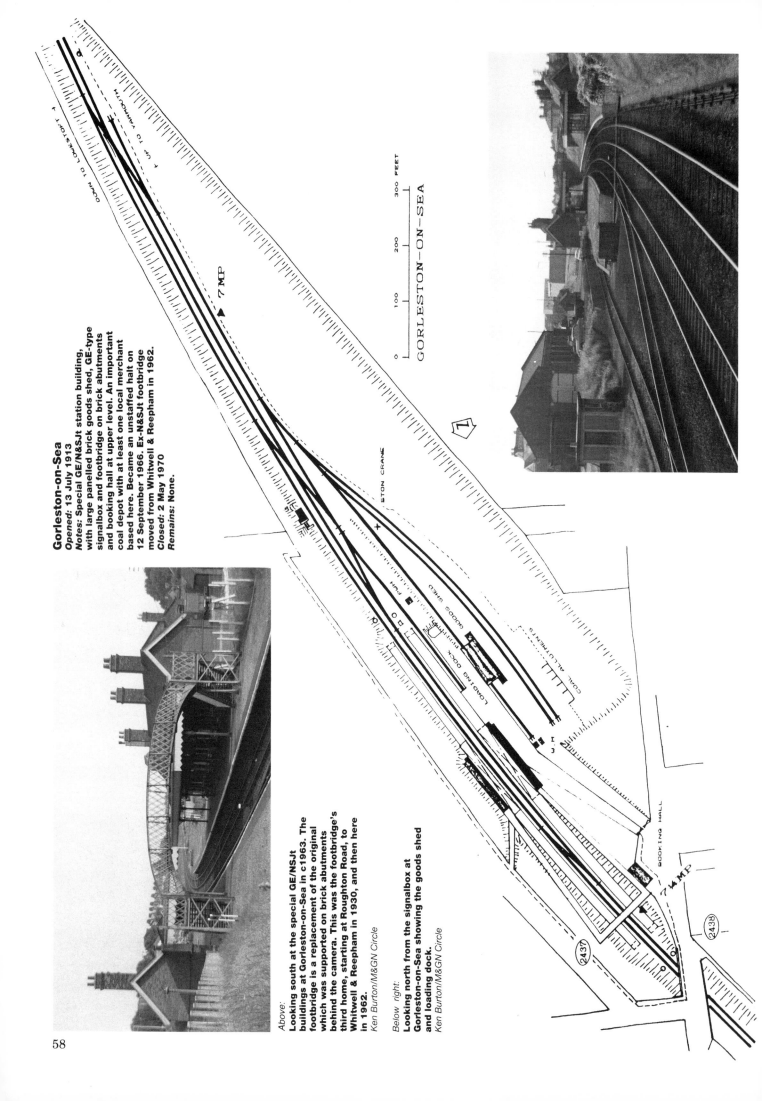

Gorleston-on-Sea

Opened: **13 July 1913**
Notes: **Special GE/N&SJt station building, with large panelled brick goods shed, GE-type signalbox and footbridge on brick abutments and booking hall at upper level. An important coal depot with at least one local merchant based here. Became an unstaffed halt on 12 September 1966. Ex-N&SJt footbridge moved from Whitwell & Reepham in 1962.**
Closed: **2 May 1970**
Remains: **None.**

GORLESTON-ON-SEA

Above:
Looking south at the special GE/NSJt buildings at Gorleston-on-Sea in c1963. The footbridge is a replacement of the original which was supported on brick abutments behind the camera. This was the footbridge's third home, starting at Roughton Road, to Whitwell & Reepham in 1930, and then here in 1962.
Ken Burton/M&GN Circle

Below right:
Looking north from the signalbox at Gorleston-on-Sea showing the goods shed and loading dock.
Ken Burton/M&GN Circle

Gorleston North

Opened: 13 July 1903
Notes: Small version of **GE/N&SJt** station, GE-type signalbox and footbridge. It was never a very successful station due to competition from trams, but was an important coal depot for the fishing fleet. It was severely damaged in air raids and closed for passengers in World War 2, but the signalbox remained open until 5 June 1950.
Closed: 5 October 1942
Remains: None

Left:
Gorleston North was a standard small GE/NSJt station with footbridge. Note the top of the supporting arches visible in the platform walls. The fences are original. The view, looking north, was possibly taken in the early 1930s.
D. Thompson

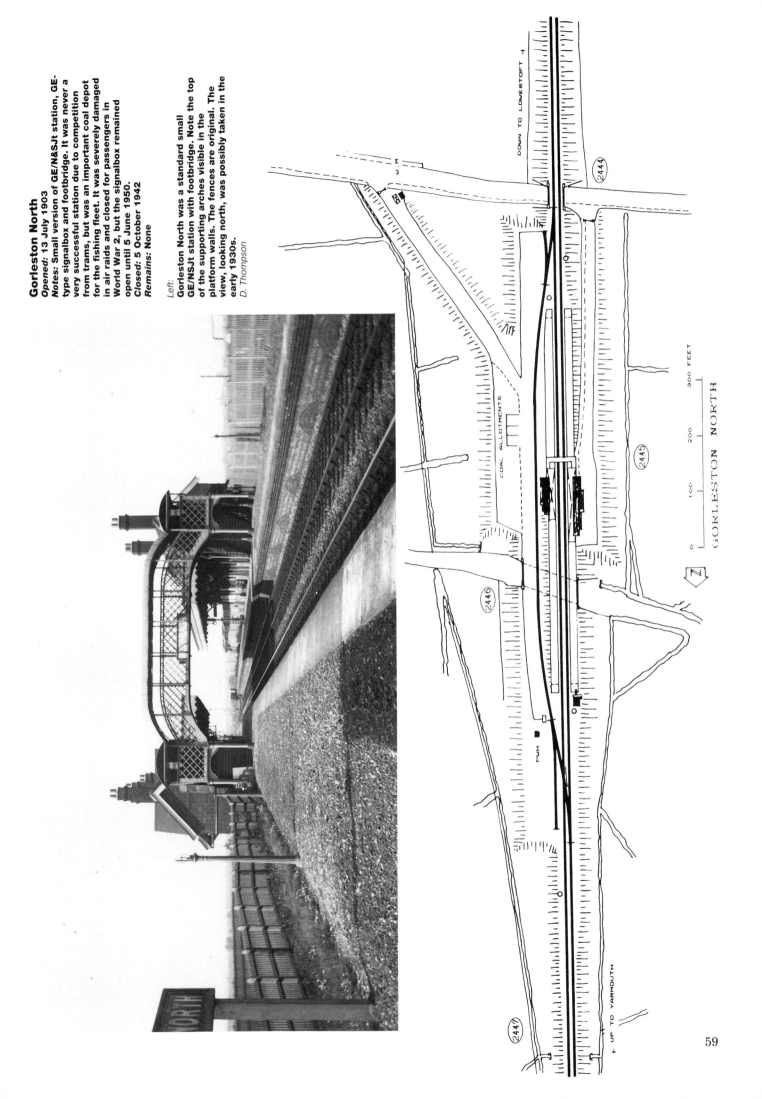

2446

2447

COAL ALLOTMENTS

PWH

UP TO YARMOUTH →

DOWN TO LOWESTOFT →

2444

2445

0   100   200   300 FEET

GORLESTON NORTH

N

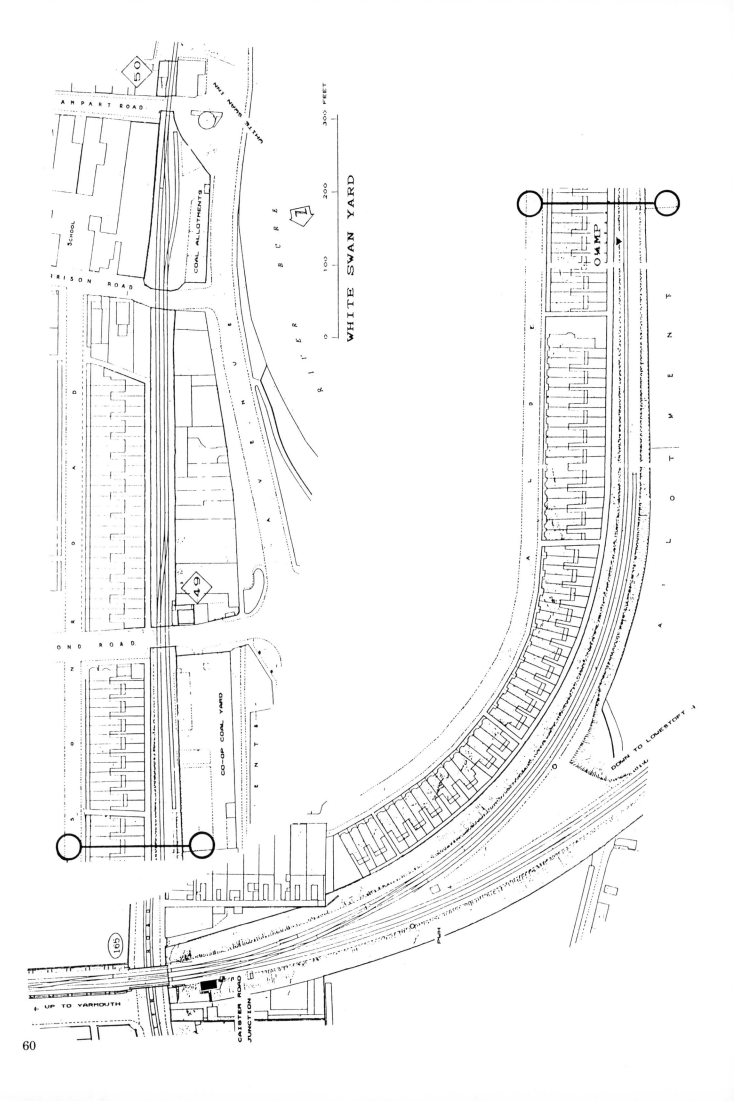

WHITE SWAN YARD

60

Yarmouth Union Line

Opened: 15 May 1882, new junction 13 July 1903

Notes: This line had brick Wilkinson & Jarvis gatehouses, except No 50 which was an adapted house, and an M&GN type 1a signalbox at Caister Road Junction. The coal sidings were added in 1902 and 1903. The line was worked by the Yarmouth Beach pilot to White Swan by train staff from Caister Road on the one engine in steam principle, then by horse to the junction with the GE tramway. After World War 1 wagons ran out onto the quay by gravity, where they were picked up by the GE tram loco from Vauxhall. The line from Beach was singled about 1953 and severed 50yd from the junction on closure. It continued in use with access from the southern end until 1970. Quay lines were lifted in 1985.

Closed: May 1970

Remains: Some fencing and gates.

Left:
Yarmouth Union: this shows the pub that gave the White Swan yard its name. Although the tramway in the foreground was still M&GN property, no loco was permitted to pass the gate until the LNER period. The house on the right is gatehouse No 50.
M&GN Circle

Below left:
White Swan coal yard, at Great Yarmouth, looking north from Rampart Road gates. The crossing in the distance is Garrison Road. Note the buffer stops constructed from E&M flat-bottom rail.
M&GN Circle

61

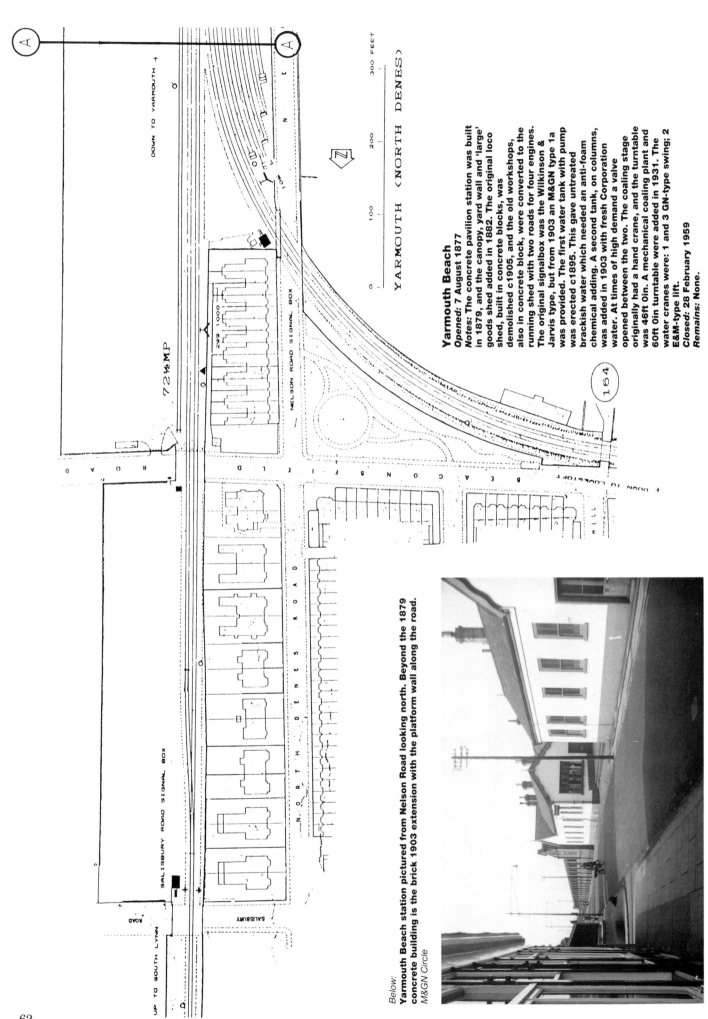

DOWN TO YARMOUTH →

72½ MP

↑ UP TO SOUTH LYNN

SALISBURY ROAD SIGNAL BOX

SALISBURY ROAD

NORTH DENES ROAD

NELSON ROAD SIGNAL BOX

BEACONSFIELD

N E

HILL

↓ DOWN TO LOWESTOFT

YARMOUTH (NORTH DENES)

0   100   200   300 FEET

A — A

Yarmouth Beach

Opened: 7 August 1877

Notes: The concrete pavilion station was built in 1879, and the canopy, yard wall and 'large' goods shed added in 1882. The original loco shed, built in concrete blocks, was demolished c1905, and the old workshops, also in concrete block, were converted to the running shed with two roads for four engines. The original signalbox was the Wilkinson & Jarvis type, but from 1903 an M&GN type 1a was provided. The first water tank with pump was erected c1895. This gave untreated brackish water which needed an anti-foam chemical adding. A second tank, on columns, was added in 1903 with fresh Corporation water. At times of high demand a valve opened between the two. The coaling stage originally had a hand crane, and the turntable was 46ft 0in. A mechanical coaling plant and 60ft 0in turntable were added in 1931. The water cranes were: 1 and 3 GN-type swing; 2 E&M-type lift.
Closed: 28 February 1959
Remains: None.

164

Below:
Yarmouth Beach station pictured from Nelson Road looking north. Beyond the 1879 concrete building is the brick 1903 extension with the platform wall along the road.
M&GN Circle

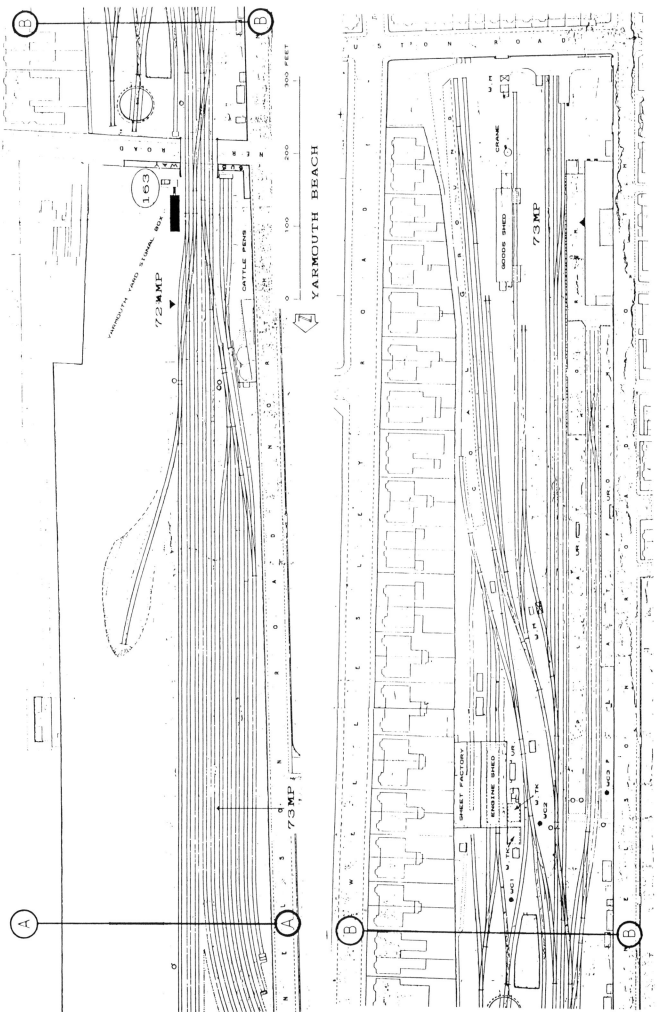

YARMOUTH BEACH

Below:
A general view of Yarmouth Beach looking towards the bufferstops, taken from the 1903 platform in 1931. The earlier station and canopy are in the middle distance, the goods shed to the left. Note the enamel nameboards, the finials of the telegraph poles, and the weighbridge cabin.
L&GRP

Bottom left:
Looking north along the original platform at Yarmouth Beach in 1959. Note the canopy with E&MR in the spandrels, and the two-lever frame controlling the crossover.
A. E. Bennett

Below right:
Yarmouth Beach possessed the largest signalbox on the Joint — an M&GN type 1a erected in 1902/1903 to replace the Wilkinson & Jarvis structure.
Ian Allan Library

Bottom right:
Yarmouth loco shed seen in c1935. One bay of the twin-arched structure of the GY&S workshops was utilised from 1905. Class A tank No 20 stands by the GN-type water crane. All engines are now in the final livery.
Lens of Sutton

Caister-on-Sea

Opened: **7 August 1877**

Notes: **A GY&S pavilion in concrete block with lavatory extension added in 1898. Not a tablet station; a small covered ground-frame controlled the crossing, the siding points and the signals protecting them. Although a small station, expresses stopped here during the summer. The express from Liverpool Street, known unofficially as 'The Camper' stopped here from c1934, as did the Saturdays only 'Holiday Camps Express' after the war.**

Closed: **28 February 1959**

Remains: None.

Left:

A view of Caister in 1955 looking north, showing the very simple facilities here. The station cabin is the small building in the foreground. Goods traffic was apparently mostly domestic coal. Horseboxes and carriage trucks could not be loaded. Rope shunting was permitted for Down trains.

D. Thompson

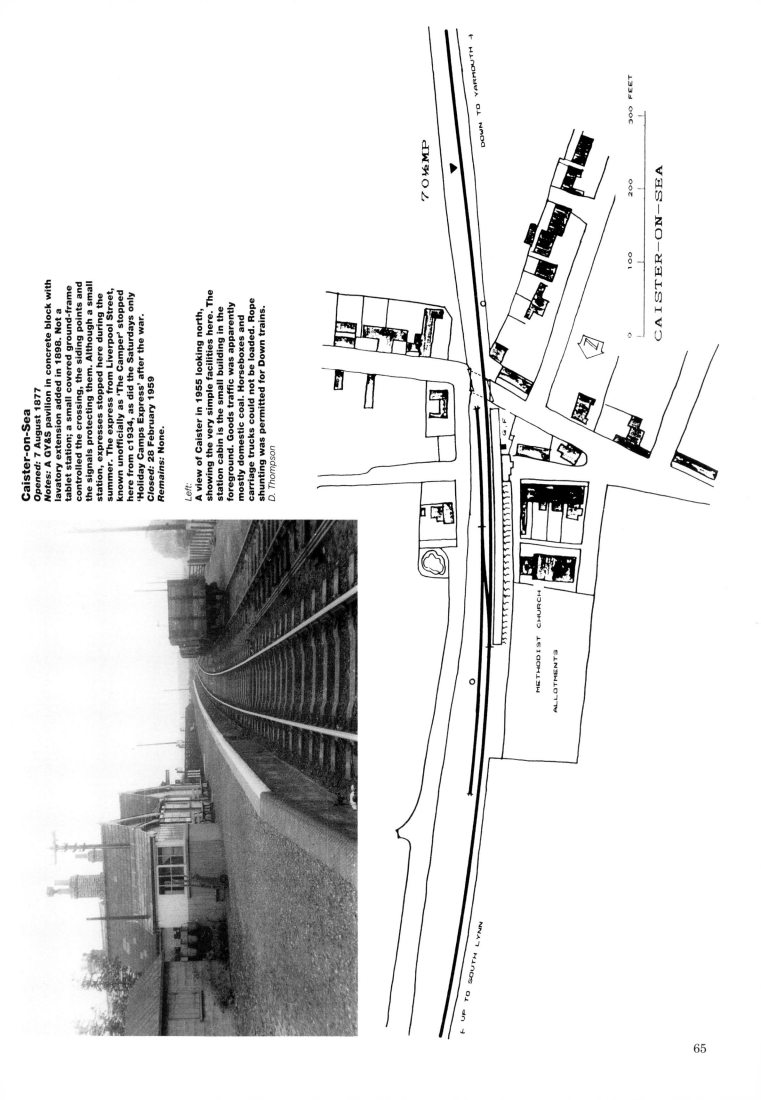

65

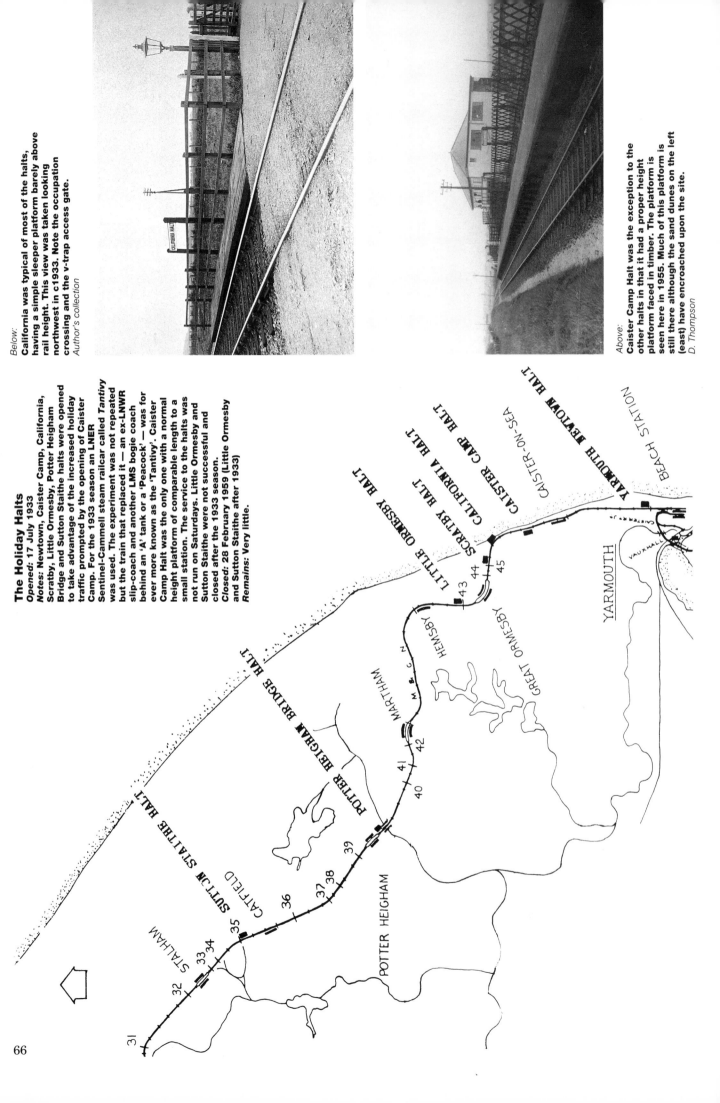

Below:
California was typical of most of the halts, having a simple sleeper platform barely above rail height. This view was taken looking northwest in c1933. Note the occupation crossing and the v-trap access gate.
Author's collection

Above:
Caister Camp Halt was the exception to the other halts in that it had a proper height platform faced in timber. The platform is seen here in 1955. Much of this platform is still there although the sand dunes on the left (east) have encroached upon the site.
D. Thompson

The Holiday Halts
Opened: 17 July 1933
Notes: Newtown, Caister Camp, California, Scratby, Little Ormesby, Potter Heigham Bridge and Sutton Staithe halts were opened to take advantage of the increased holiday traffic prompted by the opening of Caister Camp. For the 1933 season an LNER Sentinel-Cammell steam railcar called *Tantivy* was used. The experiment was not repeated but the train that replaced it — an ex-LNWR slip-coach and another LMS bogie coach behind an 'A' tank or a 'Peacock' — was for ever more known as the 'Tantivy'. Caister Camp Halt was the only one with a normal height platform of comparable length to a small station. The service to the halts was not run on Saturdays. Little Ormesby and Sutton Staithe were not successful and closed after the 1933 season.
Closed: 28 February 1959 (Little Ormesby and Sutton Staithe after 1933)
Remains: Very little.

66

Great Ormesby

Opened: 7 August 1877

Notes: A GY&S pavilion in concrete block, with 1898 lavatory extension and standard timber tariff shed. There was a coal shed for Bessey & Palmer. Originally the station was a single platform, but it was made into a passing place in 1894 when the Down platform, timber standard M&GN waiting shed and M&GN type 1a signalbox were erected. It was not a busy station, but there were quite a number of passengers commuting to Yarmouth. A noted feature was the garden in front of the building with tall hollyhocks.
Closed: 28 February 1959
Remains: Private house, including platforms and top of signalbox.

Below:
A view of Ormesby looking southeast on a summer evening in 1949. The M&GN type 1a signalbox (of five bays) and the cattle pens can be seen in the distance. Outside the main building is one of the original curved and slatted seats. The station is still completely oil-lit.
D. Thompson

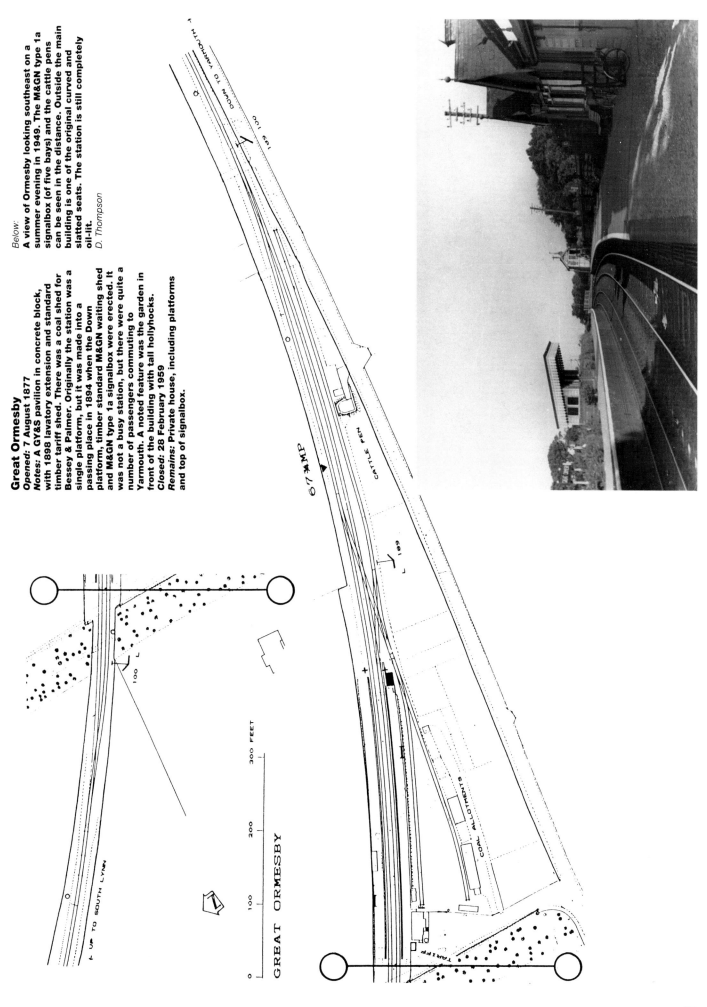

GREAT ORMESBY

Hemsby (For Winterton-on-Sea)

Opened: 16 May 1877
Notes: A short version of the W&J office design in concrete block with plain bargeboards and standard timber tariff shed. Originally there was a W&J timber signalbox on the platform, but a new box was built adjacent to the crossing c1904. The box controlled the crossing, the siding points and the signals protecting them, but was not a tablet post. Bessey & Palmer had a timber coal shed, which was later removed. Hemsby became very popular with the opening of the local holiday camp and was crowded on summer weekends.
Closed: 28 February 1959
Remains: None.

Below left:
A well-known postcard of Hemsby showing the station early in the M&GN period. The small signal cabin can be seen on the platform.
Author's collection

Below right:
Hemsby viewed in 1959, showing the replacement cabin by the level crossing. The station building was a special short version of the standard W&J design.
D. Thompson

HEMSBY STATION.

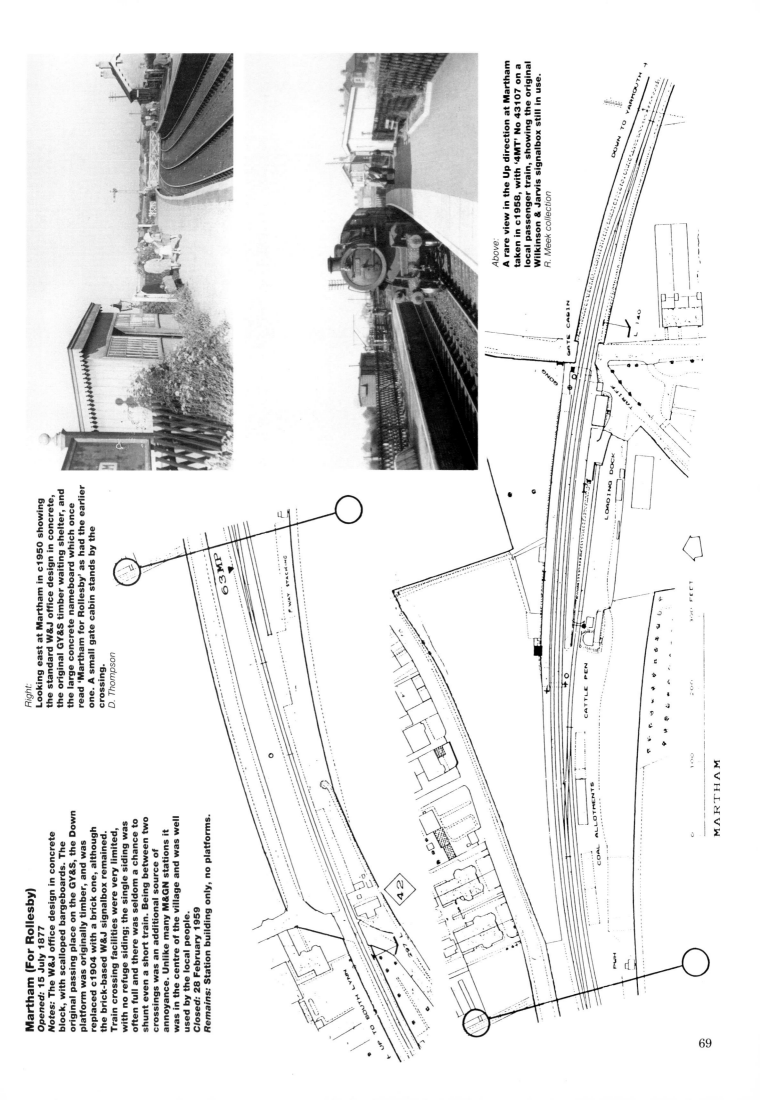

Martham (For Rollesby)

Opened: 15 July 1877

Notes: The W&J office design in concrete
block, with scalloped bargeboards. The
original passing place on the GY&S, the Down
platform was originally timber, and was
replaced c1904 with a brick one, although
the brick-based W&J signalbox remained.
Train crossing facilities were very limited,
with no refuge siding; the single siding was
often full and there was seldom a chance to
shunt even a short train. Being between two
crossings was an additional source of
annoyance. Unlike many M&GN stations it
was in the centre of the village and was well
used by the local people.

Closed: 28 February 1959

Remains: Station building only, no platforms.

Right:
**Looking east at Martham in c1950 showing
the standard W&J office design in concrete,
the original GY&S timber waiting shelter, and
the large concrete nameboard which once
read 'Martham for Rollesby' as had the earlier
one. A small gate cabin stands by the
crossing.**
D. Thompson

Above:
**A rare view in the Up direction at Martham
taken in c1958, with '4MT' No 43107 on a
local passenger train, showing the original
Wilkinson & Jarvis signalbox still in use.**
R. Meek collection

69

Broadland and Poppyland

After crossing the Thurne (or Hundred Stream) on the lattice girder bridge No 155 the line once more regained the flat Broadland fields but between Catfield and Stalham the marshy areas of Sutton Broad with their reed beds came right up to the line. After Stalham the character of the landscape begins to change and despite the northernmost arm of Broadland — the canalised River Ant — the land is beginning to rise. This is the change from Broadland to the geographical sub-region known as the 'Loam Region' whose light sandy soils form the basis for Poppyland. The landscape is more elevated in the north of the region and it was the climb to the heathy peninsula on which North Walsham was founded that formed the first serious obstruction to westbound trains, the two miles at 1 in 100 of Honing or Bengate Bank. After North Walsham the line fell on the steepest M&GN gradient, at 1 in 64, to pass beneath the GER and then fell more sedately through Felmingham to the valley of the Bure and Aylsham.

Poppyland, the name coined by the writer Clement Scott in the early 1880s, originally applied to the coastal region between Cromer and Mundesley, but on the rise in popularity of this area where the 'regal red poppies' did indeed cover the cornfields in summer, the name began to be applied to the whole of northeast Norfolk in an area from Weybourne to Happisburgh penetrating inland as far as North Walsham. The Mundesley line was first proposed in 1888 when the Poppyland boom was at its height but by the time it was opened as the Norfolk & Suffolk Joint 10 years later the boom was on the wane and when the link to Cromer was finished in 1906 it was really too late. The development hoped to follow the railway at Mundesley, Trimingham and Overstrand never came.

The Mundesley line penetrated into the lower slopes of the highest land in Norfolk known as the 'Cromer Ridge' and in consequence the earthworks were considerable and the gradients surprisingly steep, with 20% of the mileage greater than 1 in 100 inclination. Leaving Antingham Road Junction in North Walsham, where the GER and M&GN lines joined, the single track descended into the valley of the Ant at 1 in 80, climbing up to Paston & Knapton station at 1 in 87. At Mundesley the line reached the coast and then followed it, never being more than half a mile from the cliffs, climbing to Trimingham and then beginning a switchback ride through Overstrand, passing under the GER at Cromer (Norfolk's only tunnel), joining the GER again at Roughton Road Junction and then falling steeply at 1 in 80 and 1 in 100 to join the M&GN at Runton East Junction. Throughout the route there was hardly ever a portion of the line that was not in a deep cutting or on a high embankment, as it crossed the foothills of the Cromer Ridge. The whole area is based on sands and gravels, much of it uncultivated and supporting heathland and vast tracts of gorse, whose sight and scent formed part of the distinctive atmosphere of Poppyland.

Today it is easy to follow several miles of the M&GN trackbed in this section, as the main Yarmouth-North Walsham road uses it between Potter Heigham and Stalham, and from Bengate near Honing to North Walsham. The remainder between Stalham and Honing, North Walsham and Aylsham is used as part of the 'Weavers Way'. The road joins the route just before the site of bridge No 155 over the Thurne, and there are no remains of Potter Heigham station, but gatehouses Nos 39 & 38 are passed on the right. Catfield station has also gone, but the yard is used as a Council salt dump and the stationmaster's house of 1914 still stands in the far corner. The road veers off the trackbed at Stalham, where the station building and one platform can be seen and also the ex-E&M

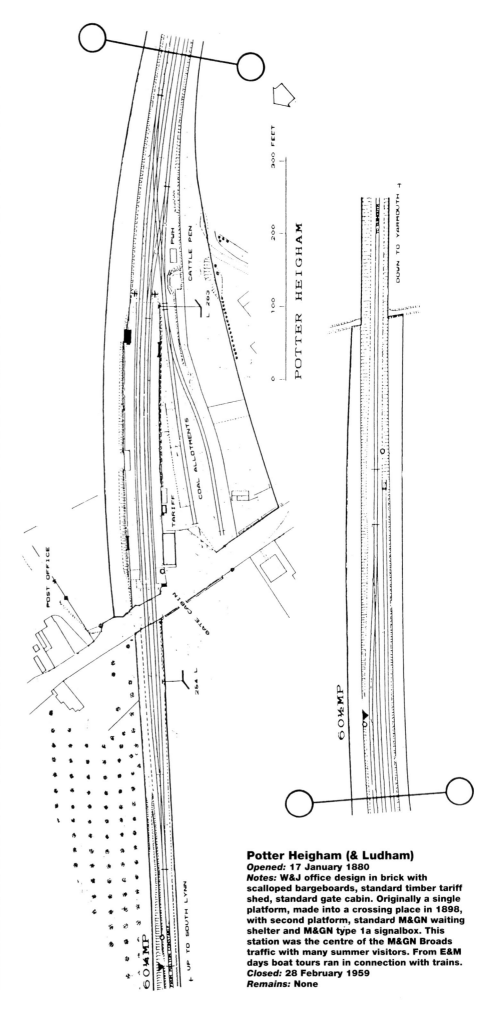

Potter Heigham (& Ludham)
Opened: **17 January 1880**
Notes: **W&J office design in brick with scalloped bargeboards, standard timber tariff shed, standard gate cabin. Originally a single platform, made into a crossing place in 1898, with second platform, standard M&GN waiting shelter and M&GN type 1a signalbox. This station was the centre of the M&GN Broads traffic with many summer visitors. From E&M days boat tours ran in connection with trains.**
Closed: **28 February 1959**
Remains: **None**

Top:
A general view of Potter Heigham in 1958 looking towards Yarmouth, showing the station building in brick, tariff shed, signalbox and standard waiting shelter.
F. Church

Above:
Class A tank No 9 on the 'Tantivy' at Potter Heigham in c1935, made up of an LMS and an LNWR coach. No 9 had her tanks cut down about 1933.
M&GN Circle

luggage brake which was used as a goods office in the 1920s. Now following the Weaver's Way, crossing houses Nos 32 & 31 still survive as do various culverts, and just before Honing the beautiful iron bridge No 146 remains. Honing station has virtually disappeared in undergrowth, but the platforms and a pumphouse are still there. Luckily Honing East signalbox was saved by Peter Bower and now resides at the Barton House Railway in Wroxham. Beyond Honing the footpath crosses the canal on a wooden bridge using the piers of No 144 to gatehouse No 30 and the site of Honing West box. Not much further on the main road joins the align-

ment and there are no remains apart from a few fenceposts right into North Walsham.

On the other side of the town the trackbed to Aylsham resumes as the Weaver's Way and is virtually complete, running through less populous countryside. It is a very pleasant walk past gatehouse No 28 and over several bridges to Felmingham station, recently renovated. The stationmaster's house is occupied and in good condition, if a little altered. After Felmingham one passes gatehouse No 27 and over the repaired bridge No 132 (wrecked in the 1912 floods), under bridge No 131 and past gatehouse No 26 to the new Aylsham bypass where a road runs on the trackbed almost up to the station itself. Nothing now remains of Aylsham except some fencing and bridge No 128.

From North Walsham towards Mundesley, new roads follow the trackbed again, passing the site of Antingham Road Junction where the link to the GE can be seen approaching from the nearby railway line to Cromer, right up to the old Mundesley Road, where elliptical bridge No 361 still stands. It is now difficult to follow the line precisely even on foot, as a lot has been cut off by removal of bridges or ploughing. Paston & Knapton station is in private hands and several bridges still stand. From here the trackbed is mostly ploughed in or built on right up to the site of Mundesley station which is now an extensive estate of bungalows.

Beyond Mundesley some of the trackbed still survives as do several bridges, the most evocative probably being No 340, a three-arch segmental bridge over the Trimingham-Gimingham road. Trimingham station has been covered with housing, but bridge No 337 still stands; the old access gates now opening on to a sheer drop instead of the wooden staircase down to the platform. The stationmaster's house and the pair of cottages are occupied and well maintained. The trackbed survives quite well from Trimingham as it is fairly constantly in cutting or on embankment, and from the site of Sidestrand Halt (reached along a lane opposite the church) to Overstrand is a well-used footpath. Overstrand station and some of the platform still exists, although the yard is, as usual, covered with housing. The subway access is still an interesting feature. The line curves round under bridge No 329 towards Cromer, but after the site of Cromer Links halt there is housing until the tunnel No 327 under Cromer GE station which is best viewed from the main road over adjacent bridge No 326. The site of Roughton Road Junction can be well viewed from the platform of the recent Roughton Road halt where the present BR line curves in from the former GE Cromer Junction. The old N&SJt line and the site of the signalbox are heavily overgrown. From Roughton Road the line is intact right into Cromer Beach.

CATFIELD

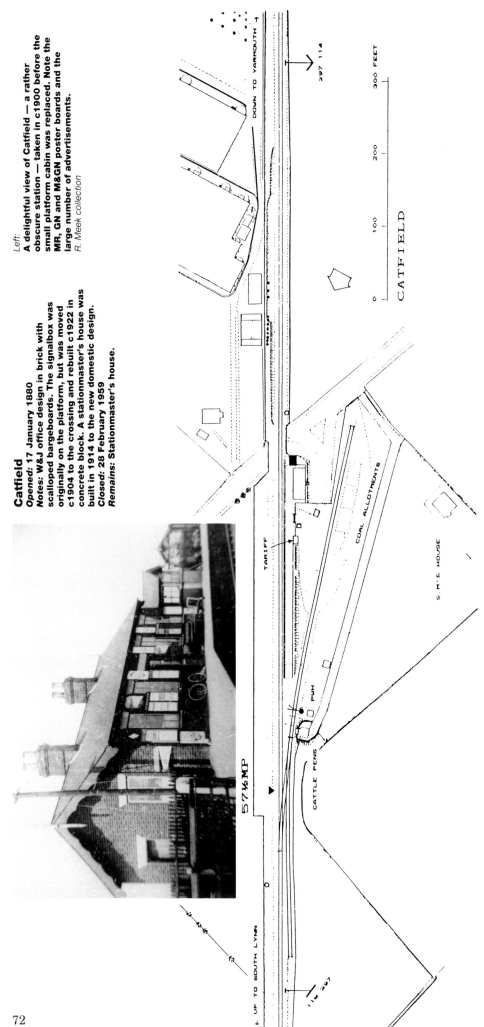

Catfield

Opened: 17 January 1880
Notes: W&J office design in brick with
scalloped bargeboards. The signalbox was
originally on the platform, but was moved
c1904 to the crossing and rebuilt c1922 in
concrete block. A stationmaster's house was
built in 1914 to the new domestic design.
Closed: 28 February 1959
Remains: Stationmaster's house.

Left:
**A delightful view of Catfield — a rather
obscure station — taken in c1900 before the
small platform cabin was replaced. Note the
MR, GN and M&GN poster boards and the
large number of advertisements.**
R. Meek collection

UP TO SOUTH LYNN

57½ MP

TARIFF

PWH

CATTLE PENS

COAL ALLOTMENTS

S. M's HOUSE

DOWN TO YARMOUTH

297 114

CATFIELD

0   100   200   300 FEET

Stalham (For Happisburgh & Palling on Sea)

Opened: 3 July 1880

Notes: W&J office design with scalloped bargeboards, timber platform shelter, monopitch timber tariff shed and two E&M-type lift water cranes. A Midland-type signalbox was installed c1907 on the Up platform opposite the old one (W&J type). A porter's room was built in 1909 and 'large stock' van bodies were added c1921 as goods offices. The yard was altered and extended in 1929, cutting off Bachelor's private siding (corn and timber). As well as local traffic, there were trippers to some of the lesser-known seaside villages, and for boating on the nearby broad. It was also a centre for the seasonal blackcurrant traffic.

Closed: 28 February 1959

Remains: Station building.

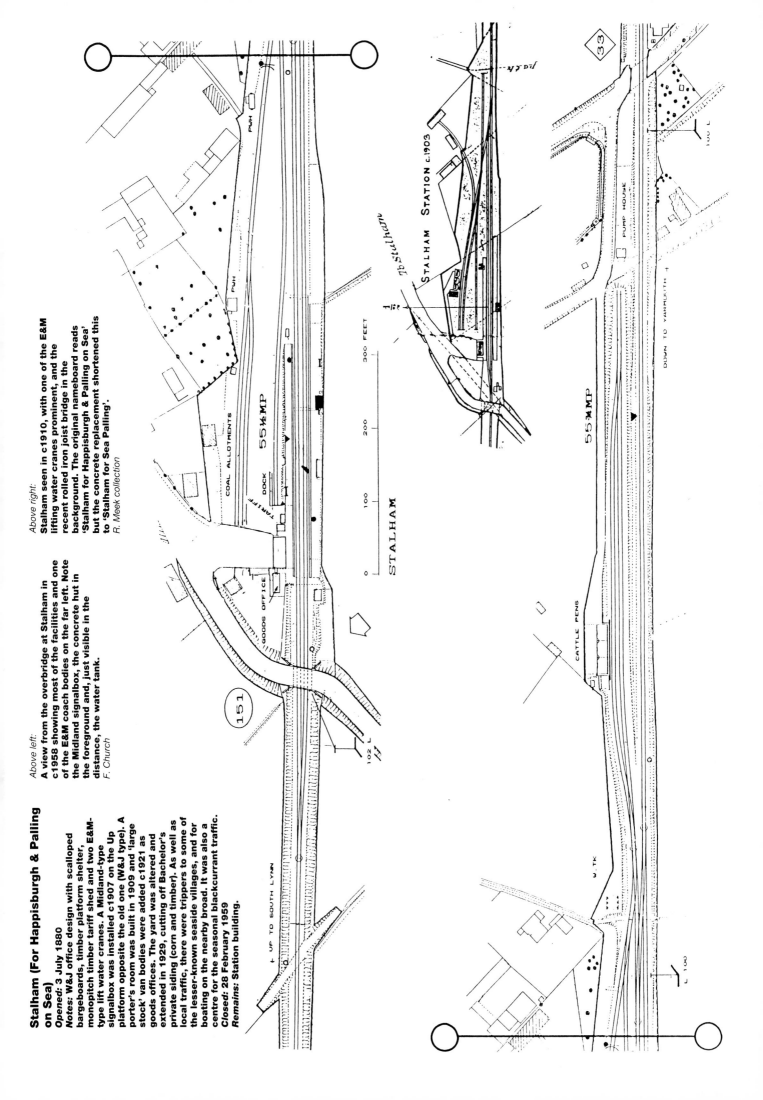

STALHAM

0   100   200   300 FEET

55½MP

COAL ALLOTMENTS

DOCK

TARIFF

GOODS OFFICE

↑ UP TO SOUTH LYNN

151

102 L

STALHAM STATION c.1903

To Stalham

33

PUMP HOUSE

55¾MP

CATTLE PENS

W.TK

DOWN TO YARMOUTH ↓

100 L

10 L

Honing for Worstead (& Dilham)

Opened: August 1882

Notes: W&J office design in brick with standard timber tariff shed. Originally a single platform with a small signalbox controlling the points and the protecting signals, became a passing place in 1901, having a long loop and East and West signalboxes and standard **M&GN** waiting shelter. The loop was capable of taking the longest train ever likely to run and was approximately halfway between Yarmouth and Melton. The West box closed on 22 June 1932 and was replaced by a gate hut and an 'Auxiliary Tablet Hut'.

Closed: 28 February 1959

Remains: Platforms only. Honing East box is now at Barton House Railway, Wroxham.

Above right:

Honing pictured looking west in 1958, with the original buildings to the left with tariff shed nearest and 1901 platform to the right.
D. Thompson

Far right:

Honing standard M&GN waiting shed, signalbox and the stationmaster's house, formerly a gatehouse, shown looking east in 1959.
K. A. Ladbury

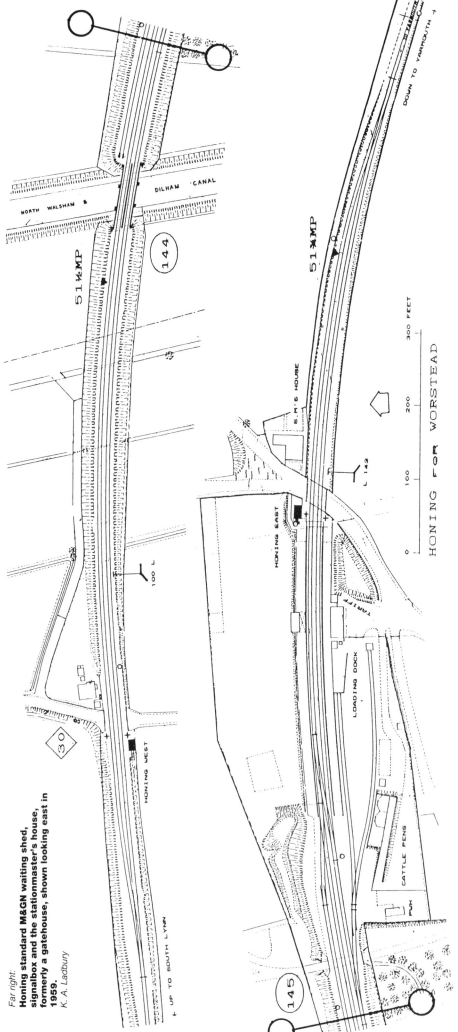

North Walsham Town

Opened: 13 June 1881

Notes: Large pavilion station in brick with timber waiting shelter, W&J-type signalbox and wooden footbridge. The goods shed was also timber. In 1897/98 the station was rebuilt by giving the main building a canopy and half-timbering in the gables, building a special 'arts & crafts' waiting room and replacing the old box with a Midland type. This was later fitted with M&GN-type front windows. Antingham Road Junction was an M&GN type 1a signalbox. The wooden

footbridge was replaced in steel in June 1910. The crossing loop was inadequate for many of the long trains over 10 bogies in length, but fortunately the refuge siding could be used for Down trains to clear the Mundesley line junction. The 1 in 64 bank was short but if a heavy Down train was held at the home signal it would have to set back to give an adequate start, or it would stall. The busy goods yard dealt with coal, timber, bricks and cattle; up to 50 wagons on peak days. The line to Antingham Road was

severed at bridge No 366 on 8 April 1958 and Antingham Road box closed on 4 May 1958. The link had not been much used in recent years, except for the 'Holiday Camps Express' in 1955. Another link to the GE was laid in 1958 south of the yard, not much used except as an access to the coal yard which remained after closure.

Closed: 28 February 1959

Remains: None.

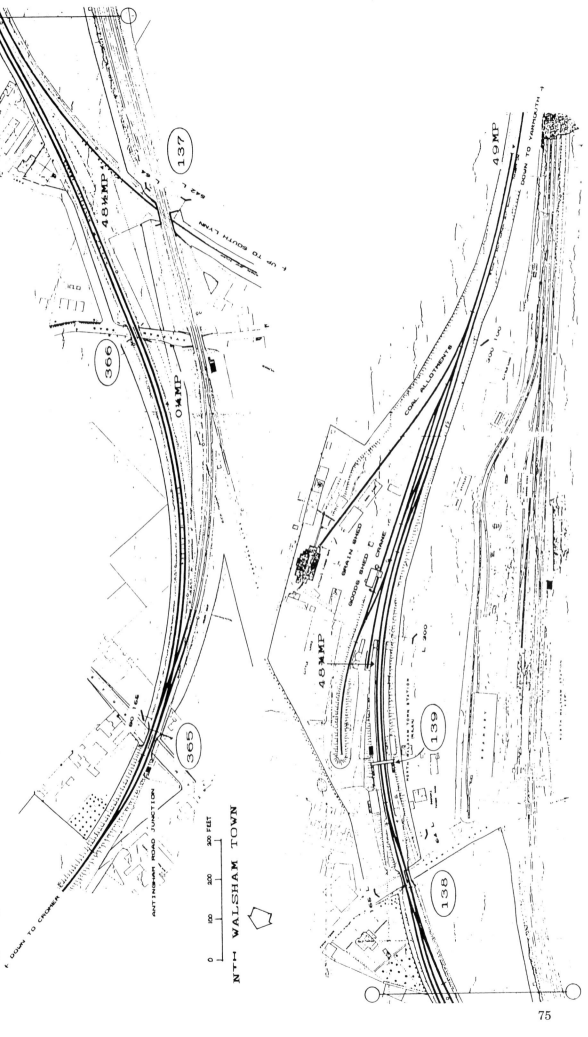

NTH WALSHAM TOWN

Paston & Knapton

Opened: 1 July 1898
Notes: A design similar to Gayton Road in 'arts & crafts' style, built by Cornish & Gaymer. Traffic was light but truckloads of mangolds, swedes and sugar beet were despatched, and it became the principal beet-loading centre for the area. There was a tablet released ground-frame in a small cabin to operate the points.
Closed: 5 October 1964
Remains: Private house.

Left:
A view of Paston & Knapton station from track level in 1964, looking towards North Walsham under girder bridge No 352. Note the concrete platform wall. Originally there were steps down from the bridge.
M&GN Circle

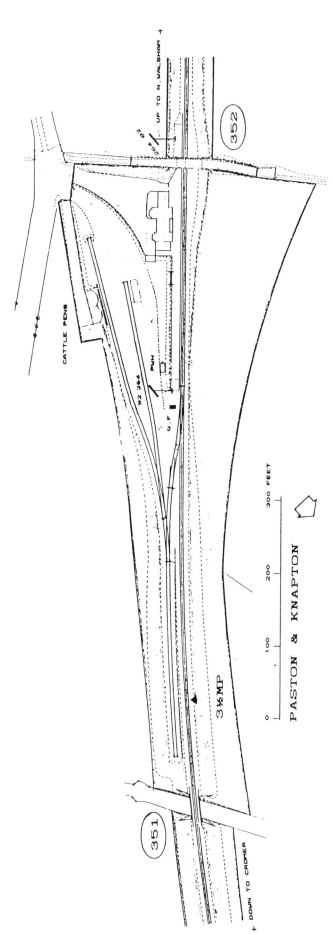

PASTON & KNAPTON

Mundesley-on-Sea

Opened: 1 July 1898

Notes: A large picturesque building in the 'arts & crafts' style, built by Cornish & Gaymer. There was a matching waiting shelter and both had large ridge and furrow canopies. There was also a large cast-iron urinal, an **M&GN**-type footbridge, an **M&GN**-type swing water crane, an **M&GN** water tower on wooden piles with twin gabled roof and a corrugated iron engine shed. Mundesley South signalbox was **M&GN** type 1a, but Mundesley North was type 1c. The latter was closed in 1930 and an 'Auxiliary Tablet Hut' supplied on the platform near the water crane, and the trackplan simplified. The station was popular in summer, especially after the opening of the Mundesley Holiday Camp in 1930. There was also a good parcels traffic, but goods traffic was light, consisting mainly of coal, Moy being the main merchant.

Closed: 5 October 1964

Remains: Row of cottages, otherwise none.

Left:

Mundesley soon after opening with a GER train in the Down platform. The station was very picturesque in the 'arts & crafts' style, both platforms having ridge-and-furrow canopies. The bay window just visible under the canopy was for the stationmaster's office.
Lens of Sutton

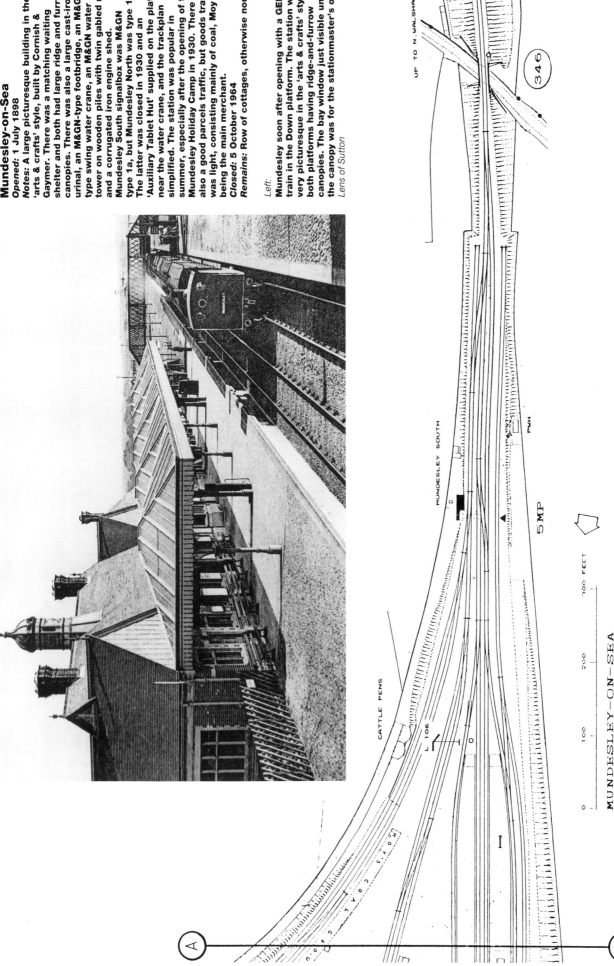

MUNDESLEY-ON-SEA

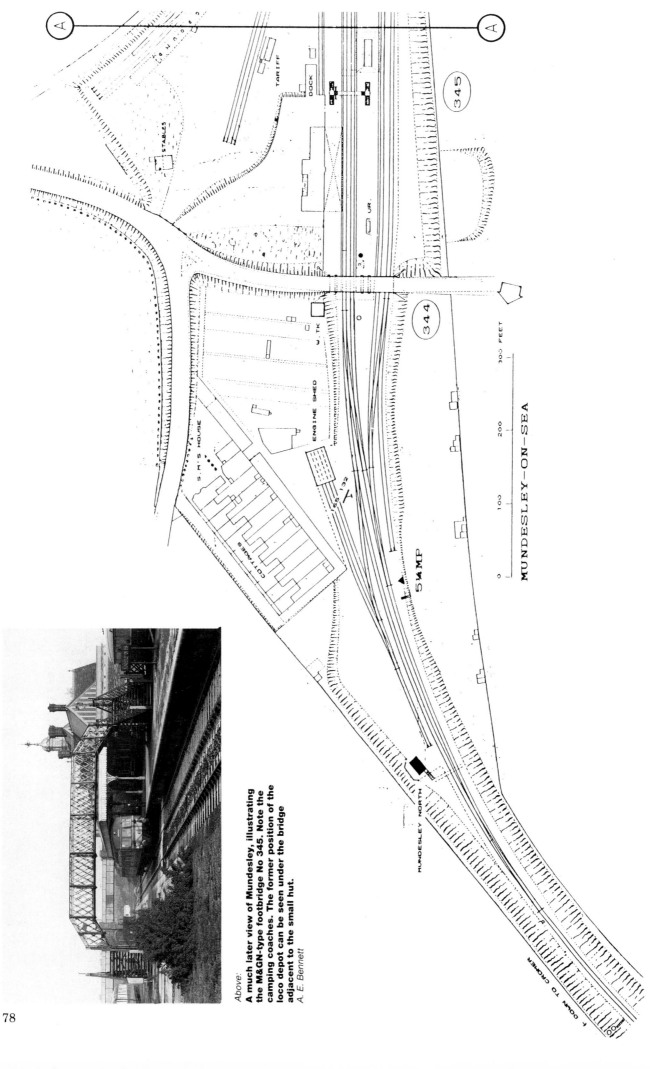

Above:
A much later view of Mundesley, illustrating the M&GN-type footbridge No 345. Note the camping coaches. The former position of the loco depot can be seen under the bridge adjacent to the small hut.
A. E. Bennett

MUNDESLEY-ON-SEA

345

344

300 FEET

200

100

0

STABLES

TARIFF

DOCK

UR

S.M'S HOUSE

ENGINE SHED

W. TK

COTTAGES

5¼ MP

MUNDESLEY NORTH

To CROMER

To N. WALSHAM

Trimingham

Opened: 3 August 1906
Notes: Island platform building in final M&GN
brick and terracotta style with enamel
nameboard and platform-mounted M&GN
type 1c signalbox. Access was from the
overbridge via wooden stairs. The yard was
never busy, nor was passenger traffic. The
signalbox closed as a tablet post in April
1922, the goods yard points being operated
by a tablet released ground-frame. The Down
loop was closed and both it and the signalbox
were removed in 1931. Between Trimingham
and Overstrand was Sidestrand Halt, opened
on 23 May 1936. It had a low, timber platform
without a shelter, and was little used except
by summer walkers.
Closed: 7 April 1953
Remains: Stationmaster's house, cottages,
bridge.

Right:
**Trimingham in 1963, showing the stairs down
from the overbridge. The building is identical
to that at Overstrand. Houses now occupy the
site.**
D. Thompson

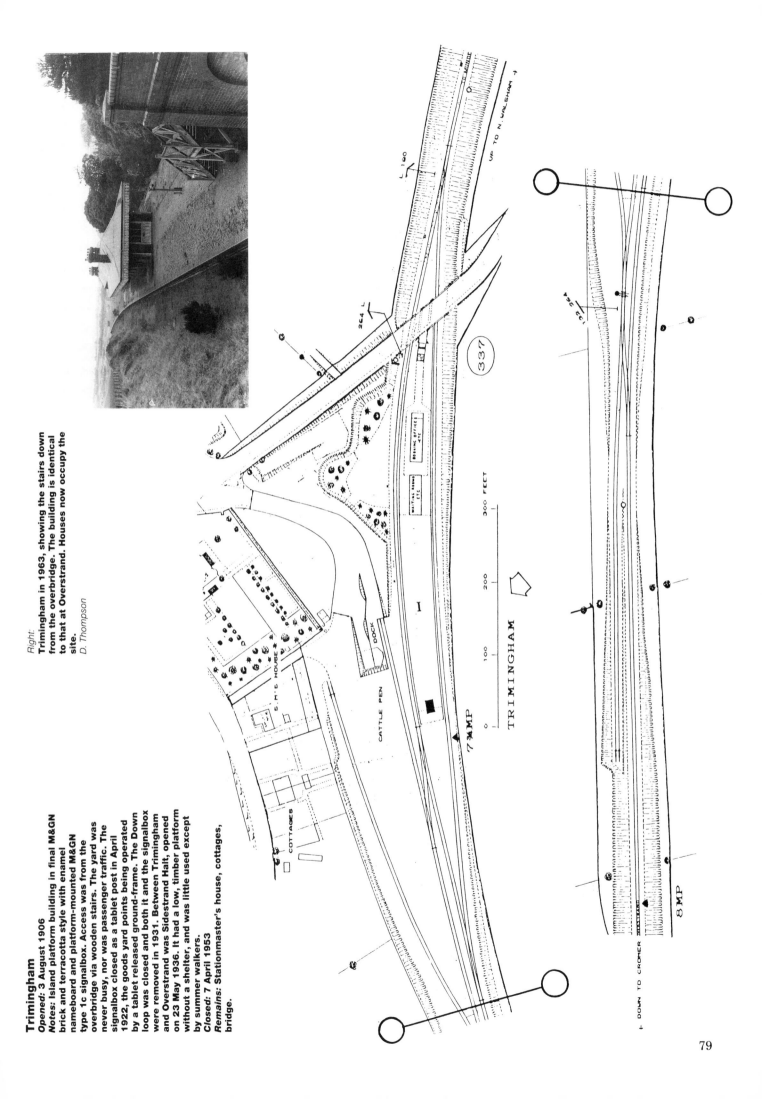

TRIMINGHAM

79

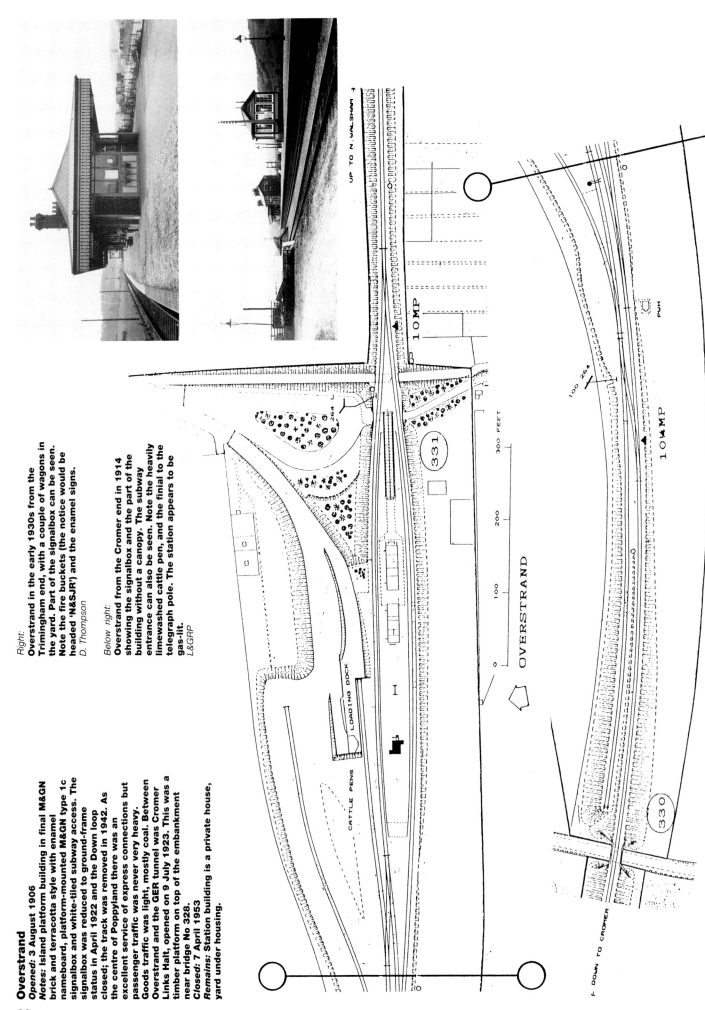

Overstrand

Opened: 3 August 1906

Notes: Island platform building in final M&GN brick and terracotta style with enamel nameboard, platform-mounted M&GN type 1c signalbox and white-tiled subway access. The signalbox was reduced to ground-frame status in April 1922 and the Down loop closed; the track was removed in 1942. As the centre of Poppyland there was an excellent service of express connections but passenger traffic was never very heavy. Goods traffic was light, mostly coal. Between Overstrand and the GER tunnel was Cromer Links Halt, opened on 9 July 1923. This was a timber platform on top of the embankment near bridge No 328.

Closed: 7 April 1953

Remains: Station building is a private house, yard under housing.

Right:
Overstrand in the early 1930s from the Trimingham end, with a couple of wagons in the yard. Part of the signalbox can be seen. Note the fire buckets (the notice would be headed 'N&SJR') and the enamel signs.
D. Thompson

Below right:
Overstrand from the Cromer end in 1914 showing the signalbox and the part of the building without a canopy. The subway entrance can also be seen. Note the heavily limewashed cattle pen, and the finial to the telegraph pole. The station appears to be gas-lit.
L&GRP

80

Poppyland

The dominant feature in this region is the so-called 'Cromer Ridge', a glacial feature crossing diagonally from Melton Constable to Cromer, where the land rises from the general 50-100ft level of east Norfolk to the 300ft contour. There is a break in this difficult obstruction in the hinterland between Corpusty and Holt, known as the Briston Gap where the land falls below the 200ft contour but, unfortunately for the M&GN, the patronage of Lord Hastings obliged the L&F to use a plot of land straddling the parish boundaries of Melton Constable with Burgh Parva and Briston over the 250ft level, involving stiff climbs from all directions. It also sloped down from west to east but nevertheless this large tract of land was developed into the important junction and works of Melton Constable.

The scenery of the area is effectively in two parts; to the south being the low-lying loamy soils covered by rolling fields of corn with pasture in the river valleys. Rising sharply to the north are the wooded hills or the heather and gorse-covered heaths of the Cromer Ridge, based on sands and gravels. These gravels were exploited for ballast at Holt, Kelling and Thurning. The ubiquitous cornfields interlaced with the 'regal red poppies' were a sight that delighted the many visitors who came to enjoy the quiet watering-places of the north Norfolk coast. As stated in the E&M opening notice for the Cromer line in 1887:

'The new line passes through one of the most beautiful and picturesque districts in Norfolk, and affords a series of magnificent views of the sea and coast.'

However these views were gained at a cost; the Cromer branch was the most steeply-graded line on the whole M&GN. The whole line was almost constantly on embankments or in cuttings, affording tantalising glimpses of the sea. Leaving Cromer Beach the double line undulated over the rolling fields, passing the Runton junctions after which it became single, falling gradually into Sheringham. From here it was almost continuous climbing for five miles up on to Kelling Heath, the steepest gradient being the two miles of 1 in 80 broken only by a short length of 1 in 264 at Weybourne. Once up on the Heath the line passed the lonely gatehouse No 53 and then fell only slightly into Holt. From Holt the surrounding land was more arable as the line plunged for two miles at 1 in 90 and 1 in 82 into the Glaven Valley, a picturesque area of wooded pastureland that penetrates deeply into the uplands. Finally came the three miles of climbing out of the valley at 1 in 80 and 1 in 93 through Briningham to Melton West Junction, the summit of the line. Although in a cutting at the junction, so elevated was the position and so steeply does the land fall away that the views from the signalbox were unrivalled, a train leaving Holt for Melton being easily followed on its way, and passing ships being visible on the distant sea.

At Melton West the Cromer branch joined the main line which itself had had to climb up to Melton. Crossing the Bure at Aylsham, the line climbed out of the valley at 1 in 100. On reaching the 150ft contour the line followed it, crossing the wooded upland at Bluestone before falling slightly again to Corpusty, perched on a ledge on the south side of the upper Bure valley. From Corpusty, apart from a slight dip over the Blackwater which flooded so disastrously in 1912, the line (now double) climbed at 1 in 150 and 1 in 100 up to the 250ft contour at Melton Constable, ignoring the lesser heights of the Briston Gap. The scenery also begins to change as the line gains the more heavily-wooded clay uplands of the sub-region known as 'Mid Norfolk'.

Cromer Beach-Sheringham is the only part of the M&GN now carrying BR passengers, but Sheringham-Kelling has been preserved by the North Norfolk Railway. The architecture and fittings are still largely *in situ* and can be experienced at first hand. Cromer was, until recently, relatively complete but the building of a Safeways supermarket on the yard caused the demolition of the engine shed, goods shed and goods office, also the train shed at the rear of the main building and so Cromer is now a shadow of its former self. Fortunately the 1920s concrete signalbox is still used, the only M&GN box to be so, and of course the platforms are in use as well.

From a Sheringham-bound train one can view the remains of the 'Runton Triangle', noting the M&GN link to the N&SJt curving away sharply to the south, and seeing where the now-abandoned arm of the N&SJt once approached from Newstead Lane Junction over the magnificent five arched viaduct No 317 to join the M&GN at Runton West Junction. West Runton station itself was always undistinguished, and is even more so now. However, the original building is still there, now boarded up, and the 1922 concrete nameboard still stands, partly obscured by a modern timetable board. Sheringham 'station' is now merely a halt positioned on the east of Station Road but the old station can be seen beyond. This is largely intact, although the East box had to be moved on to the platform to make way for road 'improvements' and the Up waiting room and footbridge have gone. Sheringham West box was unfortunately demolished but has now been replaced by a preserved GE box. Weybourne has been restored and developed as perhaps the best NNR station, but the Holt terminus has yet to be finished.

Beyond the confines of BR and the NNR, the Cromer branch has not fared too badly. The main Fakenham road now occupies the trackbed right through the site of Holt station, but the old ballast pits can be seen on the left and the large grain store still stands. A roundabout now occupies the site of bridge No 297 but the line can be seen curving away in a cutting to the west. The trackbed survives well along this stretch, passing under the Thornage road further along where only one side of bridge No 296 remains, the road having been straightened. The line can be regained near the village of Hunworth where it crosses the River Glaven and the road with two distinctive semicircular arched bridges Nos 294 and 293. However, between Hunworth and the site of Briningham Junction, two underbridges have been removed and some of the line has been ploughed in. Gatehouse No 52, once superseded by Briningham signalbox, has now outlasted it, but some housing occupies the line and the site of gatehouse No 51. Towards Melton the trackbed resumes and can be followed almost up to Melton West Junction.

Melton Constable is now a sorry sight in comparison to its former glory. The station and platform are gone, the main road has been realigned over the site of bridge No 104, and most of the cuttings around Melton West have been filled in. However, there are many other remains: the railway village on the south side of Briston Road is largely unchanged, although the gasworks has gone; the Railway Institute (now the Country Club) is still lively and Colman's shop and the Hastings Arms opposite still stand. Adjacent to Colman's is part of the original timber Yarmouth/Holt station. The goods yard has been bisected by the access to the industrial estate (Marriott Way) but the goods shed is still used. Most of the works' buildings now house local industries, although a few have been demolished. At the rear of the site, by the Hindolvestone road, the enormous 1898 water tank is a prominent landmark, and the original works entrance steps can still be seen. The site of Melton East has been altered by levelling, and part of the Norwich line has been infilled. All of the Yarmouth line cutting has been filled right up to bridge No 105. The parapet walls of the latter have been rebuilt, apparently because a Wellington bomber crashed on it in 1941!

Much of the Yarmouth line between Melton and Briston gatehouse No 23 has been lost, but after that most of it remains complete with several bridges almost into Corpusty. The station building at Corpusty is used as a sports pavilion but the yard has been levelled and grassed; a good view can be obtained from the adjacent overbridge No 115. Although at several points the formation has been incorporated into fields, in general the line survives quite well on its way to Bluestone, and can be followed along the main Corpusty-Norwich road. Bluestone station (or crossing No 23A since 1916) is in private hands and is well preserved. Although once standing on a through road to Oulton, the building of the airfield in World War 2 severed the connection, and the station now stands on a private cul-de-sac. From Bluestone almost into Aylsham the trackbed has been ploughed in, only gatehouse No 24 showing where the line once crossed the road to Oulton Street. Nearer Aylsham the trackbed becomes the Weaver's Way and crosses the Bure on girder bridge No 126 before reaching the site of the station.

81

Cromer Beach

Opened: 16 June 1887

Notes: Large 'arts & crafts' building with medium goods shed, small E&M-type engine shed, tall timber E&M-type signalbox (replaced c1922 by concrete box) and standard water tower, fitted with roof c1902. The cattle dock could hold three wagons, but after tow-roping was discontinued in 1904, two at a time were shunted by hand. Goods trains were halted at the home signal, the engine would run forward into the 'Jubilee' siding and the train would run into the reception road by gravity. Shunting was done by the train engine. The goods traffic was quite heavy, coal being important to supply the five merchants and the gas works, timber for Travis & Arnold, beer from Burton and general groceries and merchandise for local shops. Mundesley line goods traffic was only light. Passenger traffic was heavy, especially during the summer. Bridge No 316 was demolished in 1920. The station was enlarged on 19 September 1954.

Closed: 31 January 1969 (goods), still open for passenger services

Remains: Main building, platform, signalbox.

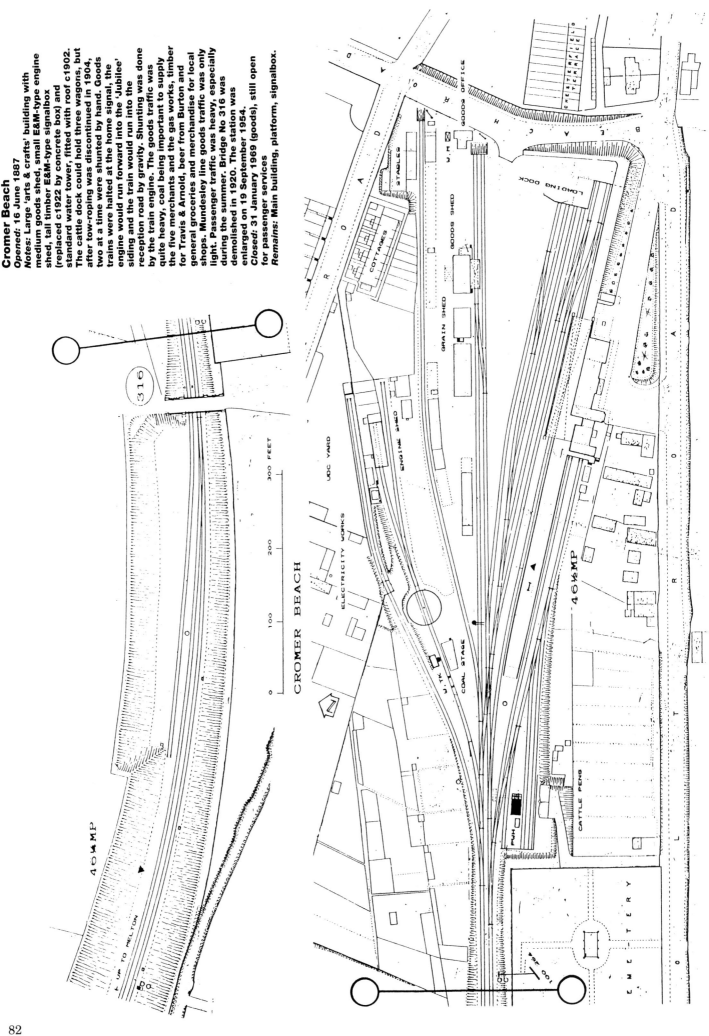

CROMER BEACH

82

Left:
Cromer station from the bufferstops in 1914. There is a variety of GN vehicles in the carriage sidings. Note the M&GN cattle wagon No 75 and the transition to flat-bottom rail in the foreground.
L&GRP

Bottom left:
Cromer pictured on a summer morning in 1910. The train in the bay is the 'Leicester' portion, made up of MR vehicles with a large stock third on the front. In the distance is a Class A 4-4-0 rebuilt with MR boiler. The signalbox is on the skyline and immediately to the right is part of the arch of bridge No 316.
Author's collection

Below:
The magnificent timber E&M signalbox at Cromer, taken before 1906, as the signalman is holding a tablet in a hand-exchange pouch. Until about 1897 a gantry extended across from this landing to a set of steps near the platform ramp. This box was replaced by a concrete one in c1920.
M&GN Circle

The Runton Triangle

Opened: 23 July 1906

Notes: Runton East and Runton West Junction boxes were M&GN type 1b, but Newstead Lane Junction and Roughton Road Junction boxes were N&SJt variant M&GN type 1c, Roughton Road having a special roof. The gas works siding was opened in June 1899 as a tablet-released ground-frame, but after 1906 controlled from Runton East. This siding was often used to store vehicles. There was coal traffic in and empties out, but other products were dispersed locally by road. The siding closed in April 1961. The Mundesley line closed on 7 April 1953; Roughton Road on 5 June 1961; West (N&SJt) curve, Runton East and West boxes closed on 21 April 1963 and lines singled to bi-directional parallel lines.

Closed: West curve 21 April 1963

Remains: largely complete, but all boxes demolished.

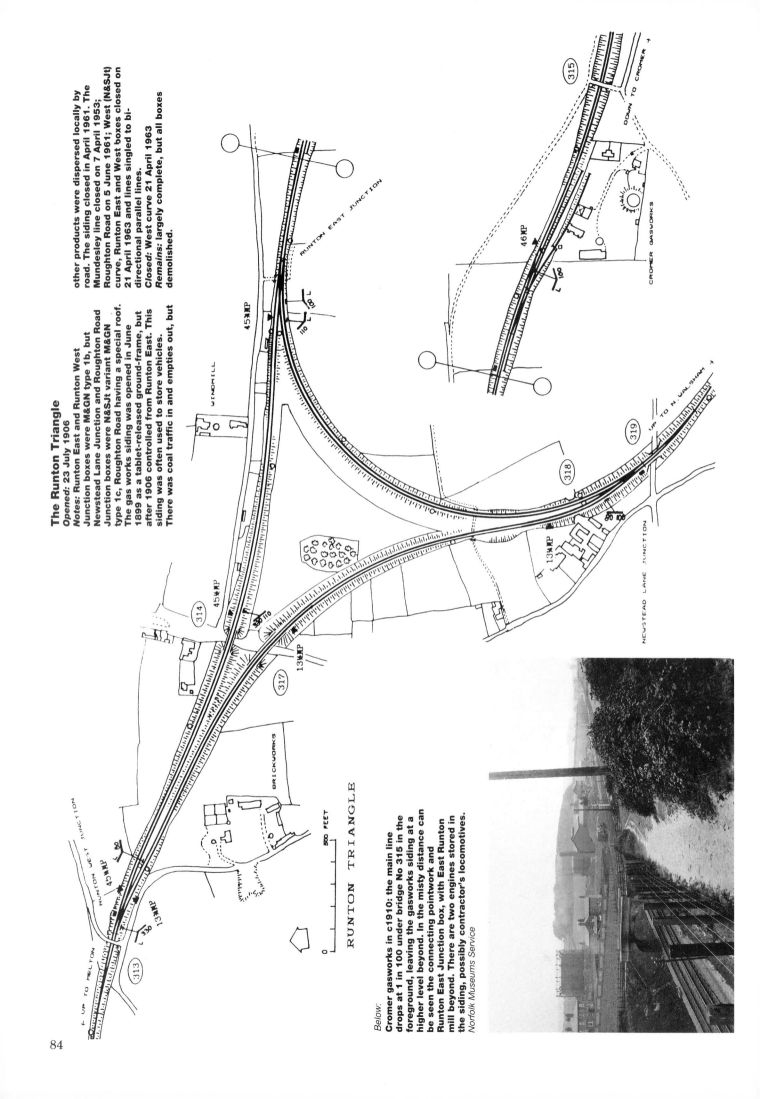

RUNTON TRIANGLE

500 FEET

Below:

Cromer gasworks in c1910: the main line drops at 1 in 100 under bridge No 315 in the foreground, leaving the gasworks siding at a higher level beyond. In the misty distance can be seen the connecting pointwork and Runton East Junction box, with East Runton mill beyond. There are two engines stored in the siding, possibly contractor's locomotives.
Norfolk Museums Service

84

Bottom left:
At the southern point of the triangle was Newstead Lane Junction, an **M&GN** type 1c box, standing high on an embankment adjacent to bridge No 319. Note the non-automatic tablet receiver; the N&SJt was all hand exchange.
R. Meek collection

Below:
At the far side of the triangle was Runton West Junction, supplied with a **M&GN** type 1b box. The line diverging to the right was the N&SJt to Newstead Lane Junction. An automatic delivering apparatus was provided, and the hand exchange stage was originally for **GE** trains to Sheringham.
M&GN Circle

Below right:
At the divergence of the two routes stood the two Runton viaducts, the further (**M&GN**) one being No 314 and the nearer (**N&SJt**) one being No 317. The latter is a masterpiece of construction, being on a curve, skew, and on a 1 in 80 gradient.
M&GN Circle

Bottom right:
The picturesque Roughton Road Junction box viewed in 1961. The route to Mundesley formerly passed in the foreground (closed in 1953), and the GER to Cromer Junction at the far side, still used today by passenger trains operated by Regional Railways.
M&GN Circle

West Runton

Opened: September 1887

Notes: A timber and corrugated iron version
of the office design. By 1909 a grounded
M&GN van body was in use as a store/tariff
shed. A concrete nameboard was erected in
1922. There was a stationmaster and in
summer a porter. Most trains stopped here,
but if any conditional stop was required a red
flag was hoisted up the flagpole. There was
considerable traffic for the adjacent golf links
and the 'Links Hotel'.

Closed: Still open but unstaffed since
2 January 1967

Remains: Complete but derelict.

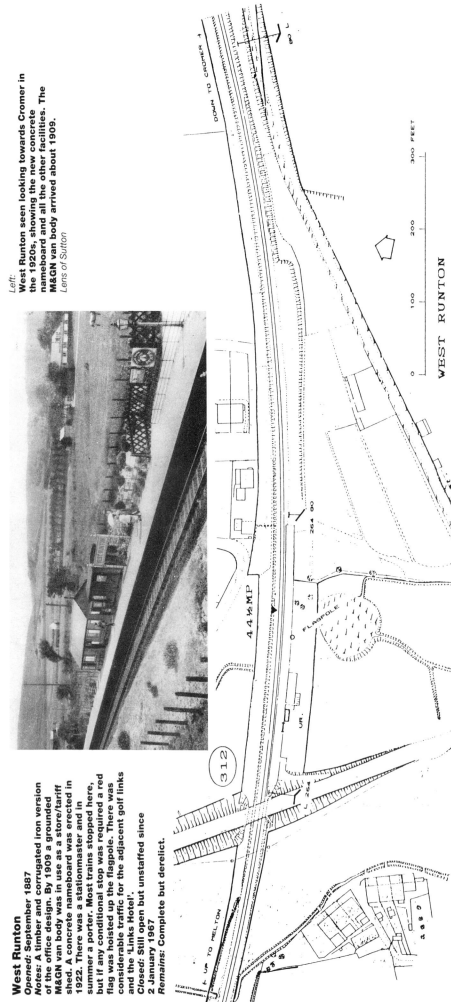

WEST RUNTON

DOWN TO CROMER →

← UP TO MELTON

44½MP

FLAGPOLE

312

0   100   200   300 FEET

Sheringham

Opened: 16 June 1887

Notes: The original station had an E&M
pavilion, E&M waiting shed, a tall E&M-type
signalbox on the Up platform and two E&M-
type lift water cranes. Bridge No 305 was
elliptical in brick. In 1896/97 the main
building was extended and an Up waiting
shelter were built to match, with 'arts &
crafts' detailing and canopies. A footbridge
was erected and the yard improved. In
1905/06 a new track layout was installed
with a new girder bridge and M&GN type 1b
East and West signalboxes. A bay platform
was used for westbound departures, and the
platforms were lengthened in 1907, as was
the footbridge. Goods traffic was general,
with some shellfish and a special traffic in
beach flints. The bay was used until February
1940 when trap points were taken out of the
goods line.

Closed: 2 February 1967

Remains: Nearly complete; now used by the
North Norfolk Railway

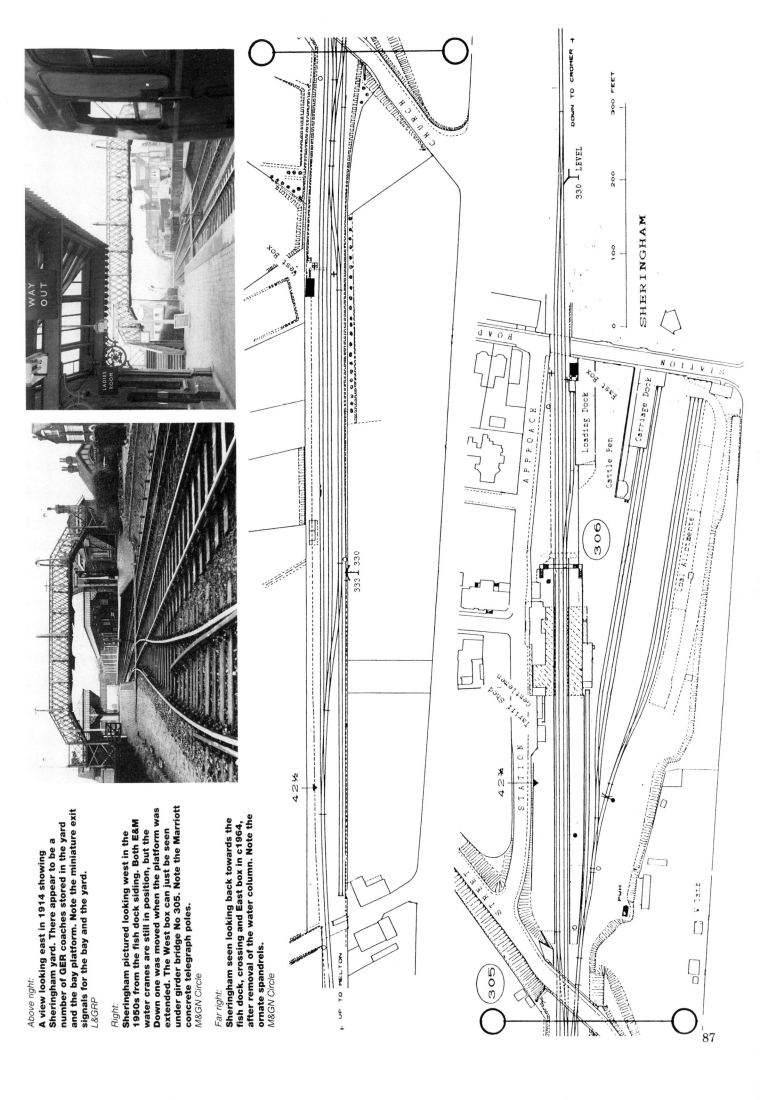

Above right:
**A view looking east in 1914 showing
Sheringham yard. There appear to be a
number of GER coaches stored in the yard
and the bay platform. Note the miniature exit
signals for the bay and the yard.**
L&GRP

Right:
**Sheringham pictured looking west in the
1950s from the fish dock siding. Both E&M
water cranes are still in position, but the
Down one was moved when the platform was
extended. The West box can just be seen
under girder bridge No 305. Note the Marriott
concrete telegraph poles.**
M&GN Circle

Far right:
**Sheringham seen looking back towards the
fish dock, crossing and East box in c1964,
after removal of the water column. Note the
ornate spandrels.**
M&GN Circle

87

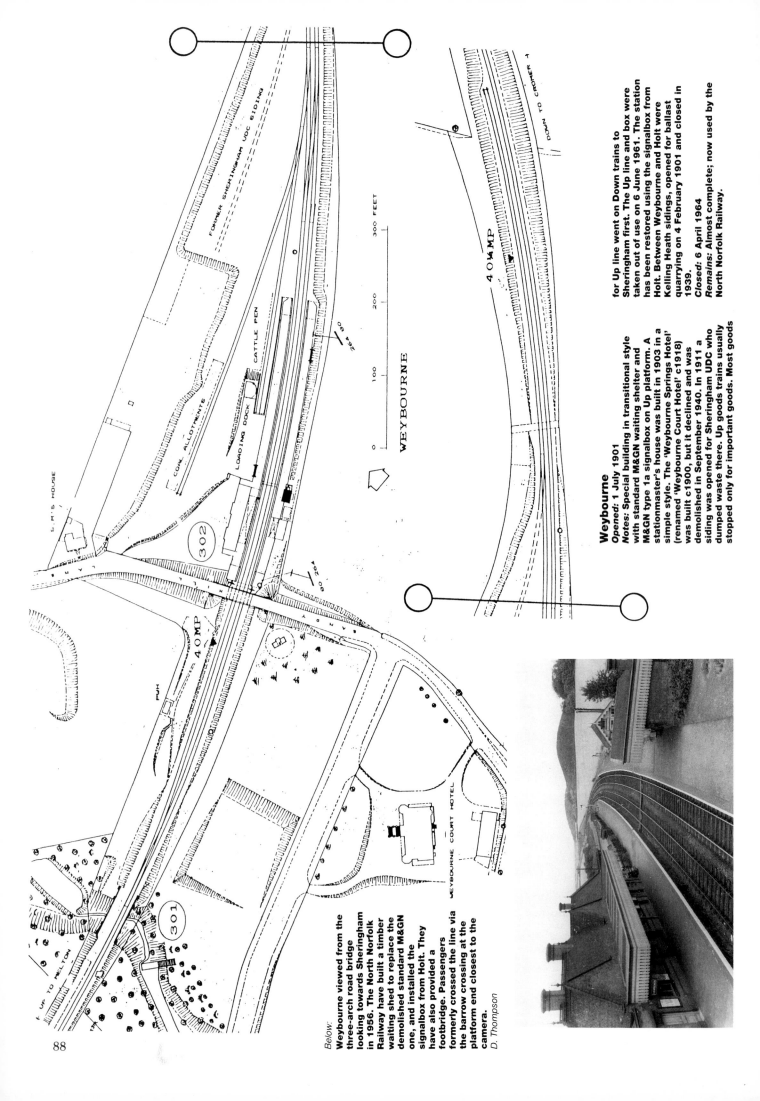

FORMER SHERINGHAM UDC SIDING

CATTLE PEN

COAL ALLOTMENTS

LOADING DOCK

DOWN TO CROMER →

302

301

40 MP

4 04 MP

S.M'S HOUSE

↑ UP TO MELTON

WEYBOURNE COURT HOTEL

PUH

WEYBOURNE

0   100   200   300 FEET

Below:

Weybourne viewed from the three-arch road bridge looking towards Sheringham in 1956. The North Norfolk Railway have built a timber waiting shed to replace the demolished standard M&GN one, and installed the signalbox from Holt. They have also provided a footbridge. Passengers formerly crossed the line via the barrow crossing at the platform end closest to the camera.

D. Thompson

Weybourne
Opened: 1 July 1901
Notes: Special building in transitional style with standard M&GN waiting shelter and M&GN type 1a signalbox on Up platform. A stationmaster's house was built in 1903 in a simple style. The 'Weybourne Springs Hotel' (renamed 'Weybourne Court Hotel' c1918) was built c1900, but it declined and was demolished in September 1940. In 1911 a siding was opened for Sheringham UDC who dumped waste there. Up goods trains usually stopped only for important goods. Most goods for Up line went on Down trains to Sheringham first. The Up line and box were taken out of use on 6 June 1961. The station has been restored using the signalbox from Holt. Between Weybourne and Holt were Kelling Heath sidings, opened for ballast quarrying on 4 February 1901 and closed in 1939.
Closed: 6 April 1964
Remains: Almost complete; now used by the North Norfolk Railway.

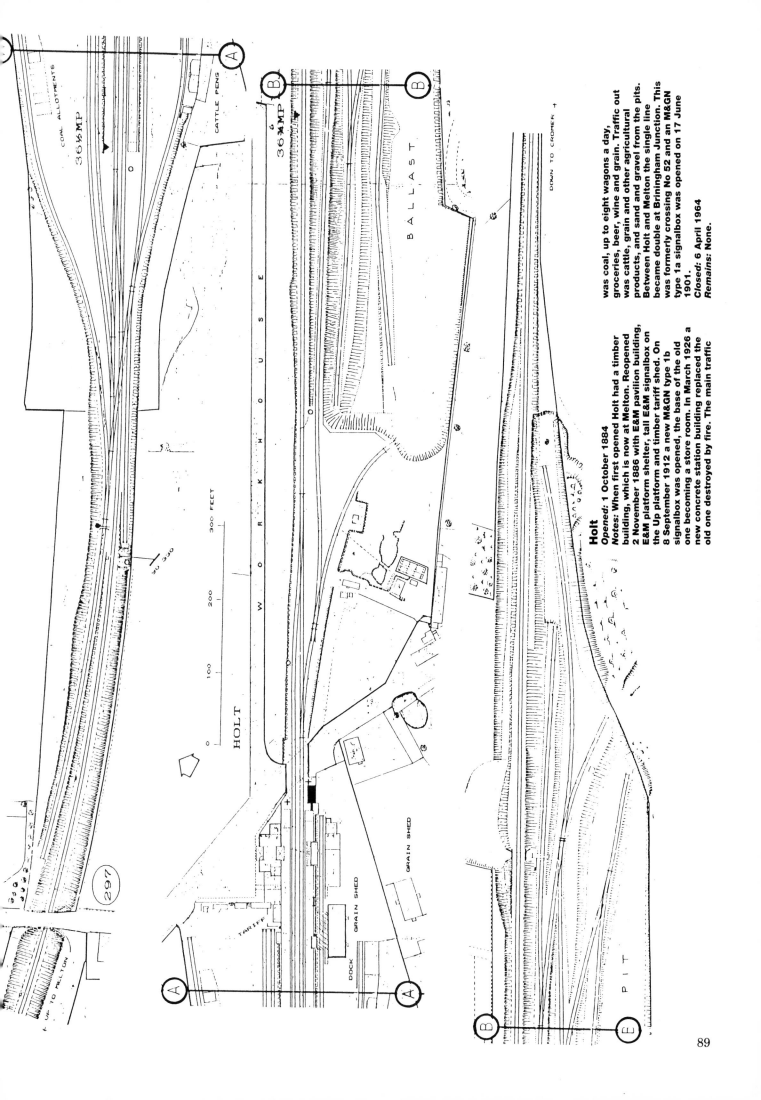

COAL ALLOTMENTS

UP TO MELTON

36¼ MP

CATTLE PENS

36¾ MP

A

B

B

A

HOLT

300 FEET

300 FEET

100 200 300

WORKHOUSE

TARIFF

DOCK GRAIN SHED

GRAIN SHED

BALLAST

DOWN TO CROMER →

E PIT

297

Holt

Opened: 1 October 1884

Notes: When first opened Holt had a timber building, which is now at Melton. Reopened 2 November 1886 with E&M pavilion building, E&M platform shelter, tall E&M signalbox on the Up platform and timber tariff shed. On 8 September 1912 a new M&GN type 1b signalbox was opened, the base of the old one becoming a store room. In March 1926 a new concrete station building replaced the old one destroyed by fire. The main traffic was coal, up to eight wagons a day, groceries, beer, wine and grain. Traffic out was cattle, grain and other agricultural products, and sand and gravel from the pits. Between Holt and Melton the single line became double at Briningham Junction. This was formerly crossing No 52 and an M&GN type 1a signalbox was opened on 17 June 1901.

Closed: 6 April 1964
Remains: None.

89

Felmingham

Opened: 5 April 1883

Notes: The last W&J office design, in brick.
Apparently, the small timber signalbox
originally controlled siding points and
protecting signals, but by 1904 this had been
converted into a tariff shed and a tablet-
controlled ground-frame installed. Rope

shunting was allowed for Down trains but this
was later stopped and Down freight had to go
to North Walsham and return on an Up train.
The stationmaster's house was built in 1913
in the new domestic style.

Closed: 28 February 1929

Remains: Almost complete.

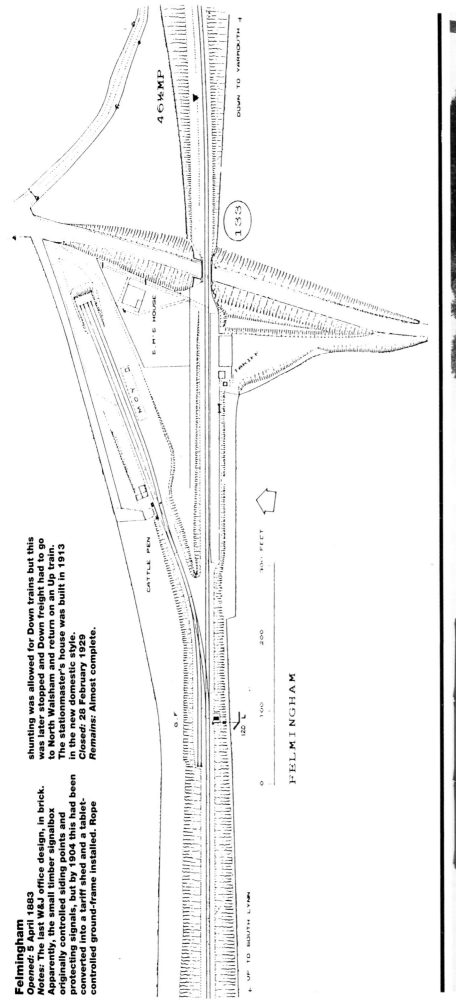

FELMINGHAM

90

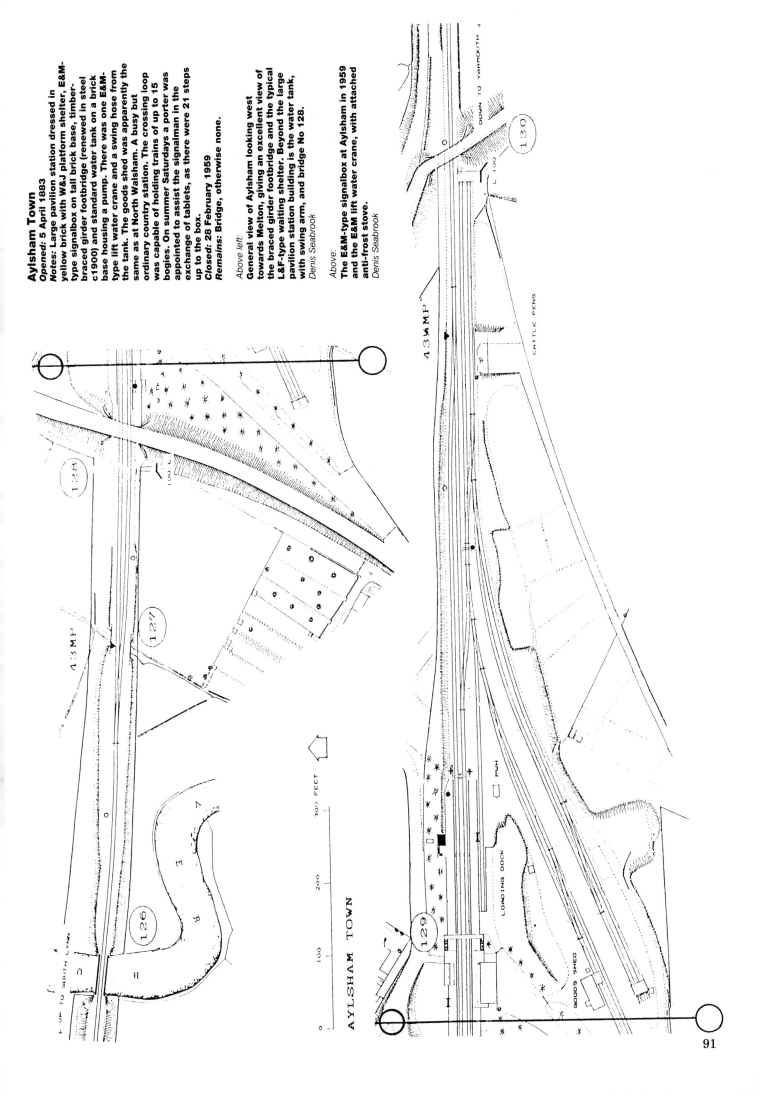

Aylsham Town

Opened: 5 April 1883

Notes: Large pavilion station dressed in yellow brick with W&J platform shelter, E&M-type signalbox on tall brick base, timber-braced girder footbridge (renewed in steel c1900) and standard water tank on a brick base housing a pump. There was one E&M-type lift water crane and a swing hose from the tank. The goods shed was apparently the same as at North Walsham. A busy but ordinary country station. The crossing loop was capable of holding trains of up to 15 bogies. On summer Saturdays a porter was appointed to assist the signalman in the exchange of tablets, as there were 21 steps up to the box.

Closed: 28 February 1959

Remains: Bridge, otherwise none.

Above left:
General view of Aylsham looking west towards Melton, giving an excellent view of the braced girder footbridge and the typical L&F-type waiting shelter. Beyond the large pavilion station building is the water tank, with swing arm, and bridge No 128.
Denis Seabrook

Above:
The E&M-type signalbox at Aylsham in 1959 and the E&M lift water crane, with attached anti-frost stove.
Denis Seabrook

AYLSHAM TOWN

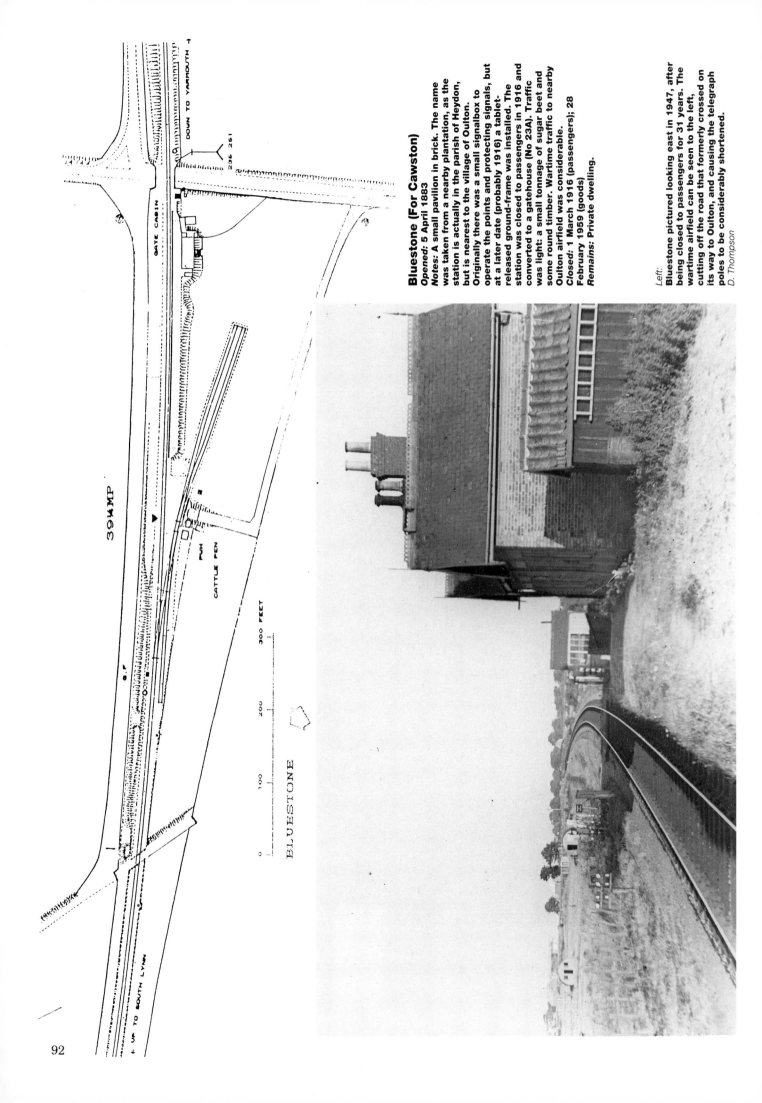

Bluestone (For Cawston)

Opened: 5 April 1883

Notes: A small pavilion in brick. The name was taken from a nearby plantation, as the station is actually in the parish of Heydon, but is nearest to the village of Oulton. Originally there was a small signalbox to operate the points and protecting signals, but at a later date (probably 1916) a tablet-released ground-frame was installed. The station was closed to passengers in 1916 and converted to a gatehouse (No 23A). Traffic was light: a small tonnage of sugar beet and some round timber. Wartime traffic to nearby Oulton airfield was considerable.

Closed: 1 March 1916 (passengers); 28 February 1959 (goods)

Remains: Private dwelling.

Left:
Bluestone pictured looking east in 1947, after being closed to passengers for 31 years. The wartime airfield can be seen to the left, cutting off the road that formerly crossed on its way to Oulton, and causing the telegraph poles to be considerably shortened.
D. Thompson

BLUESTONE

394MP

GATE CABIN

DOWN TO YARMOUTH

UP TO SOUTH LYNN

CATTLE PEN

235 261

0   100   200   300 FEET

Corpusty & Saxthorpe

Opened: 5 April 1883

Notes: A small pavilion in brick, with W&J
brick-based shelter and E&M-type signalbox
on tall brick base. The double line was
opened to here on 20 May 1901. A busy
station, being near the centre of the village.
Goods traffic was mainly agricultural: feeds,
fertilisers (including fish manure) and sugar
beet. Between Corpusty and Melton was
Thurning siding, first opened for ballast
quarrying in 1895, but supplied with an
M&GN type 1a signalbox in 1901. It was
usually only opened for ballast trains or to
increase train occupation capacity in the
summer. The sidings were removed in 1935
and the box taken out of use in December
1938.

Closed: 28 February 1959
Remains: Main building and bridge No 115.

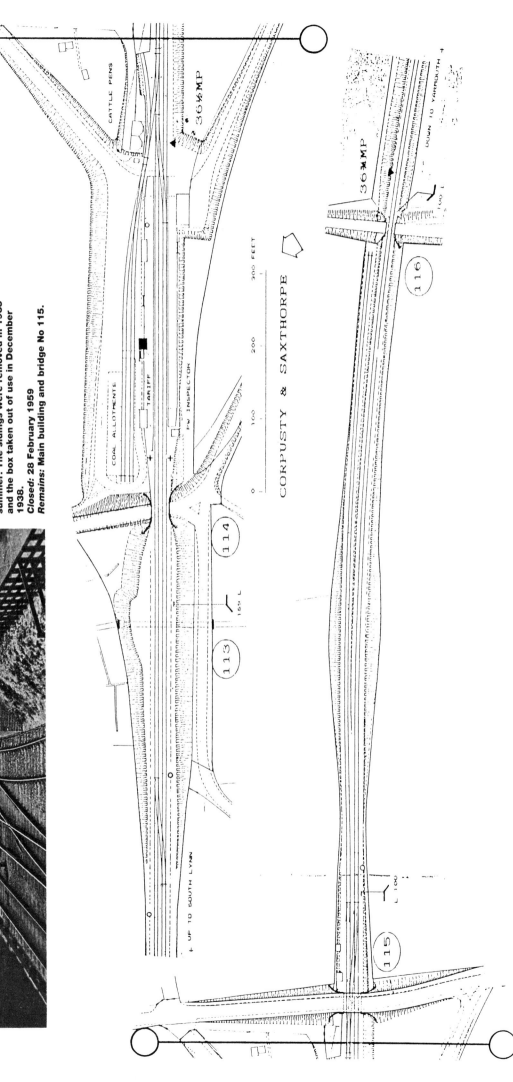

Left:
Corpusty viewed looking west from the road
bridge in c1914, showing many typical
features. Note the L&F waiting shelter with
no canopy. A GN cattle wagon is at the
limewashed cattle dock. The two white
circles above are elevated ground discs,
raised to be seen from the E&M signalbox.
M&GN Circle

CORPUSTY & SAXTHORPE

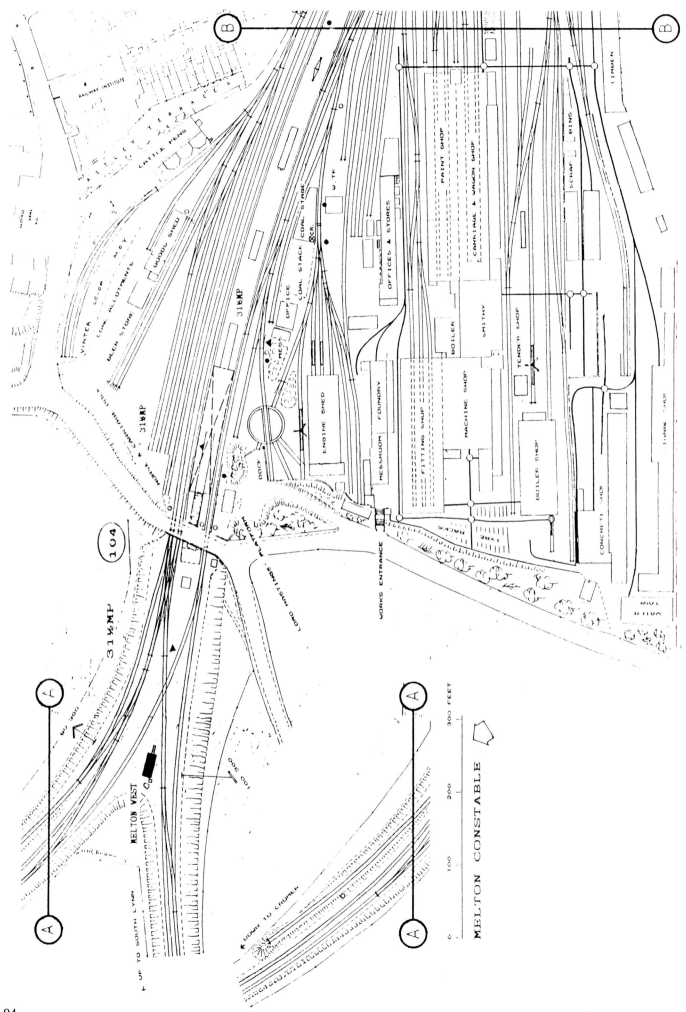

MELTON CONSTABLE

94

Melton Constable

Opened: 19 January 1882

Notes: Island platform with station building in yellow brick with red brick dressings, under a large canopy with CNR spandrels. Lord Hastings' private platform had a very small version of the pavilion. Originally the East and West signalboxes were of the E&M type with tall brick bases and the bridge was rolled iron joist with brick masonry. Other structures were the three-road engine shed for nine locomotives, the brick-based water tank, coal stage with hand crane and the Locomotive & Carriage Works. The Yarmouth line was doubled on 20 May 1901, the Lynn line on 2 June 1901 and the Cromer line on 17 June 1901. Two new M&GN type 1a boxes were opened at the same time at Melton West Junction and Melton East Junction. The lines between were worked on the 'permissive block' system, allowing two trains

to occupy them. The bridge was reconstructed in 1915/16 in concrete with wider spans, allowing a Down relief line to be laid. The very large water tank at the rear of the site was added in 1898 (100,000gal) and also supplied the village. The Yarmouth and Lynn lines were closed on 28 February 1959, but the others remained. The Norwich line closed on 12 September 1960 and the West box on 1 January 1961.

Water colums:
1 M&GN-type swing Hastings platform (Up)
2 M&GN-type swing Down platform
3 L&F-type standpipe turntable road
4 E&M-type lift loco road
5 Hose from tank loco road

Closed: 6 April 1964
Remains: Extensive, but incomplete.

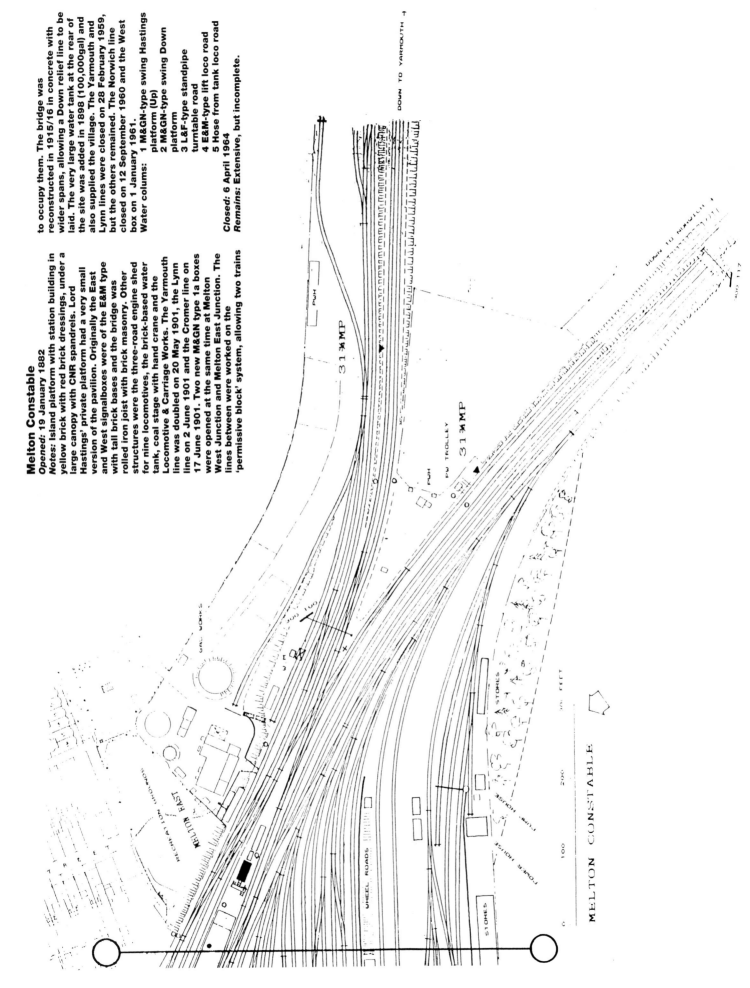

MELTON CONSTABLE

Right:
Looking east along the Down platform at Melton from the bridge in c1958, with the loading dock in the foreground. The hatch in the canopy roof was for access to the signal gantry which cantilevered over the main and goods lines at that point prior to 1916.
Denis Seabrook

Centre right:
Looking east along the Up platform at Melton from the bridge in c1958 showing the canopy roof, Melton East box in the distance, coaling stage (with later roof), water tank, messroom and 'wicka', and drawing office. In the foreground is the Hastings platform with adapted M&GN water crane, and above it the L&F type standpipe.
Denis Seabrook

Below right:
Melton loco shed in 1932 with unidentified Class A tank, Class A, Class C, and Class C No 47 present. The foundry is on the left. Note the shear-legs on the right.
A. G. Ellis

Bottom left:
Looking west along Melton's Down platform towards the bridge in c1958. Note the 'CNR' of the Central Norfolk Railway in the spandrel, and the M&GN concrete bracket signal equipped with upper quadrant arms and electrical route indicators.
Denis Seabrook

Bottom right:
A view from the west at Melton of the original bridge, showing work beginning on the rebuilding, and the main entrance to the station. Note the large, painted telegraph pole, and the bracketed Up starter signals, which were replaced in 1916 by two separate posts.
Author's collection

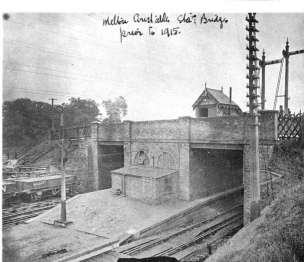

96

Mid-Norfolk and the Wensum Valley

The area of land whose northernmost bastion forms the hill upon which Melton Constable stands is the sub-region known as 'Mid-Norfolk'. The soil here is a heavy boulder clay on a chalk base and supports extensive oak woods. Although mainly a featureless plateau at about the 150ft contour, the east and south of this sub-region is bisected by wide river valleys, the major one being that of the Wensum. This river winds its way down from a source on the west Norfolk chalk ridge, passing Fakenham and crossing between Reepham and Dereham to Norwich. The valley bottom is filled with pasture and woodland and towards Norwich becomes almost a ravine, being quite narrow and restricted.

Norwich City station was built on a low island between the Wensum and a flood channel, just outside the old city wall and within sight of the Cathedral. As part of the arrangement with the city the L&F had to build two bridges and an approach road on to the island. The site seems to have been a bit unstable as the main entrance arch showed signs of cracking by c1900. A siding was laid across the station road into a riverside Corporation depot, eventually used to load coal destined for Norwich gasworks into barges via a jetty.

Although part of the original L&F construction, the Norwich branch was well-engineered and did not follow the terrain like the earlier GY&S. Leaving City station the single line crossed the Wensum on the first of three distinctive 'A frame' bridges and followed the river plain on nearly level gradients to Hellesdon where there was a second 'A frame' bridge, and on to Drayton and the third bridge. At Drayton the line left the valley and climbed steeply at 1 in 100 over a promontory left by the meandering river, falling again through Attlebridge back to the river valley at Lenwade. Here the L&F had to build two bridges and an approach road to the station for the convenience of Viscount Canterbury. The line then left the main valley and followed a small tributary of the Wensum, climbing at 1 in 100 through Whitwell &

Reepham on to the mid-Norfolk plateau. Apart from a slight dip into the head of the Blackwater valley the line climbed steadily through Guestwick (borrowed by Trollope) and Hindolvestone to join the main line at Melton East Junction.

For the station largest in area on the M&GN surprisingly little remains of Norwich City today, especially since track still remained here until 1969, but the pressure on available land in the city is very high. The major part of the platforms and site of the station building are taken up by the roundabout and approaches of the inner ring road. The bridge over the Wensum erected by the L&F and made by Barnard, Bishop & Barnard of Norwich is still used but there is little else to inform the modern traveller of the former use of the site. A strange survival are the rails crossing New Mills Yard where the old riverside coaldrops were situated. Most of the main station area is taken up by an industrial estate but alongside the river at the rear of the warehouses a footpath follows the route of the main lines. Near the roundabout the buffer wall of the central pair of platform roads can be seen and further along the route the base of the engine shed and the 52½ milepost. A wooden footbridge replaces the first 'A-frame' bridge which unfortunately was recently demolished, and the footpath follows the intact trackbed all the way to Hellesdon, which is the official start of 'Marriott's Way', having a car park. Much of the route can be followed by use of minor roads, but by far the most pleasant method is to walk the entire length. Only the platform remains of Hellesdon station, with the cattle pens and lairage, featuring a lot of half-round sleepers. Apart from some bridges, the trackbed is largely intact and used by Marriott's Way all the way past Whitwell & Reepham. The only significant deviation is at Drayton, where three bridges have been demolished and the station covered with an industrial estate. Attlebridge is in private hands and has been significantly altered, Lenwade also survives in private hands but mostly intact, and the footpath deviates around both these properties, before passing gatehouse No 22 on the way to Whitwell & Reepham station. It is intended to restore Whitwell & Reepham, at

the time of writing rather derelict, and make it into a visitors' centre. The yard and goods shed is presently in use as a garage for a private bus operator.

A few miles further towards Melton is an interesting area at Themelthorpe where not only do two abandoned lines cross each other (the GE Wroxham-County School line passing under the M&GN), but the abandoned curve of the BR link line built in 1960 can also be seen and this is the route taken by Marriott's Way, following the GE trackbed into Aylsham where one can join the Weaver's Way. Sandwiched between the two routes is gatehouse No 21. The GE line under the M&GN has now been ploughed, leaving the abutments of the M&GN bridge in the middle of a field. Passing gatehouse No 20 the traveller comes upon Guestwick station which is intact and inhabited. The platform-mounted signalbox still exists, as do the two railwaymen's cottages. Beyond Guestwick a lot of the trackbed has been ploughed but gatehouses Nos 19 and 18 can be seen from the Hindolvestone road. Hindolvestone is in private hands and slightly altered, and the cottages, gatehouse No 17 and the adjacent gate box also survive. Between Hindolvestone and Melton Constable most of the line is privately owned.

By virtue of the Norwich branch having stayed open for goods after the main closure (the section from Themelthorpe to Lenwade surviving until the early 1980s), it is perhaps the most complete stretch of abandoned M&GN trackbed with the highest concentration of remaining architecture and artefacts.

Below:
The impressive exterior of Norwich City station taken from Station Road in c1906. Tram lines are just visible in the cobbled surface of the street. The boys are lounging outside the entrance to their school and to the right is the bridge over the Wensum flood channel.
M&GN Circle

Norwich City

Opened: 2 December 1882

Notes: The station building was a large Italianate brick structure with a central entrance under a portico, two main platforms and two large canopies bearing 'E&MR' in the spandrels. There was also a large three-road engine shed and two E&M-type signalboxes — Norwich North and Norwich South. The connection into the goods yard was singled in 1926 and the North box abolished in March 1934, its function being divided between the South box and an 'Auxiliary Tablet Hut' with ground-frame. A new 60ft 0in turntable was brought into use on 30 January 1931. The main building was destroyed in an air raid on 27 April 1942 and was replaced by a 'temporary' building adapted from LNER sectional concrete huts which lasted until closure. Norwich was the premier station on the line with express connections to London and the Midlands and North. There was a substantial volume of sundries, minerals and, especially, coal; it was quite common for four coal specials to leave South Lynn for Norwich in one morning. Cattle was handled in large numbers, sometimes over 100 wagons per day. The remaining signalbox was abolished on 31 October 1962.

Closed: 28 February 1959 (passengers); 3 February 1969 (goods)

Remains: Very little.

Above right:
This interesting view of the platforms at Norwich City was taken in 1914 and shows the twin canopies, M&GN open and covered carriage trucks, and the original nameboard.
L&GRP

Below right:
The same aspect of Norwich City station taken from further back in c1930, showing all four platform faces (the middle pair were used mainly for storage) and the water tank and enginemen's messroom to the left. Note the 3mph limit board and the signals for both directions of running on one post.
M&GN Circle

Far right:
A view of Norwich City looking towards Hellesdon in the 1950s: the E&M signalbox was originally Norwich South, Norwich North being similar. The loco shed is the LNER post-1942 replacement and the line in front of the box leads to the 1931 turntable.
M&GN Circle

NORWICH CITY PLAN DATE 1920

500 FEET

COAL MERCHANTS

1. WALPOLE
2. HASTINGS & STERRY
3. WILLIMENT
4. PLUMMER
5. BARBER
6. BESSEY & PALMER
7. BETTS
8. BUSH
9. RUDD
10. BETTS
11. GOULD
12. TAYLOR
13. SELLEX
14. SAVAGE
15. BELL
16. JONES
17. HASTINGS & ST.
18. WEBSDALE
19. GOULD
20. WEBSDALE
21. FULCHER

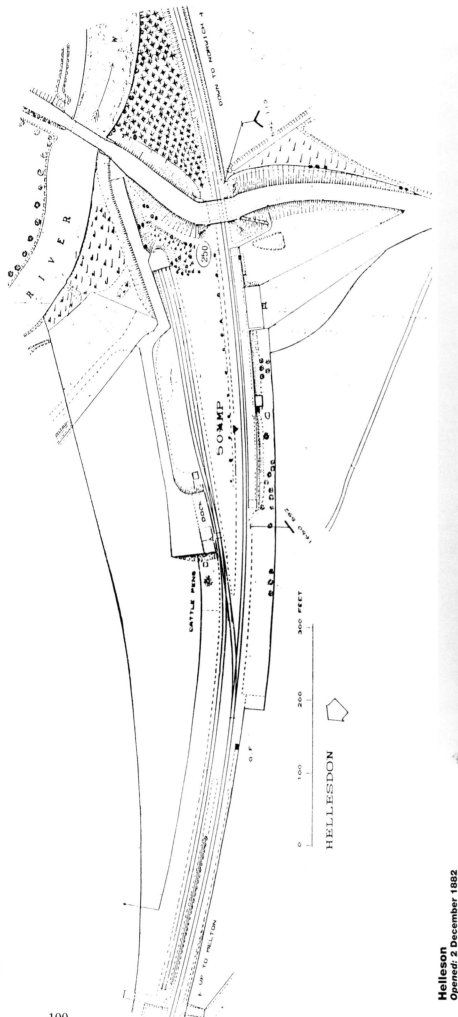

HELLESDON

RIVER

DOWN TO NORWICH →

UP TO MELTON →

CATTLE PENS

DOCK

50 MP

250

G.F.

0   100   200   300 FEET

Helleson

Opened: **2 December 1882**
Notes: **Large pavilion station in brick with
E&M-type signalbox on a tall brick base.
Never a block post, the box was abolished
c1901 and a tablet-released ground-frame
installed at the siding points. The old box
survived as a porter's room into the 1920s.
Where conditional stops were required a red
flag or red lamp was shown. The major traffic
was livestock from Ireland or from Norwich
market for lairage on the adjacent marshes.
Later, roadstone was delivered here for
Norfolk County Council.**
Closed: **15 September 1952 (passengers); 3
February 1969 (goods)**
Remains: **Platform and cattle dock.**

Right:
**A view of Hellesdon taken at an unknown
date, although the poster boards read LMS,
LNER and M&GN. The E&M-type 'signalbox'
stood by the telegraph pole on the platform
beyond the nameboard.**
D. Thompson

100

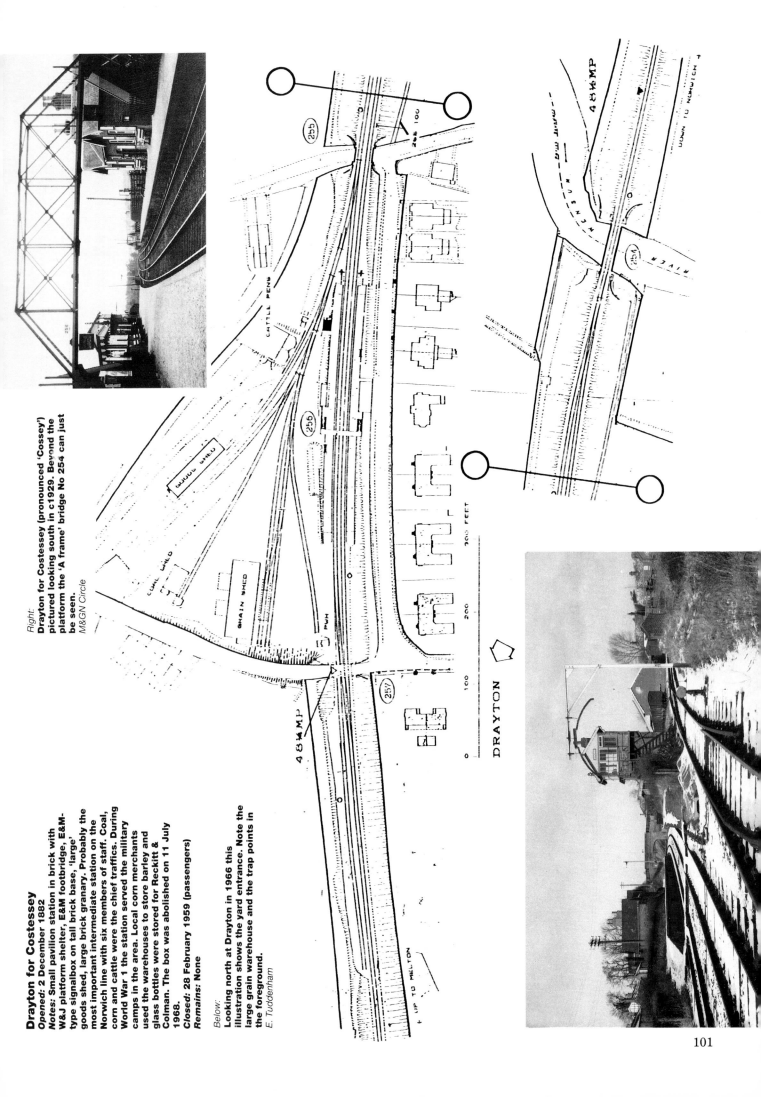

Drayton for Costessey

Opened: 2 December 1882

Notes: Small pavilion station in brick with
W&J platform shelter, E&M footbridge, E&M-
type signalbox on tall brick base, 'large'
goods shed, large brick granary. Probably the
most important intermediate station on the
Norwich line with six members of staff. Coal,
corn and cattle were the chief traffics. During
World War 1 the station served the military
camps in the area. Local corn merchants
used the warehouses to store barley and
glass bottles were stored for Reckitt &
Colman. The box was abolished on 11 July
1968.

Closed: 28 February 1959 (passengers)
Remains: None

Right:
Drayton for Costessey (pronounced 'Cossey')
pictured looking south in c1929. Beyond the
platform the 'A frame' bridge No 254 can just
be seen.
M&GN Circle

Below:
Looking north at Drayton in 1966 this
illustration shows the yard entrance. Note the
large grain warehouse and the trap points in
the foreground.
E. Tuddenham

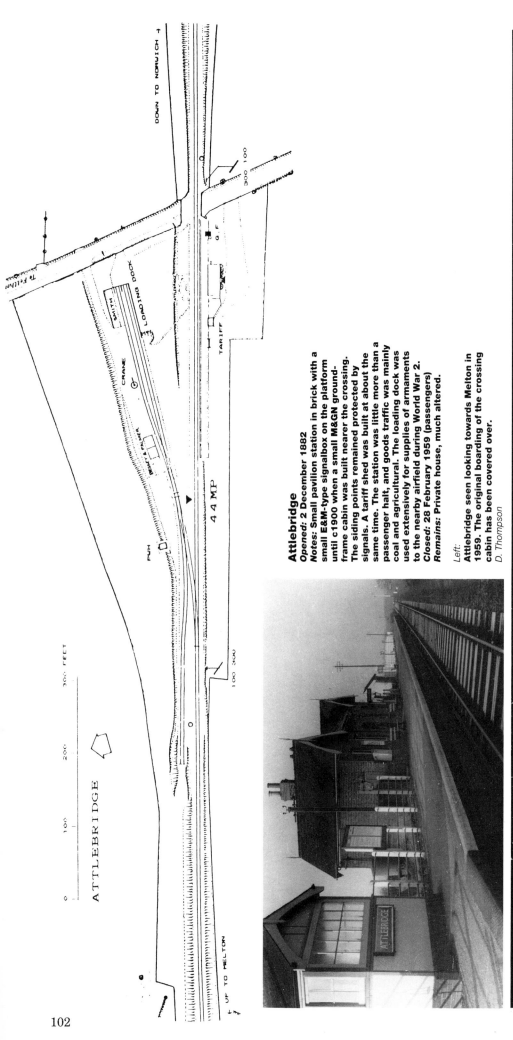

ATTLEBRIDGE

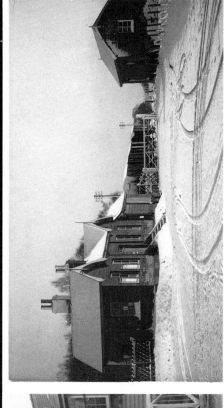

Attlebridge
Opened: 2 December 1882
Notes: Small pavilion station in brick with a
small E&M-type signalbox on the platform
until c1900 when a small M&GN ground-
frame cabin was built nearer the crossing.
The siding points remained protected by
signals. A tariff shed was built at about the
same time. The station was little more than a
passenger halt, and goods traffic was mainly
coal and agricultural. The loading dock was
used extensively for supplies of armaments
to the nearby airfield during World War 2.
Closed: 28 February 1959 (passengers)
Remains: Private house, much altered.

Left:
Attlebridge seen looking towards Melton in
1959. The original boarding of the crossing
cabin has been covered over.
D. Thompson

Lenwade
Opened: 1 July 1882
Notes: Small pavilion in brick with 'medium'
goods shed and small E&M-type timber
platform signalbox. Made a tablet station in
1895 and could cross passenger trains using
the refuge siding. The ballast sidings were
also added c1895. The signalbox was
renewed in 1912 with an M&GN type 1b box
on a concrete block base. The old box was
replaced by a timber monopitch tariff shed
rebuilt shortly after in concrete block. Traffic
was considerably boosted by the opening of
the Anglian Building Products siding in 1957.
The firm supplied concrete components. The
line stayed open to serve this siding although
the box was demolished in 1974.
Closed: 28 February 1959 (passengers);
15 June 1983 (goods)
Remains: Fairly complete.

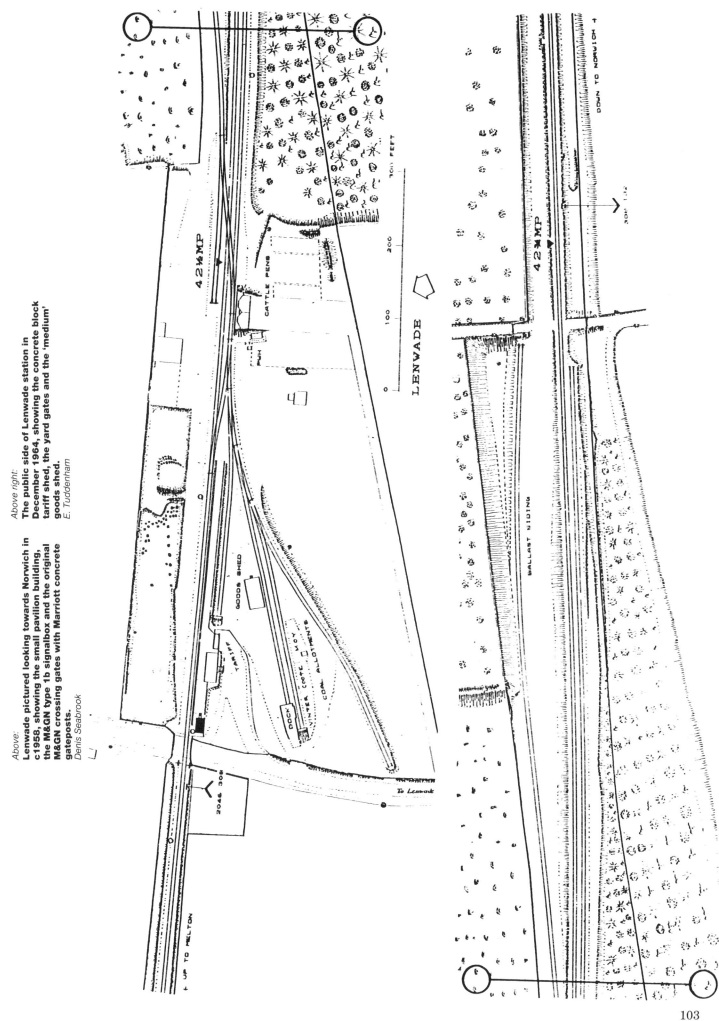

Above:

Lenwade pictured looking towards Norwich in c1958, showing the small pavilion building, the M&GN type 1b signalbox and the original M&GN crossing gates with Marriott concrete gateposts.
Denis Seabrook

Above right:

The public side of Lenwade station in December 1964, showing the concrete block tariff shed, the yard gates and the 'medium' goods shed.
E. Tuddenham

LENWADE

42¼ MP

42¼ MP

↑ UP TO MELTON

DOWN TO NORWICH ↑

To Lenwade

CATTLE PENS

PUH

GOODS SHED

TARIFF

DOCK

WINTER COTE

MOY

COAL ALLOTMENTS

BALLAST SIDING

2046 308

300 FEET

200

100

0

Whitwell & Reepham

Opened: 1 July 1882

Notes: Large pavilion station in brick with W&J waiting shelter, E&M-type signalbox on tall brick base, 'large' goods shed and E&M footbridge. A small cottage was purchased for the stationmaster in 1919. The footbridge was replaced by an ex-N&SJt example (No 323) from Felbrigg Woods in 1930. The station served a purely agricultural area and suffered from competition with Reepham GE, particularly in the sugar beet season. The signalbox was closed on 5 December 1966.

Closed: 28 February 1959 (passengers)

Remains: Quite complete, but derelict.

Above right:
Whitwell & Reepham viewed from the south in 1959. Note the replacement footbridge and the two sets of combined receiving/delivering tablet apparatus.
H. C Casserley

Right:
A later view of Whitwell & Reepham in 1967 showing the yard's entrance, the large goods shed and the cattle pens. Note the Engineer's Department trolley on its side road.
E. Tuddenham

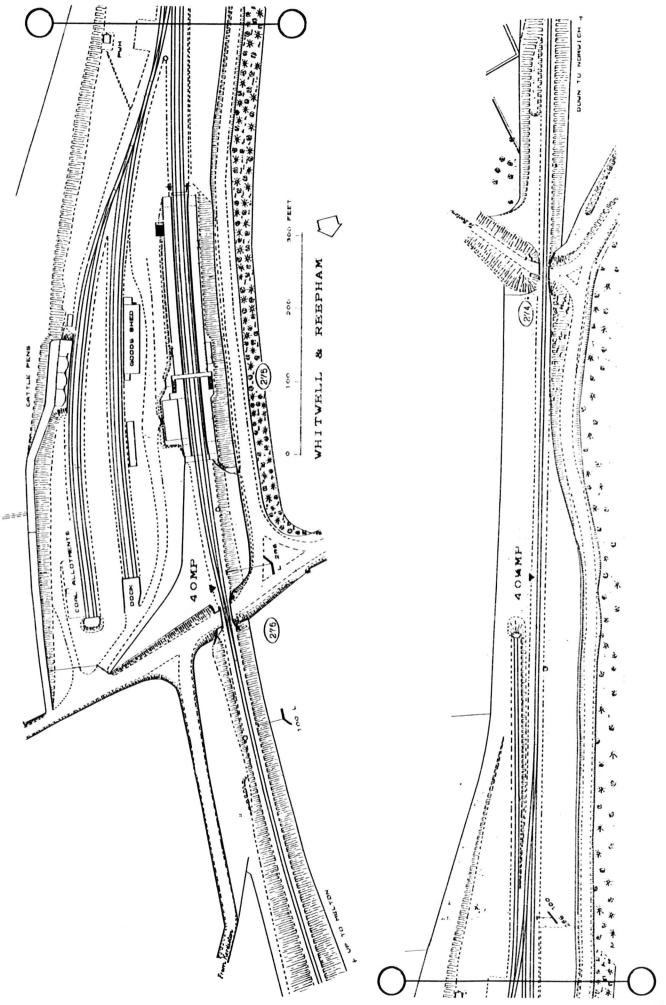

WHITWELL & REEPHAM

CATTLE PENS

GOODS SHED

COAL ALLOTMENTS

DOCK

400 FEET

300

200

100

0

2'5

2'6

40 MP

From Foulsham

UP TO MELTON

404 MP

2'4

GOODS TO NORWICH

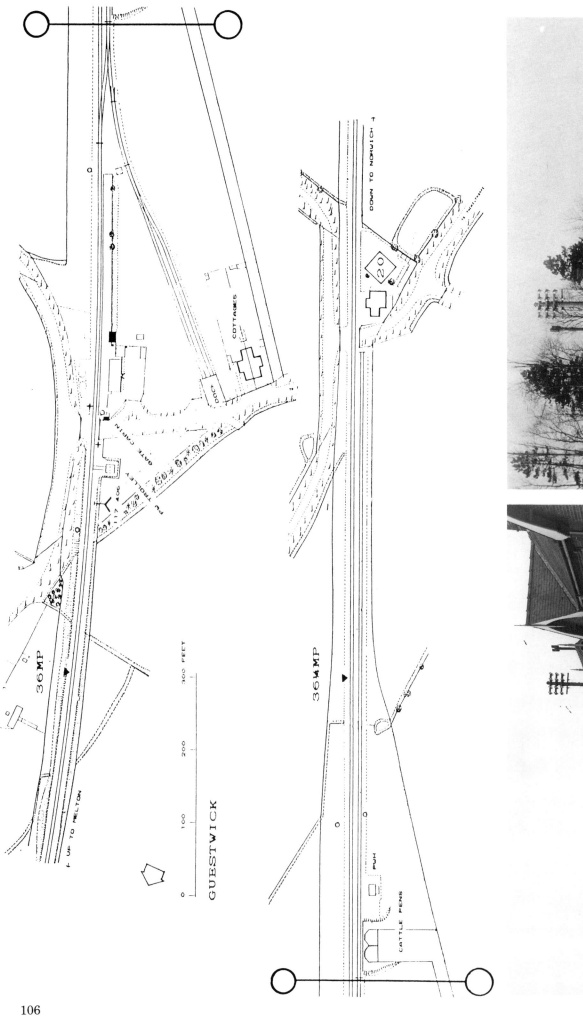

GUESTWICK

36 MP

36¼ MP

UP TO PELTON

DOWN TO NORWICH

COTTAGES

DOCK

GATE CABIN

TROLLEY

CATTLE PENS

PGH

0   100   200   300 FEET

Guestwick

Opened: 19 January 1882

Notes: Small pavilion station in brick, with pronounced window arches and keystones. The cottages were built in the simple style in 1902. The M&GN type 1a signalbox was built in 1895 when it became a tablet station, passenger trains being crossed in the refuge siding. A standard gate cabin controlled the crossing.

Closed: 28 February 1959 (passengers); 12 September 1960 (goods)

Remains: Quite complete, now a private house.

Above left:
Looking south at Guestwick towards Norwich, showing the yard points and a close-up of the tablet apparatus out of use.
Denis Seabrook

Above:
Guestwick seen viewed towards Melton in 1959. Note the original slatted seat, the crossing cabin and the bracketed miniature on the Down home signal.
H. C. Casserley

Hindolvestone

Opened: 19 January 1882

Notes: Small pavilion in brick with pronounced window arches. Standard timber tariff shed. Originally there was a small timber E&M-type box on the platform but this was replaced c1903 by a tablet-released ground-frame. Gatehouse No 17 had an M&GN type 1a gate box. The cottages were built in the 'arts & crafts' style in 1899.

Closed: 28 February 1959 (passengers); 12 September 1960 (goods)

Remains: Station is now a private house and the signalbox still stands.

Left:
Hindolvestone in c1959 viewed towards Norwich, showing the single siding, the 1902 'arts & crafts' cottages, and no less than two original slatted seats.
M&GN Circle

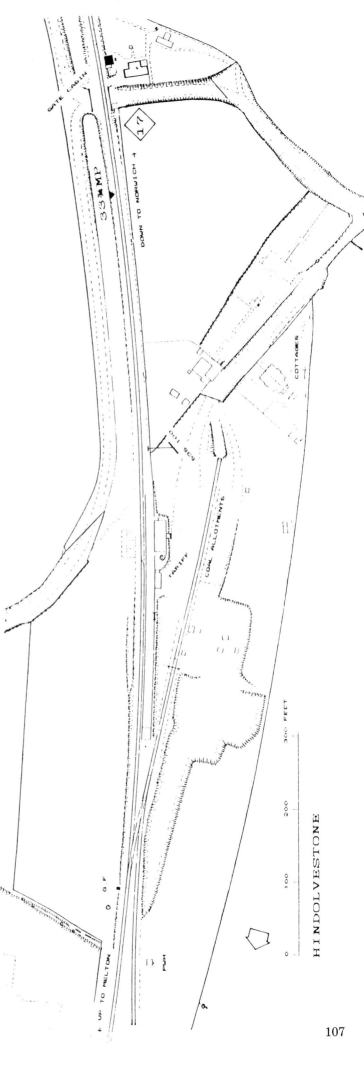

HINDOLVESTONE

High Norfolk

This is not the title of a true sub-region of Norfolk but is a traditional name and is certainly applicable from a purely physical point of view. The difficulty lies in the fact that the MR Distance Diagram for the Fakenham district spans the junction between two sub-regions: 'Mid-Norfolk' to the east and 'the Good Sands' to the west. The picture is further complicated by the deep penetration of the Wensum valley into the two areas. As already described, Mid-Norfolk is largely a plateau area of heavy soils, considerably wooded. The Good Sands are an area of chalk downland, largely above the 200ft contour, dealt with more fully in the next section.

From Melton Constable the double main line climbed considerably at 1 in 100 mostly in cuttings, passing under Pigg's Grave bridge No 102 and reaching the summit of the whole M&GN (312ft above Ordnance Datum) at Gunthorpe crossing No 16. The climb out of Melton could sometimes be a serious obstacle for a heavy westbound train, and it was here that the only official instance of banking was allowed; the station pilot (usually a Melton 0-6-0T) doing the honours up to the Lynn line advance starter signal for trains on the Up main, but only as far as the overbridge for Up trains leaving from the Down platform. There followed five miles of almost continuous descent at 1 in 100 through Thursford down to the levels of the Wensum valley at Langor Bridge goods station. This bank, often called 'Barney Bank' due to the proximity of a small village of that name, was undoubtedly the most serious obstruction to heavy eastbound trains on the whole line. It was also difficult taking a loose-coupled goods train down it, split trains apparently being a common occurrence.

The line now closely followed the river almost on the level, under the GER Wells line to Fakenham, the original terminus of the L&F. Here there had been the L&F's running shed and turntable and although the shed was used only for storage during the M&GN period, the turntable was retained as it was the practice for newly-shopped engines to be run to Fakenham, turned, and run back to Melton to detect any faults. From Fakenham the line still followed the river through delightful meadows to Raynham Park. This station was actually in the parish of Helhoughton but since the owner of nearby Raynham Hall, the Marquis Townshend, was a director of the L&F the name was a foregone conclusion!

On investigating the remaining trackbed between Melton and South Lynn one finds that unlike the eastern lines, several parts of it have been bought privately and are thus closed to further investigation, and others are under cultivation or roads. Leaving Melton where the cutting by Melton West has been filled in, the line can be seen parallel to the Thursford road, bridge No 102 being a landmark where the Holt road crosses it at Pigg's Grave. The route continues on embankment for a short way but then is lost to agriculture until gatehouse No 16, still with its distinctive M&GN gate box. Beyond, more of the trackbed survives until gatehouse No 15 when a new stretch of road begins, occupying the formation right through the site of Thursford station to the main Fakenham road. At Thursford the goods shed remains as a council depot and the road from the village that crossed the line here has been stopped off, leaving only the road to Barney accessible. From Thursford what is left of the trackbed strikes off across country and can only be intercepted on minor roads at bridge No 96 near Kettlestone and, by taking a very small road indeed, one can find gatehouse No 14. However, Langor Bridge stands on the main Norwich-Fakenham road. The two cottages are still there, as is the signalbox (at the time of writing). This box replaced the former gatehouse No 13 in 1898, when it was demolished and

the cottages built. Between here and Fakenham part of the line is used as access to gravel workings, and more has been absorbed into the Pensthorpe Wildfowl Trust.

In Fakenham itself (or more strictly Hempton) there is very little to show the presence of a large station here. The approach on embankment from the east to the site of the East box is used as the access road to a golf club. Opposite, only the end of the Down platform with a small plaque commemorating the L&F can be seen, the rest of the site being occupied by an industrial area. Even 'The Grove' has been demolished although the garden fence and gates remain. Further along Hempton Green beside the long line of cottages the entrance to the cattle droveway is still there as is a concrete hut and at the site of Fakenham West box a concrete stop block.

Leaving Hempton on the Shereford road the trackbed can be seen running along the river bank, passing under bridge No 85 at Shereford. The line turns southwest here, still following the river and crosses a minor road at concrete gatehouse No 12. Looking north here from the train one would have seen an old E&M carriage doubling as Dunton-cum-Doughton Methodist Church. The trackbed can be crossed again at the site of gatehouse No 11, now rebuilt, and the Helhoughton road passes Raynham Park station. This remains largely complete, having been restored by the owners, with standard M&GN platform shelter and signalbox, as well as standard Wilkinson & Jarvis 'office' building.

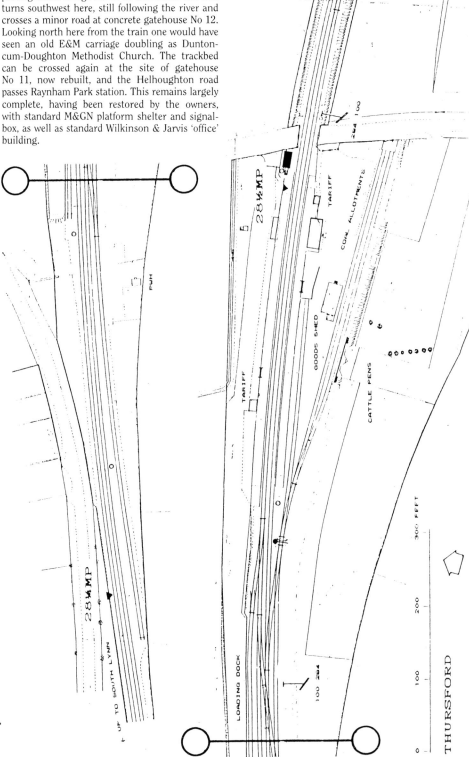

Thursford

Opened: 1 January 1882

Notes: Small pavilion in brick, with W&J shelter, 'medium' goods shed and E&M-type signlbox on a brick base on the Down platform, replaced by an M&GN type 1a when the line was doubled on 2 June 1901. The base of the old one was converted into a tariff shed. There was also a timber monopitch tariff shed of the Stalham pattern on the Up platform. The horse dock was extended in 1929/30 and there was some other work done to the dock in the yard at about the same time. The station served a wide and rich agricultural area. The passenger traffic was relatively light but the goods traffic was not, receiving sand, roadstone, bricks, feedstuffs and coal. Outward traffic was grain and sugar beet between September and January. Thursford held the record for sugar beet, averaging 15,000 tons per annum.

Closed: 28 February 1959

Remains: Goods shed only.

Right:
Thursford pictured looking towards Fakenham in c1958. On the far left is the tariff shed. The '4MT' 2-6-0 is hauling an express passenger past the typical L&F waiting shelter.
M&GN Circle

Below right:
Thursford looking towards Melton, showing the signalbox. Note the enamel 'Gentlemen' sign.
M&GN Circle

Langor Bridge

Opened: 1 July 1898

Notes: Originally the end of the double line from Fakenham, the M&GN type 1a signalbox replaced gatehouse No 13, which was demolished. The box came under the control of the Fakenham stationmaster, the two signalmen resided in the nearby cottages. All Up traffic went through to Fakenham and returned on the roadside goods next morning.

All outward traffic went to Thursford or Melton for attachment to the appropriate trains. There was a small regular coal traffic, but from 1913 a considerable tonnage of sugar beet.

Closed: 28 February 1959

Remains: Quite complete, including signalbox.

25MP

COTTAGES

COAL ALLOTMENTS

PUM

93

↑ UP TO SOUTH LYNN

DOWN TO YARMOUTH →

0   100   200   300 FEET

LANGOR BRIDGE

Fakenham Town

Opened: 6 August 1880

Notes: Large pavilion station in brick with W&J/L&F waiting shelter, 'large' goods shed and E&M-type signalbox, which was replaced in 1894 by two M&GN type 1a boxes — Fakenham East and West — when the loop was extended and the footbridge erected. The base of the old box was retained as a store. The line to Langor Bridge was doubled on 1 July 1898, and to Raynham Park on 4 July 1899. The engine shed appears to have been similar to that at Yarmouth. There was a standard M&GN water tank on columns, an L&F-type water standpipe on the Down platform under the footbridge, and an E&M-type lift crane at the exit of the Up sidings. The station was known locally as Hempton and was an important one. The passenger traffic was good, particularly on the Thursday market day, and for the races or agricultural shows. Parcels and milk traffic were regular, as was grain and flour traffic generated by the nearby water mill. Coal and coke for domestic use and the gas works was heavy, as was sugar beet traffic. On

Thursdays it was not unusual for 60 or 70 livestock wagons of cattle, sheep and pigs to be loaded. In the 1920s there was an oil company depot on the Down sidings, and when an oil tank was detached from a Down train the wagon was manhandled onto the buffer stops.

Closed: 28 February 1959

Remains: End of Down platform, otherwise very little.

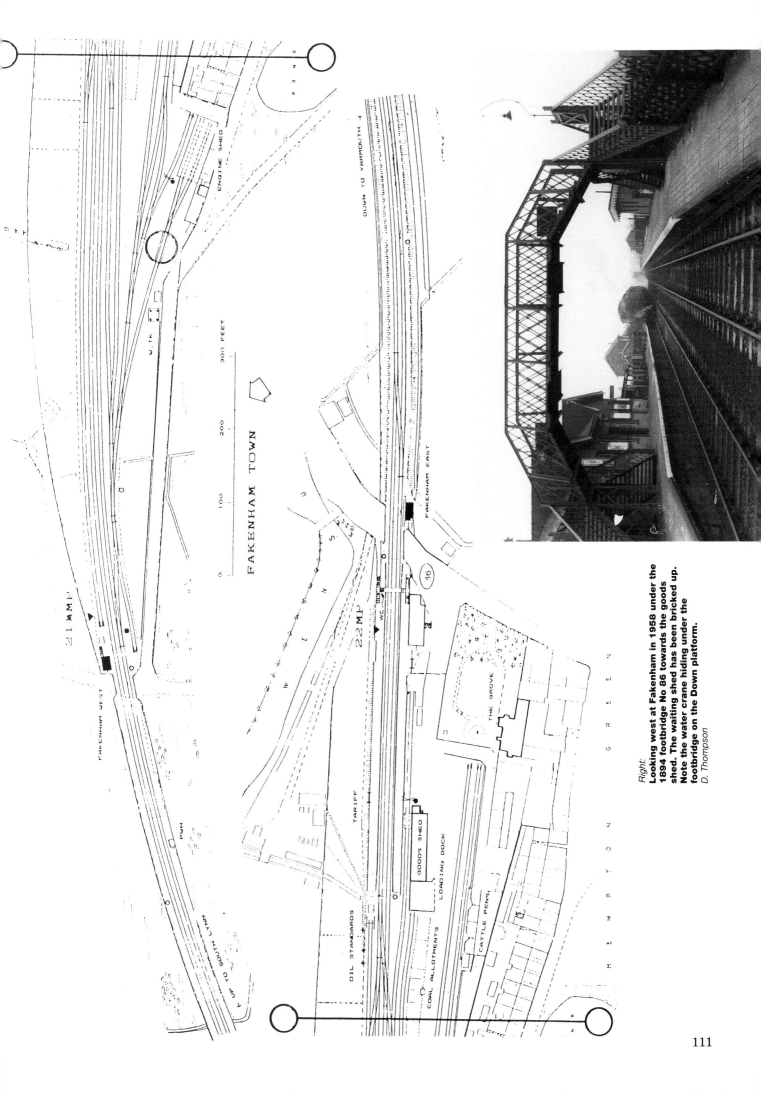

FAKENHAM TOWN

0   100   200   300 FEET

21¼MP

FAKENHAM WEST

W.TK.

ENGINE SHED

UP TO SOUTH LYNN

DOWN TO YARMOUTH

FAKENHAM EAST

22MP

WC

36

OIL STANDARDS

GOODS SHED

LOADING DOCK

COAL ALLOTMENTS

CATTLE PENS

TARIFF

THE GROVE

GREEN

HEMPTON

Right:
Looking west at Fakenham in 1958 under the 1894 footbridge No 86 towards the goods shed. The waiting shed has been bricked up. Note the water crane hiding under the footbridge on the Down platform.
D. Thompson

Raynham Park
Opened: 6 August 1880
Notes: The office design in brick. When the double line was opened on 4 July 1899 a second platform, standard M&GN waiting shed and M&GN type 1a signalbox were supplied. The 'luggage room' was added c1899. The house adjacent had been leased in 1886 but had apparently been given up by 1900.
Closed: 28 February 1959
Remains: Complete and well preserved.

Right:
The buildings at Raynham Park pictured after closure. The furthest portion is the 'Luggage room' added in c1900.
Denis Seabrook

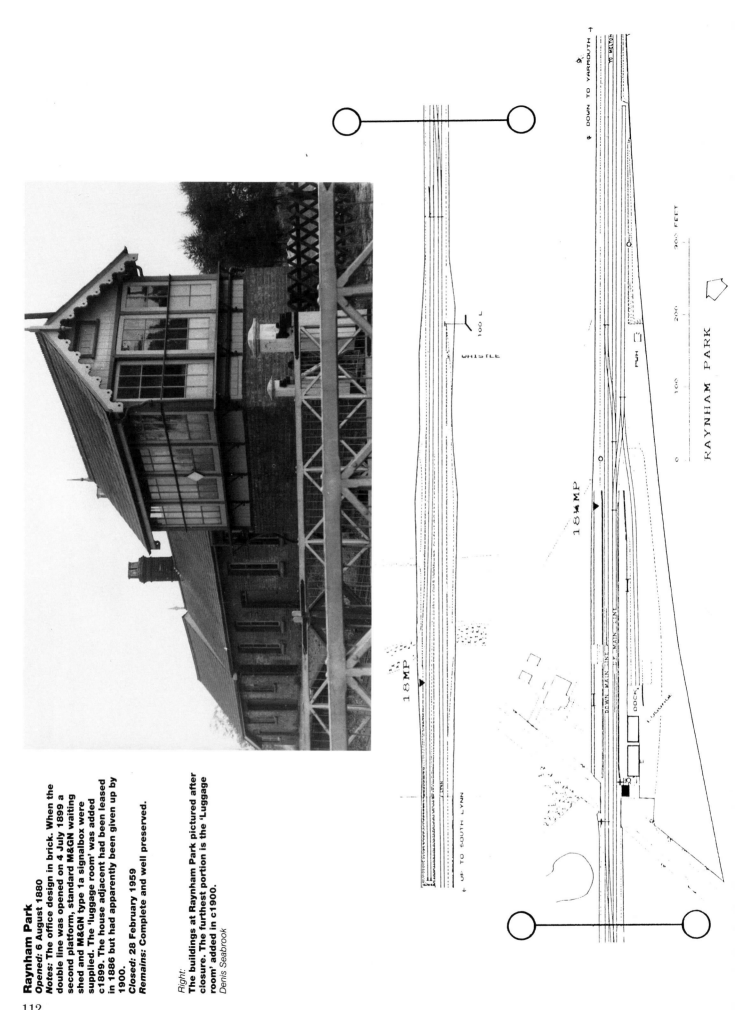

West Norfolk

This is again a general name as the Midland diagram spans two sub-regions: the 'Good Sands' and the 'Greensand Belt'. The Good Sands region was named by 18th century agriculturalist Arthur Young and was conspicuous for its agricultural improvements in the 17th and 18th centuries. The geological base is chalk, the end of a band extending from the North Downs, and the topography here is also open downland mostly above 200ft, with typical chalkland coombes and dry valleys. The soil is either chalky or a light loam and although some areas were cultivated, a lot remained as grassland until recently, with the occasional tract of heathland on sandy pockets. The Greensand Belt is geologically complex but in essence is based on a band of brown sandstone (carstone) forming a hilly ridge to the west of the chalk downland at around the 50-100ft contour. The soil is mainly sandy and supports extensive heaths, commons and birch woods.

From Raynham Park station the main line, now single, left the valley and climbed steeply for 1½ miles at 1 in 90 on to the west Norfolk downs at East Rudham. Although in the parish of that name, the station was over a mile away from the village. During the last war it acted as the railhead for West Raynham airfield and became very busy dealing with personnel and armaments. Skirting the higher ground to north and south the line wound across West Rudham Common, passing three lonely gatehouses to Massingham, the home of the Reverend Brereton, progenitor of the L&F. Massingham station, actually in the parish of Little Massingham was the last Wilkinson & Jarvis construction in concrete block, and was originally the only crossing place between Grimston Road and Fakenham. From Massingham the line fell at 1 in 100 to gatehouse No 7 over the Peddar's Way, a Roman road. Here there was a private siding, closed in 1915 but later reopened, to serve an Air Ministry petrol dump. The gatehouse was originally timber, like all those between Lynn and Fakenham, but was rebuilt in concrete blocks in 1915. As the line rose slightly and then fell into Hillington it passed into the greensand area. The full name of 'Hillington for Sandringham' proclaimed the hope cherished by the Company that Royalty would use the station as it was only a quarter mile further from Sandringham House than the rival GER Wolferton station, and indeed it was used several times by members of the family or their guests but on the whole Wolferton was still considered to be the Royal station. Nevertheless some 'Royal' waiting rooms were added to Hillington in 1896.

Again falling, the line passed near the village of Roydon, but the station built here was called Grimston Road; Grimston was a much larger parish and settlement just to the east, of which Roydon could be said to be a satellite community. The line had been doubled to Grimston Road from Lynn in 1882. Crossing Roydon and Grimston Commons, a landscape typical of this area, the double line fell gradually to Bawsey Sidings, where there had been private sand sidings from the very earliest days. There had even been a plan for a paint factory using the natural iron oxide to be found amongst the sand on Grimston Warren. At this point the original line turned sharply to the west and followed the Gaywood River (or River Gay) on the level past the lost village and ruined church of Bawsey, where gatehouse No 2 stood, crossed the Wootton Road at gatehouse No 1 and met the GER Hunstanton line at Gaywood Junction, thus gaining access to Lynn station. This line was abandoned in 1886 but the gatehouses still remained railway property. The E&M's Lynn avoiding line carried on from Bawsey in a southwesterly direction and passed under the Gayton road, hence the name of Gayton Road for the station serving the remains of the lost communities of Bawsey,

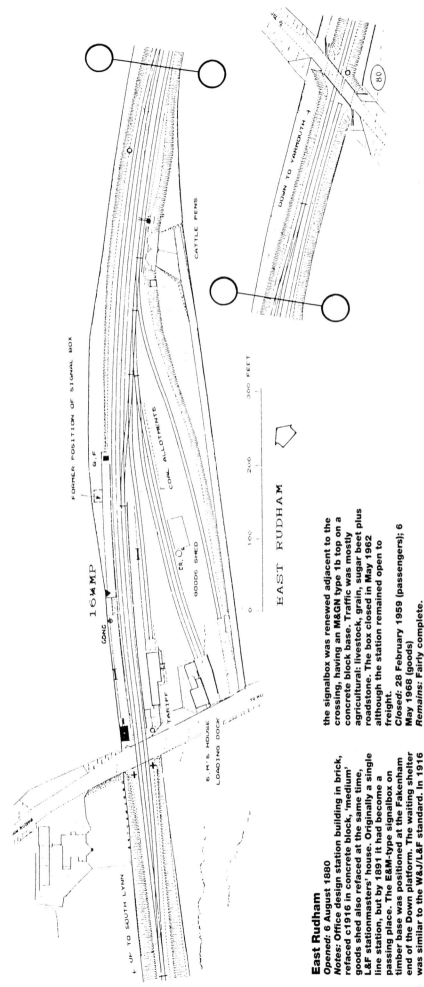

East Rudham
Opened: 6 August 1880
Notes: Office design station building in brick, refaced c1916 in concrete block, 'medium' goods shed also refaced at the same time, L&F stationmasters' house. Originally a single line station, but by 1891 it had become a passing place. The E&M-type signalbox on timber base was positioned at the Fakenham end of the Down platform. The waiting shelter was similar to the W&J/L&F standard. In 1916 the signalbox was renewed adjacent to the crossing, having an M&GN type 1b top on a concrete block base. Traffic was mostly agricultural: livestock, grain, sugar beet plus roadstone. The box closed in May 1962 although the station remained open to freight.
Closed: 28 February 1959 (passengers); 6 May 1968 (goods)
Remains: Fairly complete.

Mintlyn and Leziate, but chiefly the extensive sand workings on Bawsey Warren, also served by the GER from Middleton Towers station. After a slight hump the line crossed the GER Swaffham line and fell gradually towards Lynn and the Fens.

Leaving Raynham Park today, the trackbed is quite well defined across Helhoughton Common and the intervening fields to East Rudham. This station is relatively complete, having stayed open for goods traffic until 1968, and the goods shed, station building and platforms still stand as does the L&F stationmaster's house. Concrete overbridge No 80 can be seen in the background. From East Rudham the trackbed seems to be used as a farm track but minor roads also cross it for exploration by vehicle. Concrete gatehouses Nos 9 & 10 can be found in this way, also gatehouse No 8; still timber but recently rebuilt. Massingham station is a fortunate survivor, the station building, platforms, tariff shed, signalbox and stationmaster's house are all still intact; they are now privately owned. Between Massingham and Hillington the trackbed runs close to the main Lynn-Fakenham road, and although the portion between concrete gatehouses Nos 7 and 6 is still in existence, for the 2½ miles from there to Hillington it has mostly been ploughed in or used for road realignment. Gatehouse No 5 has recently been rebuilt but the adjacent two pairs of 1914 cottages are still unaltered although derelict. Hillington station remains virtually complete except for the signalbox but the yard has been covered with housing.

The line now veers away from the main road and can be rejoined at Grimston Road where the station building is now the centre of a small industrial area. Opposite the station is the carstone-built stationmaster's cottage. From Grimston the trackbed crosses Roydon Common and can be intercepted at the site of gatehouse No 4 on the Lynn road, and at the end of a narrow road from Pott Row where timber gatehouse No 3 stands. Beyond this point the line becomes rather inaccessible. Until relatively recently the old L&F alignment was still visible as a farm track as it crossed the Lynn bypass, but now the entire route has been ploughed in and its position is revealed only by the line of electricity poles which follow it and the ruin of Bawsey Church on the nearby hill.

From the Gayton road there is little to betray the position of Gayton Road station except the nearby 'Sand Boy' pub as bridge No 72 over the line 150yd to the west has been demolished to straighten the road. However, the platforms can just be made out, complete with rodding tunnel showing the position of the signalbox. Beyond Gayton from bridge No 71 much of the line has been absorbed into the sand workings, although further along the embankment and the abutments of bridge No 66 over the single ex-GE goods line to Middleton Towers can be seen from the Lynn bypass.

Massingham
Opened: 16 August 1879
Notes: Office design station building in concrete block with L&F waiting shelter, L&F stationmaster's house, small brick goods shed and E&M footbridge. The tariff shed was added c1900. The original W&J type signalbox was replaced by a Midland type in c1895. The crossing gates were worked from a gate cabin. Goods were mainly agricultural and coal. Horse boxes were usually attached to Up passenger trains by hand. The box was closed in April 1942.
Closed: 28 February 1959 (passengers); 6 May 1968 (goods)
Remains: Fairly complete.

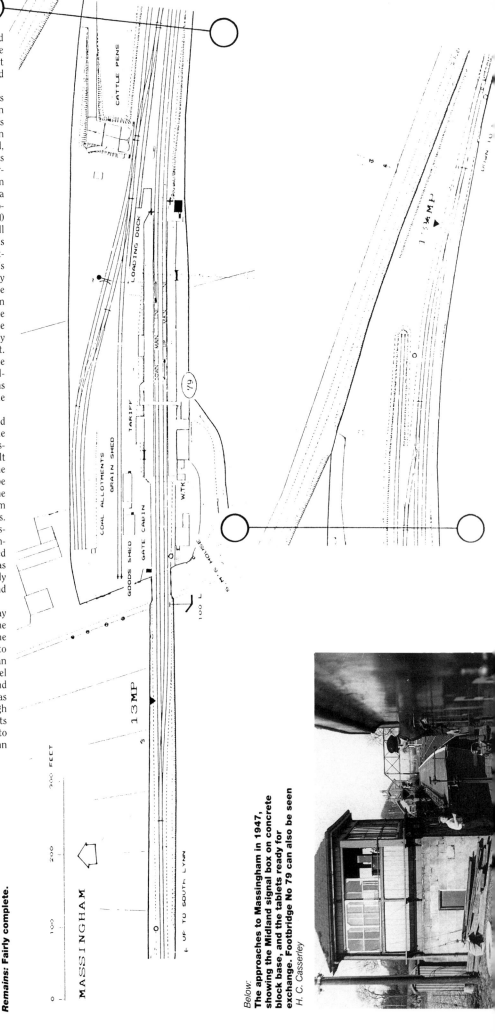

MASSINGHAM

Below:
The approaches to Massingham in 1947, showing the Midland signal box on concrete block base, and the tablets ready for exchange. Footbridge No 79 can also be seen
H. C. Casserley

Hillington for Sandringham

Opened: 16 August 1879

Notes: Small pavilion in yellow brick and red brick dressings with L&F stationmaster's house. Originally single line but made a passing place in 1896 with M&GN type 1a signalbox and special 'Royal' waiting rooms in 'arts & crafts' style. The tariff shed was built c1900. The signalbox was moved to the crossing in 1927, where there had been a small gate cabin. Goods traffic was mainly vegetables and cattle, and an increasing amount of sugar beet. Passenger traffic was quite good, being near the village, and being the starting station of 'Rail and Drive' tours to Sandringham House. The station was used several times by the Royal Family, particularly King Edward VII when Prince of Wales, and later when King it is believed that

he entrained here for Poppyland. A red carpet was rolled on to the platform on these occasions. When Sandringham was occupied the London newspapers were sent up first train from Peterborough.

Closed: 28 February 1959 (passengers); 6 May 1968 (goods)

Remains: Fairly complete, but yard covered with housing.

Right:
The Down platform at Hillington in 1936 showing the enamel nameboard, the other 'Royal' waiting room and the signalbox. The L&F type stationmaster's house is just visible over the waiting room.

H. C. Casserley

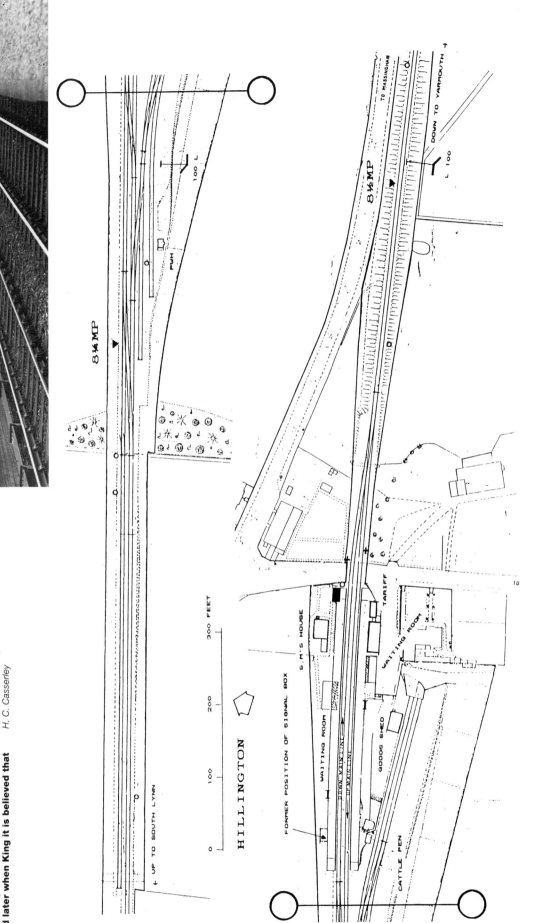

HILLINGTON

**A good view of the facilities at Grimston Road
viewed towards Fakenham in 1937. Note the
enamel nameboard and the Midland signalbox
on an M&GN type 1a base.**
L&GRP

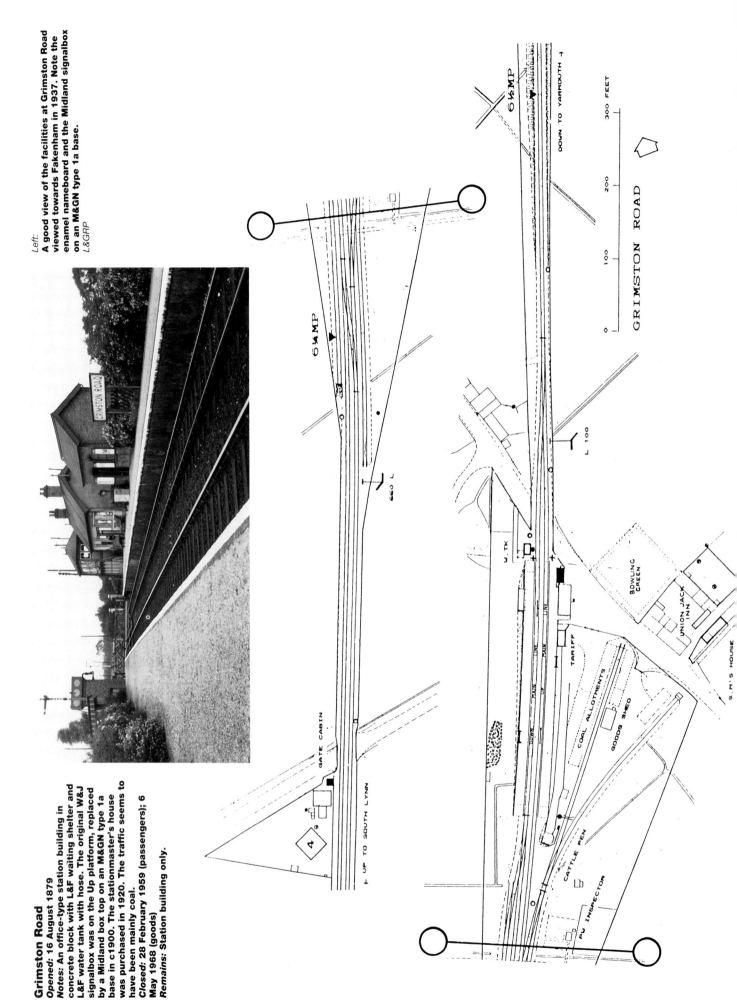

Grimston Road

Opened: 16 August 1879
Notes: An office-type station building in
concrete block with L&F waiting shelter and
L&F water tank with hose. The original W&J
signalbox was on the Up platform, replaced
by a Midland box top on an M&GN type 1a
base in c1900. The stationmaster's house
was purchased in 1920. The traffic seems to
have been mainly coal.
Closed: 28 February 1959 (passengers); 6
May 1968 (goods)
Remains: Station building only.

116

Gayton Road

Opened: 1 January 1886

Notes: Transitional design similar to Paston & Knapton with open-fronted waiting shelter and E&M-type platform box. An old E&M coach was provided for a porters' room c1921. An immaculate station, winning the 'Best Kept Station' award in 1937. The first sand siding was provided in 1887, another in 1897, connected to narrow gauge railways, but the second siding was closed in 1929. Sand was thus the main traffic, perhaps 100/200 tons a day. On a good day an engine and brake were sent from South Lynn to make a special. There was also some coal and sugar beet.

Closed: 28 February 1959 (passengers); 6 May 1968 (goods)

Remains: Platforms only.

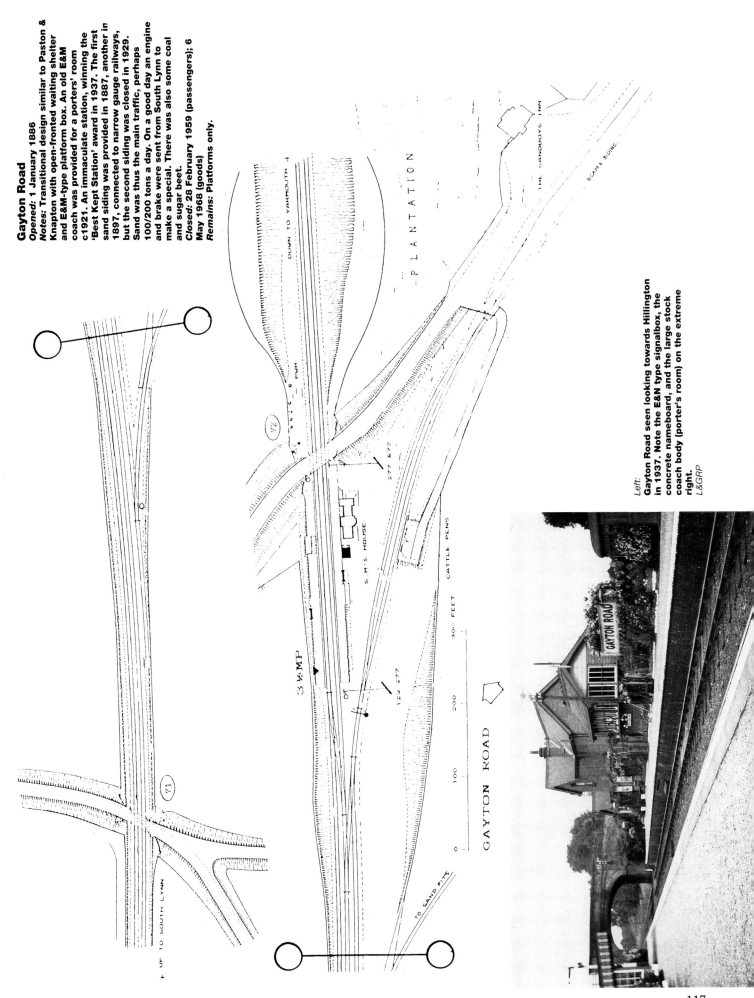

Left:
Gayton Road seen looking towards Hillington in 1937. Note the E&N type signalbox, the concrete nameboard, and the large stock coach body (porter's room) on the extreme right.
L&GRP

Lynn and the Fens

For the 32 miles between King's Lynn and Bourne stretches a flat, fertile plain — the Fens. Although very interesting historically, particularly in the construction of the many drainage channels and the gradual reclamation of farmland from the tidal marshes of the Wash, to the eye it is a featureless desert, relieved only by groups of trees around clusters of habitation and the church steeples rising above them. The scenery of the area is one of miles of flat fields broken by very few significant features. The dark soil was planted with potatoes and other vegetables, and many acres of flowers for bulbs and cutting; this whole district as far as Holbeach was often referred to as 'Little Holland'.

King's Lynn was an important town to the M&GN, not least because its headquarters were there in an old merchant's house on Austin Street. The town's history is a complicated one and need

not concern us here; suffice it to say that it owed its prosperity to the sea, both as a port for foreign trade and as a base for a large fishing fleet. Thus when the first railway reached Lynn in 1846 (the East Anglian Railway) a harbour branch was seen as essential. The branch left the main line from Ely a mile south of Lynn at Harbour Junction and served the quays of South Lynn. When the Lynn & Sutton Bridge Railway was opened in 1866 to a junction just to the south, it was given running powers over the branch, passed on to the E&M and then the M&GN. The quaysides to the north of the town had to wait until the construction of the Alexandra Dock in 1869 before they were connected to the railway, now the GER, by the Docks Branch. This was actually a separate company with representatives from the MR, GN, GE and the town. When the L&F was opened to Gaywood Junction in 1879 and obtained running powers to the GE Lynn Town station, they were also included

in the Dock Railway scheme and passed their powers to the E&M and the M&GN. A second dock, the Bentinck, was opened in 1883. The L&F also had designs on the north of the town as a branch was built from Salters Road Junction, just to the south of Gaywood Junction, to a junction and crossing of the Docks line and finally to a goods station at Austin Street, not far from the Tuesday Market Place in Lynn. After much uncertainty it is now known that the line was built in 1882/83 but never opened. The merchant's house purchased with the land for the goods station was retained as the offices of the L&F, becoming the headquarters of the E&M and M&GN. The goods shed, all that remained of the station when the track was lifted in 1885, was used for storage of stationery and old paperwork.

Throughout the existence of the railway the GER station in the town was considered the prime M&GN passenger station, but on the opening of

South Lynn

Opened: 1 January 1886
Notes: The first passenger station was on the east side of Saddlebow Road and made entirely of timber, with a Midland-type signalbox. The new South Lynn was opened on 14 April 1901 on the west side of the road with a new double-span rolled iron joist bridge No 49. Access was from the road through a covered stairway. The building was in the 'arts & crafts' style under a flat canopy. An M&GN-type footbridge, No 48, spanned across to the wooden 'local' platform, which had only a small waiting room. Part of the original station survived as a First Aid classroom. The signalboxes: South Lynn Junction and South Lynn West were M&GN type 1a; but South Lynn Single Line Junction and West Lynn were Midland types, being survivors of the earlier layout. The goods sidings were divided into West and East yards, and the West yard was provided with cattle pens and a timber two-road tranship shed. The main function of the yards was the storage and interchange of traffic from each section of the M&GN, being open 24hr for this purpose, each yard with a shunting engine. The timber engine shed, with four roads, could hold 10 engines and was expanded to this size in 1895, when the large water tank was also installed. There was also an enclosed timber coaling stage and 47ft 0in turntable. In 1930/31 South Lynn was expanded with reception roads at the West yard, new sidings to hold 60 wagons in the East yard, a new steel and corrugated iron coal stage, electric coaling plant, 60ft 0in turntable, and a new concrete brick and block goods shed.

Hardwick Road was a small goods station a mile towards Gayton Road, with two sidings and a cattle dock, on the Up side of the line between bridges Nos 59 and 60. There was no connection to the Down line, traffic from the west having to go to Gayton or Grimston first.
Closed: 28 February 1959 (passengers); South Lynn is still open for goods
Remains: Nothing of the passenger station.

Above right:
The eastern approaches to South Lynn viewed towards Fakenham, possibly before 1908. Class Da No 86 (?) shunts while a Class D stands at the original coaling stage. An ex-E&M horsebox stands on the right.
Bucknall collection/IAL

Right:
South Lynn viewed towards the west on the Down side during the 1930/31 improvements. The cattle docks and old goods shed (in the smoke) are to the right above the carriage & wagon department's shed. The Midland diamond arrangement of nameboards is just visible by the West box.
Author's collection

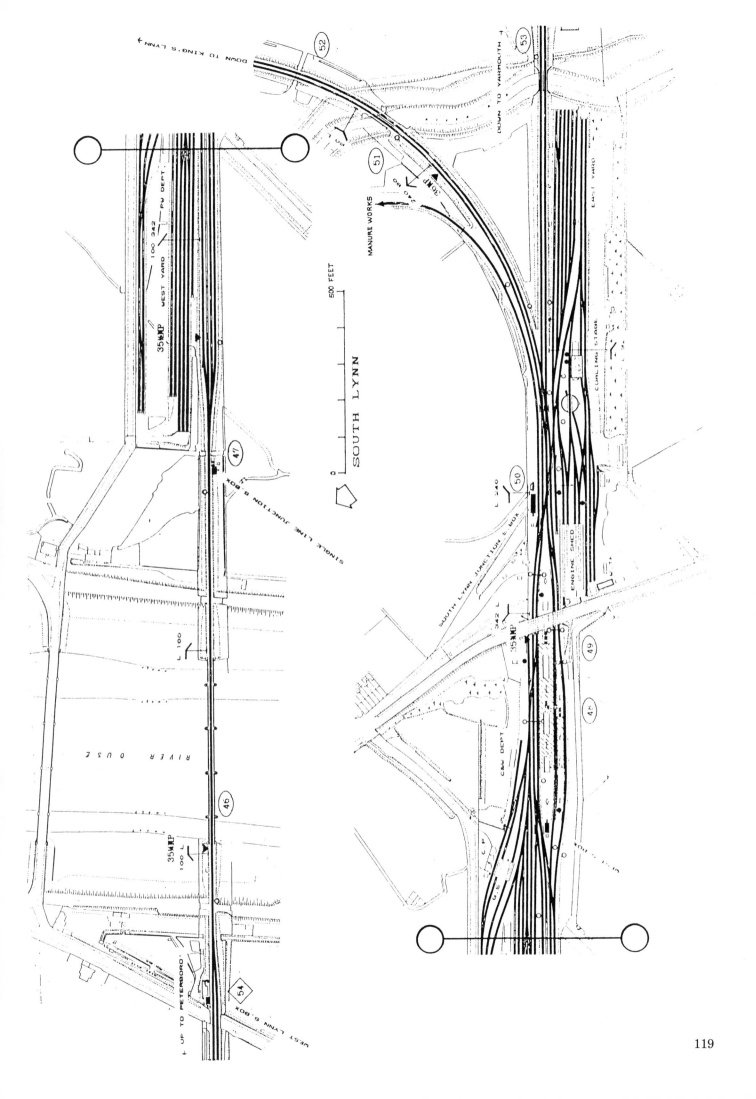

DOWN TO KING'S LYNN →

52

51

50

53

DOWN TO YARMOUTH →

MANURE WORKS

30MP

140 80

140 80

35MP
100 342
WEST YARD   PW DEPT.

EAST YARD

COALING STAGE

342

47

SINGLE LINE JUNCTION B BOX

SOUTH LYNN

0   500 FEET

SOUTH LYNN JUNCTION B BOX

ENGINE SHED

342

35MP

49

48

RIVER OUSE

L 100

C&W DEPT

G.B

46

35MP
100 L

G.F

54

← UP TO PETERBORO'

WEST LYNN B.BOX →

the Lynn avoiding line the new South Lynn station assumed greater importance as a goods exchange yard and locomotive depot. Many of the expresses called only at South Lynn, passengers to and from Lynn having to use a connecting shuttle service, but most stopping and semi-fast trains used King's Lynn.

Descending from Gayton Road the Lynn avoiding line reached the levels of the River Nar. About a mile outside South Lynn, sandwiched between the Swaffham and the Ely road bridges (Nos 59 & 60) was Hardwick Road siding, a small goods station and cattle loading area. After passing gatehouse No 1A and a short but severe hump over the GE Ely line and the River Nar, the line ran into South Lynn where it was joined at South Lynn Junction by the original alignment from Harbour Junction. South Lynn was positioned on the edge of Fenland and the lines to the west, apart from certain exceptions were largely level. The exceptions were several bridges over waterways requiring gradients on each side, the Spalding avoiding line which contained the second steepest gradient on the M&GN at 1 in 66, and eventually the rise into higher country in the far west. Thus after the climb out of South Lynn at 1 in 98 to pass over the single line Ouse bridge No 46 and the 1 in 100 fall on the other side, there was no appreciable gradient encountered by the double line through Clenchwarton, Terrington and Walpole until the 1 in 100 climb to the Cross Keys bridge No 32 eight miles later. Just over half a mile before the

swing bridge, at the foot of the gradient was Wingland signalbox, an intermediate block post abolished in 1913. The line was single track over Cross Keys bridge and each end was controlled by signalboxes interlocked with the control cabin on top. Sutton Bridge had an island platform and was the third station on the site, the goods yard being developed from the original Norwich & Spalding station yard. To accommodate the 1 in 110 gradient up to the swing bridge, the station canopy was stepped down at intervals to maintain its level. The gradient coupled with the very sharp curves necessary to bring the alignment to the more southerly position of the 1897 bridge made it a difficult station to traverse and there was a 10mph speed limit right through from East box to Sutton Bridge Junction.

Today the remains of the M&GN around South Lynn are quite extensive, if incomplete, and there are also some to be found in King's Lynn itself, but the major loss has been the entire line between South Lynn and Sutton Bridge under the new A17 trunk road. The Lynn avoiding line approaches South Lynn as a farm track over open fields to the site of Hardwick Road sidings, which has been affected by tipping of spoil from the works associated with the bypass, but bridge No 60 stands on the Swaffham road and the cattle dock and buffer stops are adjacent, reached by the cattle drove descending from the road. Bridge No 59 has gone and the cutting towards gatehouse No 1A is being filled, but from the Hardwick industrial estate the trackbed is relatively complete, with bridge No 53 over the Nar still standing. The Lynn bypass bridges the Lynn main line right over Harbour Junction. The GE signalbox was demolished some years ago but a single track still uses the M&GN formation to South Lynn to service the sugar beet

factory sidings and some storage silos on the East Yard, and thus is the oldest part of the M&GN still carrying track. The bypass now occupies the site of South Lynn station and an overhead roundabout gives access to Saddlebow Road, but the BR line still passes under the latter in approximately the same position as the M&GN once did to reach the ladder of sugar beet sidings installed in 1927. The 1958 replacement engine shed stood on the east side of the road until recently but this has been demolished and a gypsy site established here. The east end of the platform can still be seen just nosing out from under the road embankment. There is an industrial estate on the site of the West Yard, but the 1930 concrete goods shed still stands by the access road.

King's Lynn station itself has been refurbished but the wooden building on Platform No 5 used by the M&GN staff has been demolished and most of the platform removed in recent alterations. At Austin Street, found by leaving Tuesday Market Place by the northeast corner and passing to the south of St Nicholas's Chapel with its tall steeple, one can see that it has been considerably altered and cut into two by a new road slicing across Austin Fields. The Traffic Manager's Office has been replaced by the DSS offices and the site of the goods shed is occupied by an industrial estate. The Docks line is still in use but now only single track, and the right of way over footbridge No 52A has reverted to a foot crossing, although the base of the central pier can still be seen. A footpath from Kettlewell Lane crosses the Docks line at the point where the E&M line joined it, and by following the path along the river to Loke Road (formerly Salters Road) one can find gatehouse No 0. Across the road from the gatehouse the trackbed is used as access to a farmyard, but the last 100yd to Salters Road Junction where it joined the Hunstanton line are obscured. The GE route is now a footpath and cycle way to the Lynnsport Centre which stands on the site of Gaywood Junction. Little now remains of the L&F line here except the abutments of the first bridge over a drainage channel. A small shop now stands on the site of gatehouse No. 1 where Marsh Lane joins the Wootton Road.

Returning to South Lynn, the bypass crosses the River Great Ouse at exactly the same point as the old West Lynn bridge and as the A17 follows the trackbed to Sutton Bridge one can see not a single railway structure has been left standing and only strips of land alongside the road at the sites of Clenchwarton and Terrington station yards are left as clues. Only Terrington weighbridge hut was left unscathed but even that has recently been demolished. However, Cross Keys bridge is still in use nearly 100 years after its installation and has been refurbished and sensitively altered to allow more headroom. There is very little left of Sutton Bridge station except some trellis fencing and the hydraulic tower for the swing bridge, there being industrial premises on the site of the platforms and the new roundabout giving access to the bridge lying where the older buildings once stood.

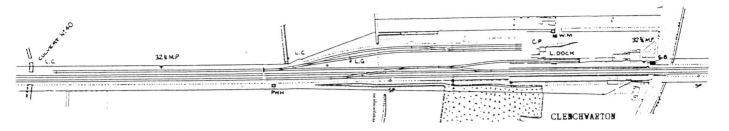

Clenchwarton

Opened: 1 March 1866
Notes: Originally single line with a Midland signalbox opposite the platform by the crossing, the line was doubled on 15 December 1898 with an MR box by the platform, a second platform and standard M&GN waiting shelter. It was a busy station dealing with potatoes, grain, hay and clover, and a great deal of fruit.
Closed: 28 February 1959
Remains: None

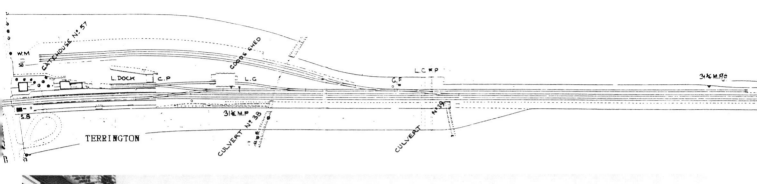

Terrington

Opened: 1 March 1866
Notes: Made a passing place in 1890 with East and West Midland-type signalboxes, but after doubling to Clenchwarton on 15 December 1898 and to Walpole on 27 March 1899 only one box was required, by the crossing. Goods traffic was heavy, particularly in the fruit and flower season when fitted wagons were required for the strawberries, plums and apples. There were also potatoes and a large quantity of sugar beet.
Closed: 28 February 1959
Remains: None.

Standard L&SB building at Terrington pictured in c1910 and showing clearly the open area by the booking hall, later enclosed. Note the MR signal and the goods shed.
Lens of Sutton

121

Walpole

Opened: 1 March 1866
Notes: Originally single line but doubled on 27 March 1899. A timber grain shed was built in 1898. A busy station, there being three coal merchants in the yard and plenty of hay and clover, but it was the fruit season that was the busiest. Often an engine and brake would have to be sent to make a special train, since the station could send up to 60 wagons a day of strawberries.
Closed: 28 February 1959
Remains: None.

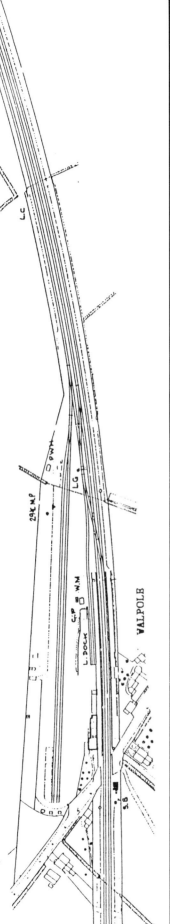

VALPOLE

Sutton Bridge

Opened: 3 July 1862 and 1 March 1866
Notes: First and second stations superceded by the third (1897) island platform with Midland footbridge No 31, large panelled brick goods shed, cattle dock and 42ft 0in turntable. The Junction signalbox was MR type 1, Station and East boxes MR type 2b. Cross Keys swing bridge dated from 1897 and is dealt with in Chapter 5. As well as considerable passenger traffic, there was heavy goods traffic. Enormous quantities of vegetables, soft fruit and cut flowers were handled. There was also timber from Scandinavia and occasionally grain by the shipload.
Closed: 28 February 1959 (passengers); 1 May 1965 (goods)
Remains: Swing bridge, little else.

Right:
The eastern approaches to Sutton Bridge viewed towards the east in c1910. Cross Keys swing bridge dominates the view, protected at the far end by Sutton Bridge East box (just visible) and the station box in the foreground. Most of the equipment is unashamedly Midland!
Lens of Sutton

122

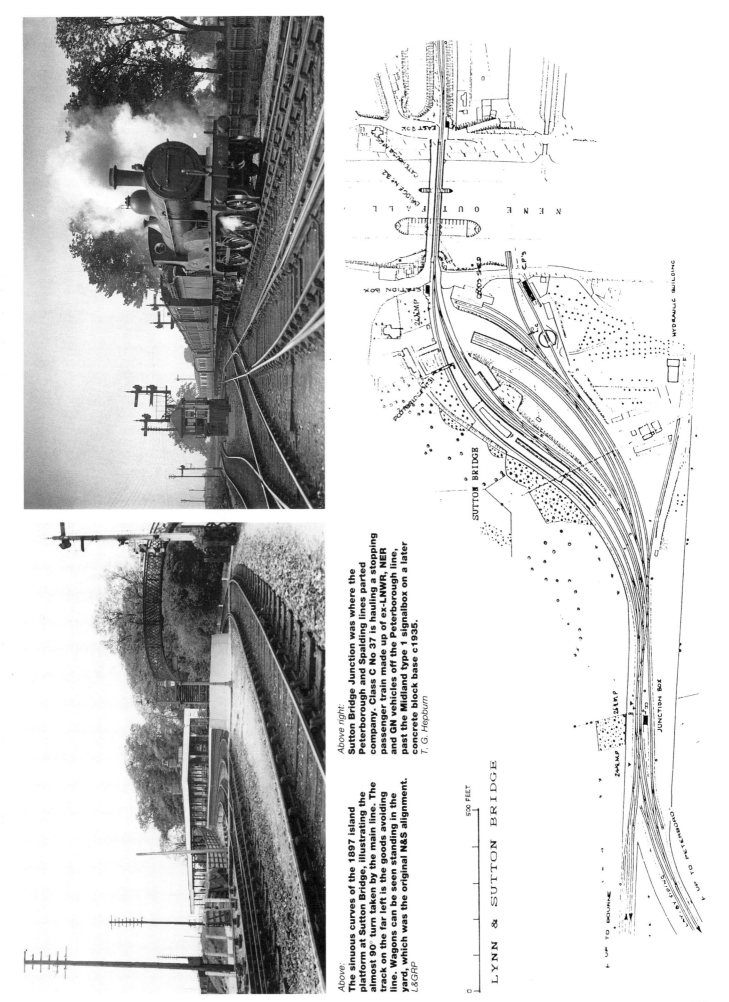

Above:

The sinuous curves of the 1897 island platform at Sutton Bridge, illustrating the almost 90° turn taken by the main line. The track on the far left is the goods avoiding line. Wagons can be seen standing in the yard, which was the original N&S alignment.
L&GRP

Above right:

Sutton Bridge Junction was where the Peterborough and Spalding lines parted company. Class C No 37 is hauling a stopping passenger train made up of ex-LNWR, NER and GN vehicles off the Peterborough line, past the Midland type 1 signalbox on a later concrete block base c1935.
T. G. Hepburn

LYNN & SUTTON BRIDGE

500 FEET

SUTTON BRIDGE

EAST BOX

NENE OUTFALL

STATION BOX

JUNCTION BOX

HYDRAULIC BUILDING

UP TO BOURNE

UP TO PETERBORO

123

Peterborough and the West

Although it was the line through Spalding and Bourne that reached the Midlands, the route through Wisbech to Peterborough was always regarded as the M&GN's main line, and Peterborough was the premier point of exchange for goods traffic to the GN and MR for destinations in London and the North. The landscape is once again intensely cultivated flat fenland, but to the south-west are low islands of clay supporting a brick-making industry on which Peterborough was founded. Wisbech is the other important settlement on the line, and as well as being a major inland port, was and is the centre of a large area of hard and soft fruit cultivation. One of the major obstacles to the railway was thus not the negotiation of difficult terrain but the bridging of the

Tydd
Opened 1 August 1866
Notes: Originally single line, became a crossing place in 1896 with a new timber Down platform and narrow timber waiting shed. The M&GN 1a signalbox was at the north end of the Down platform with a gate cabin to operate the gates. Beyond bridge No 27 was the double crossing of Foul Anchor, two sets of gates controlled from one central gate cabin. The southern crossing also had gatehouse No 66 and, c1923, the northern crossing was demoted to an occupation crossing and the gate cabin closed.
Closed: 28 February 1959
Remains: Main building (extended) and platform.

Ferry
Opened 1 August 1866
Notes: A new timber waiting room was built on the single platform in 1892, and a Midland-type signalbox provided about the same time. The yard points were released by Annett's Key. The loading dock siding was laid in 1894. The box was abolished in 1919 and a tablet-released ground-frame installed. Traffic was agricultural — grain, fruit and potatoes.
Closed: 28 February 1959
Remains: House only.

Wisbech
Opened: 1 August 1866
Notes: The site was controlled by Horse Shoe Lane, Leverington Road, Station and Barton Lane signalboxes, all of which were MR type 2a. The line was doubled from Horse Shoe Lane through Wisbech to Barton Lane in 1892. From Horse Shoe Lane, a Harbour branch became a street tramway worked by horses into the Old Market near the Nene Bridge. Between Horse Shoe Lane and Leverington Road boxes was Wisbech goods station, which had a panelled brick goods shed (extended in 1890), loading dock and timber fruit stages. There was a large volume of fruit traffic, about 50% plums and apples, the rest strawberries loaded in 4lb 'Chip' baskets. Both the GN and MR sent men, horses and vehicles to help, and in the 1930s a motor fleet was built up, starting a collection service in 1934. The passenger station was very MR in flavour, having a Midland water tank, pair of water cranes and footbridge.
Closed: 28 February 1959 (passengers); 4 January 1965 (Harbour); 31 October 1965 (goods)
Remains: None.

Top left:
Tydd viewed towards Sutton Bridge from the crossing in c1958 with '4MT' 2-6-0 No 43094 on a stopping passenger to Peterborough. The signalbox can be seen at the far end of the 1896 platform, an awkward position for controlling the crossing.
F. Church

Above left:
Ferry pictured towards Sutton Bridge from the crossing, showing the station house divorced from the platform. The siding formerly ran right into the loading dock.
F. Church

Left:
Wisbech goods station was situated between Horse Shoe Lane signalbox and Leverington Road box. Note the typical PW&S goods shed, and the former crossing gatehouse in the foreground.
E. L. Back/M. Back

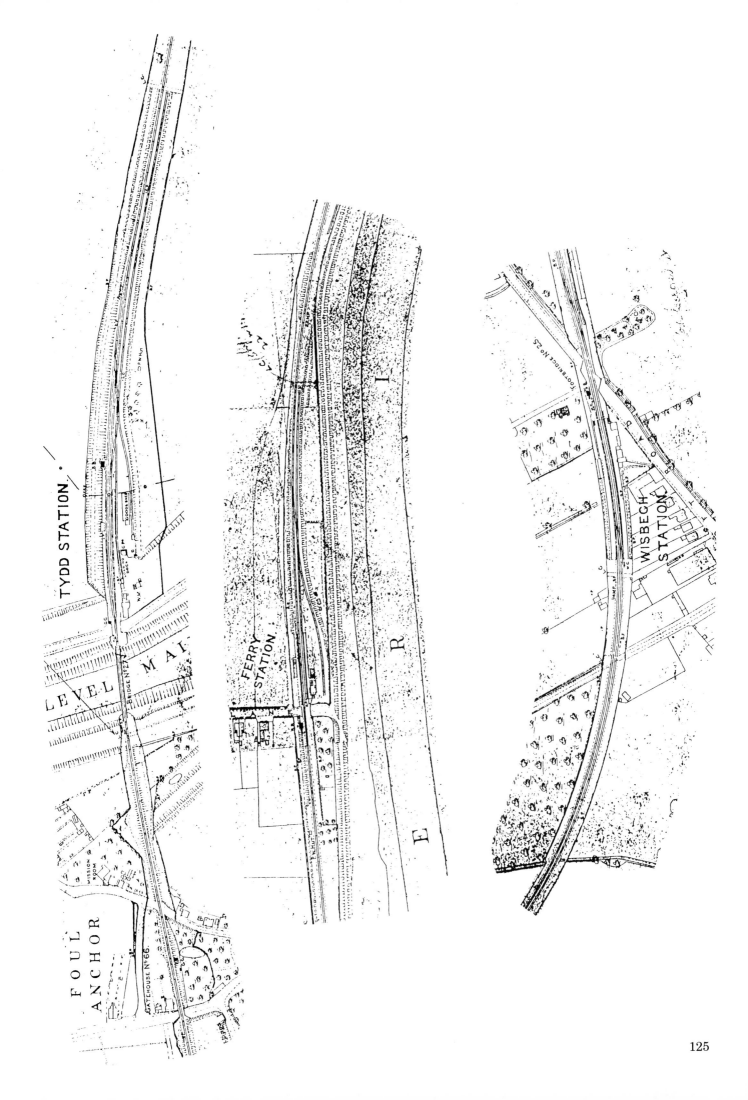

TYDD STATION

FOUL ANCHOR

LEVEL MAI

FERRY STATION

WISBECH STATION

E R I

125

many drainage channels and rivers, some of which required spans of considerable length, and approach gradients.

Leaving Sutton Bridge Junction (formerly Midland Junction) the single line followed the bank of the River Nene and rose and fell in a hump over the South Holland Main drain (bridge No 28). A mile further on it did so again to cross the North Level Main Drain on bridge No 27, passing through Tydd station. Tydd was made a passing place in 1896. Just beyond Tydd was the double crossing of Foul Anchor; two road crossings five chains apart controlled from one small signalbox, although there was also gatehouse No 66. This arrangement was abolished in c1922. From this point the line settled down to a largely level profile which lasted nearly 20 miles to Eye Green, being only slightly disturbed by minor undulations along the way. The formation was very close to the Nene all along this stretch, having the high embankment to the east of the track all the way to Wisbech, passing several picturesque gatehouses and through the single platform station of Ferry. Through Wisbech from Horse Shoe Lane signalbox and goods station the line was double, passing Wisbech St Mary station (known as 'Polly') to Murrow (pronounced 'Murrer') where it singled again in time to cross the GN&GEJt March-Spalding line on the level. Between Murrow and the crossing station of Wryde was Turf Fen Crossing, an intermediate tablet post, but not a crossing place, with a small Midland signalbox. The tablet post was abolished in 1929. The next station from Wryde was Thorney, where the double line resumed and continued all the way into Peterborough, passing Eye Green and Dogsthorpe Siding. From Eye Green the line began to rise from the general 6-12ft level of the fens to the 50ft level of Peterborough. However, the gradients were still only gentle, rising at 1 in 200 and 1 in 309 to a level at Dogsthorpe brickworks before the climb at 1 in 100 and 1 in 140 to 'Rhubarb Bridge', M&GN No 1, over the GN and MR main lines. The remaining half mile to Wisbech Junction was at a fall of 1 in 235.

The western section has not fared at all well in the years since closure. In fact most of the actual trackbed has gone except in inaccessible places, eg along the bank of the Nene. However, most of the architecture survives in the form of gatehouses and stations, but all the large steel bridges have been removed. It would be tedious and unnecessary to reiterate details of remains which have already been covered in other publications (see Bibliography) and so only a brief catalogue will be given here.

As we have seen, all the line between King's Lynn and Sutton Bridge has been lost. On the Peterborough line the best preserved stretch is that along the bank of the Nene where several gatehouses of the PW&S type survive as do parts of Tydd and Ferry stations. Very little remains in Wisbech until the gatehouses resume on the other side, and Wisbech St Mary is fairly complete. Murrow has recently been demolished and unfortunately a road has been built on the trackbed between Thorney and Peterborough.

Wisbech St Mary
Opened: 1 August 1866
Notes: Originally single line, it was doubled on 19 February 1901. The Midland signalbox released the ground-frame at the far end of the goods yard. An unremarkable station, handling mostly fruit, agricultural produce and coal.
Closed: 28 February 1959 (passengers); 31 October 1965 (goods)

Right:
Wisbech St Mary (Polly) in 1954 is seen viewed towards Wisbech from under the canopy of the standard M&GN waiting shelter.
R. E. G. Read

Murrow

Opened: 1 August 1866

Notes: The station passing loop was first installed in 1892 with a Midland box controlling the level crossing on the Down side. Doubling reached here from Wisbech on 19 February 1901, but the M&GN type 1b box was not provided on the Up side until January 1912. The timber Up waiting room was built in 1901. Goods traffic was based mainly on fruit and other agricultural produce. Beyond the GN&GE crossing was Turf Fen a small Midland box controlling crossing No 76. It was a tablet post, but not a passing place. It opened in 1891 and closed in 1929.

Closed: 28 February 1959 (passengers); 31 October 1965 (goods)

Remains: None.

Murrow station viewed towards Wisbech in 1956. The timber Up waiting shelter is apparently a Midland design.
R. E. G. Read

The M&GN crossed the GN&GEJt on the level just outside the GN&GEJt station at Murrow, seen here looking south towards March. Trains leaving Murrow M&GN for Peterborough would have crossed from left to right. The tablet section between Murrow and Turf Fen was also a block section with this signal box.
Author's collection

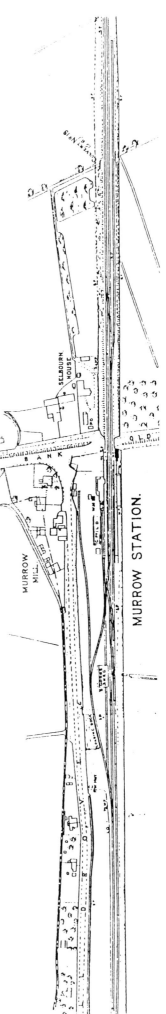

MURROW STATION.

Wryde

Opened: 1 August 1866

Notes: Originally single line with a Midland signalbox, the station was made a crossing place in 1906 with an M&GN type 1b signalbox. The grain shed and possibly the timber waiting room were built in 1890. Goods traffic was mainly grain and potatoes with some fruit.

Closed: 2 December 1957 (passengers); 18 April 1966 (goods)

Remains: Fairly complete.

Thorney

Opened: 1 August 1866

Notes: In 1892 the station had a long loop with East and West MR-type signalboxes, but when the line was doubled to Peterborough on 27 February 1900 only the East box by the crossing was required. The original goods shed was panelled brick and the standard timber grain shed was erected in 1892/93. The western end of the goods yard was controlled by a ground-frame in a cabin, released from the signalbox. The original timber Midland-type waiting shelter survived on the Down platform. The goods yard was busy, dealing with grain, potatoes, fruit and beer.

Closed: 2 December 1957 (passengers); 18 April 1966 (goods)

Remains: None.

Eye Green (For Crowland)

Opened: 1 August 1866

Notes: The station had a long loop from 1891 with East and West MR-type signalboxes, but after doubling on 24 June 1900 only one box was required, another MR-type erected next to the old East box. A ground frame dealt with the west end of the station until 1935. The siding to Northam's Brickworks (later LBC & Forders Ltd) was opened in 1898 and bricks were the lifeblood of the station. Other outward traffic was principally potatoes, with sugar beet and grain. Inward traffic was mainly large quantities of coal, both for the merchant in the yard and small coal for firing the brick kilns. Passenger traffic was very light.

Closed: 2 December 1957 (passengers); 18 April 1966 (goods)

Remains: None

Top left:
Wryde photographed in 1958, viewed towards Peterborough.
D. Thompson

Top right:
Thorney is pictured in a view looking towards Peterborough from beside the 20ft Midland signalbox, with the typical large PW&S station and goods shed. The date is c1959.
D. Thompson

Above:
A view of the station and yard at Eye Green, viewed towards Thorney from the overbridge.
D. A. Digby

128

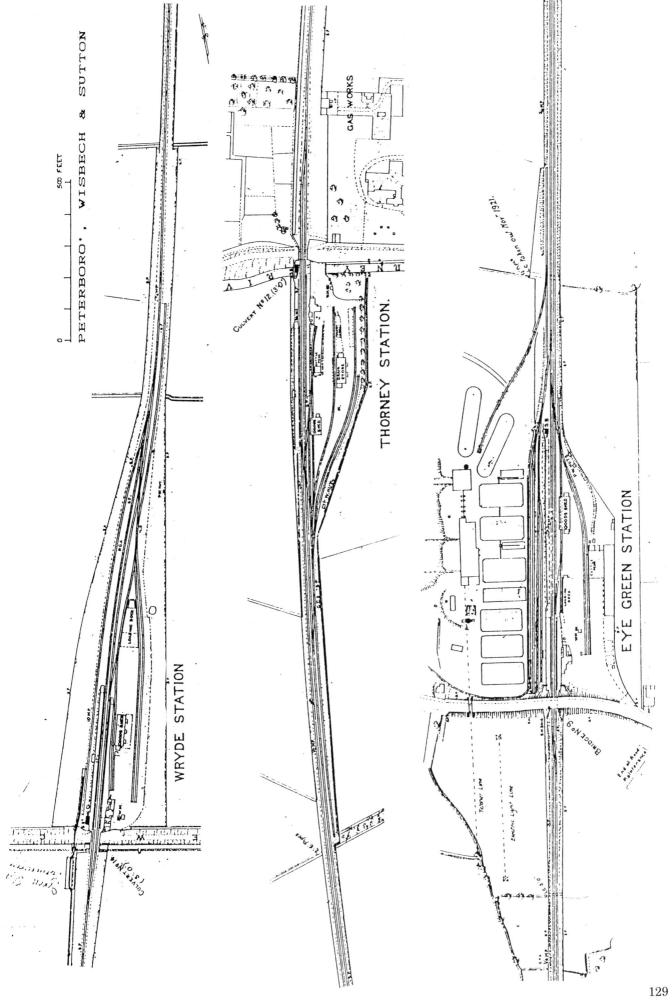

PETERBORO. WISBECH & SUTTON

500 FEET

WRYDE STATION

THORNEY STATION.

GAS WORKS

CULVERT Nº 12 (3'0")

EYE GREEN STATION

BRIDGE Nº 9

129

Peterborough

Opened: 12 June 1848 (MR), 7 August 1850
(GNR), 1 August 1866 (PW&S)
Notes: The M&GN joined the Midland Railway
at Wisbech Junction, an MR box but 50% of
the working expenses were paid by the
M&GN. There was a linking line to the Great
Northern at Westwood Junction, and M&GN
passenger trains used the GE station. Trains
continued to the GE station until 1904, after
which most platforms at Peterborough GN
were used. M&GN locomotives were serviced
at the MR Spital or GN New England sheds.
The M&GN presence at Peterborough was
restricted to Wisbech Sidings East signalbox,
an MR-type for which the MR paid 50% of the
working expenses. This box gave access to
the MR's Wisbech sidings, where much of the
M&GN freight was marshalled. Other freight
was handled at the GN Westwood sidings
and, to a lesser extent, the several other
goods depots of the MR and GN. The M&GN
crossed all the lines north of Peterborough on
bridge No 1, officially 'New England' but
known as 'Rhubarb Bridge'.
Closed: (M&GN) 28 February 1959
Remains: Very little of M&GN interest.

Right:
**The M&GN approached Peterborough over
New England bridge No 1, also known as
'Rhubarb Bridge', seen here from the north.**
M&GN Circle

Below right:
**The M&GN merged with the Midland at
Wisbech Junction, the signalbox to the left,
and trains then used the link line to
Westwood Junction on the GN, in the
background.**
E. L. Back/M. Back

Bottom far right:
**On a summer's morning in 1938 Class C
4-4-0 No 050 with G6 boiler and in LNER
livery waits to take out an express passenger
from Peterborough for the M&GN.**
H. C. Casserley

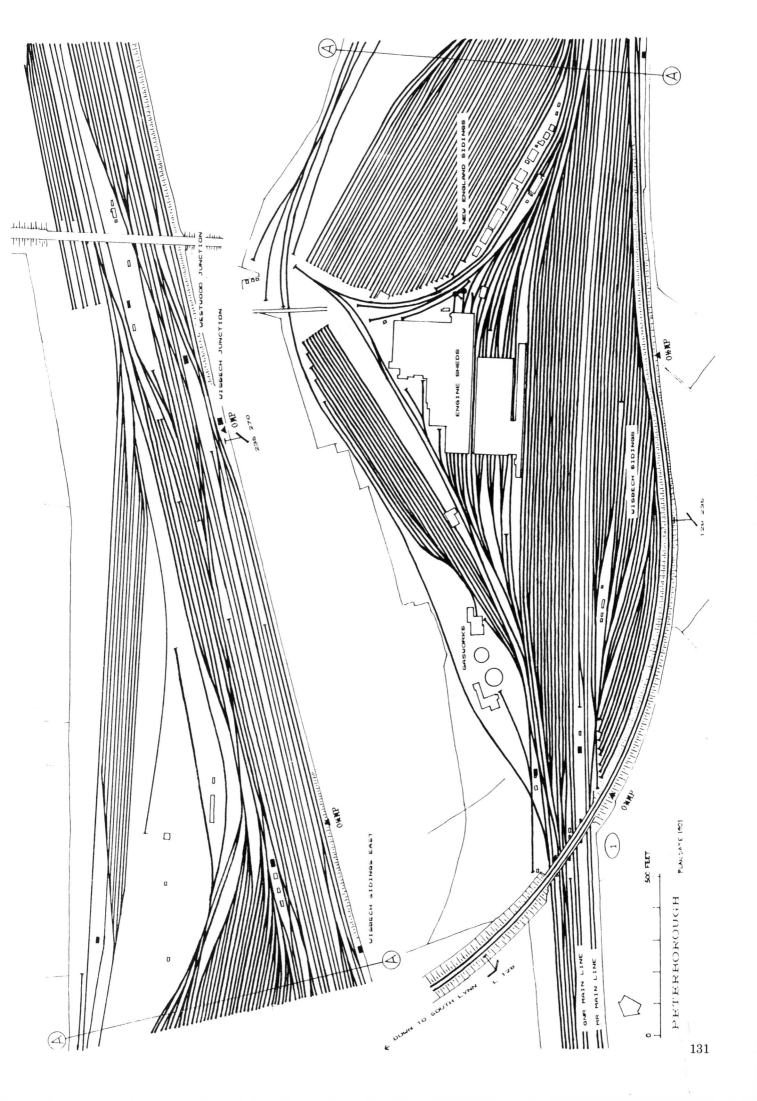

WESTWOOD JUNCTION

WISBECH JUNCTION

O MP
235 270

NEW ENGLAND SIDINGS

ENGINE SHEDS

WISBECH SIDINGS

O MP
128 235

GASWORKS

WISBECH SIDINGS EAST

O MP

O MP

DOWN TO SOUTH LYNN

L 128

PETERBOROUGH   PLAN DATE 1901

500 FEET

GNR MAIN LINE

MR MAIN LINE

131

Spalding and the West

Although the Peterborough route was considered the main line, the old Norwich-Spalding and the Spalding-Bourne lines were probably the most productive in terms of goods traffic on the whole M&GN, certainly from Long Sutton to Moulton where enormous quantities of potatoes, peas, fruit and flowers were dispatched from this area in their due season. This line also had a different character. The PW&S followed the River Nene and crossed open fenland, but the Spalding line passed through quite densely populated areas and cut across the 'grain' of the land, where the drainage process had left numerous roads, lanes and droves running roughly north-south. This can be illustrated by the fact that whereas the whole PW&S had 15 gatehouses, there were 22 between Sutton Bridge and Spalding alone.

Leaving Sutton Bridge Junction, the line singled at Dock Junction (crossing No 81) where the branch came in from the quayside. The dock had been abandoned in 1881. As on the Peterborough line there was little to interrupt the level gradient over the fertile fenland. For the 15 miles to Spalding there was no posted gradient at all, although the diagrams do show some very slight ones. The seven stations were all close together; first was Long Sutton, a tablet station since 1911 but with only a goods loop. A mile later came Gedney, a passing station, then Fleet which had been a tablet station with goods loop since 1909. Fleet and Gedney were architecturally identical. Holbeach was the original passing station, being approximately halfway between Spalding and Sutton Bridge. It had a long loop with East and West signalboxes. Whaplode was a simple single platform and less than a mile later came the passing place of Moulton. Weston was another simple platform although the building was extended in 1895. Just before Spalding the line was doubled at Cunningham's Drove signalbox and crossing, and passed Clay Lake box and siding before crossing the river where the line split at Welland Bank Junction to Spalding or the avoiding line. The latter was the

only significant feature that interrupted the flat gradient profile, rising with startling abruptness at 1 in 131 and 1 in 66 to clear the GN&GEJt and the GN and then falling at 1 in 95 and 1 in 200 to Cuckoo Junction.

Spalding itself was a GN station with several platforms, some of which the M&GN used for its local trains. The M&GN also had a small loco depot and the Midland had a goods shed, both situated by the double line coming in from Bourne which paralleled the GN main line. Each line had separate gates at the crossing over Winsover Road and the hold-ups to road traffic at 'Eight Gates', as they were known locally, were legendary. The Bourne line turned to the west, crossing Hawthorn Bank at gatehouse No 103 where there was a small gate cabin and a footbridge, and again on the level reached Cuckoo Junction where the avoiding line joined it. Now single, the line passed the lonely fenland stations of North Drove and Counter Drain, reaching Twenty where it doubled again into Bourne. On its way the line had to cross South Drove Drain on lattice bridge No 216, North Drove Drain on plate girder bridge No 217, Counter Drain on bridge No 223 and the River Glen on plate girder bridge No 225, very similar to No 27 at Tydd. Finally between Twenty and Bourne came the Bourne Eau, bridge No 229. At Bourne, actually a GN station, the M&GN had another loco depot, also used by the Midland engines from Saxby. The climb into the hills of west Lincolnshire began at 1 in 100 almost from the end of the island platform, as the double line had to assault a 150ft ridge only a mile to the west. This ridge was penetrated by Toft Tunnel No 237 (the only tunnel on the M&GN proper) and a deep cutting until the land fell away to the valley of the Lound Beck, crossed by a magnificent five-arch viaduct (No 239). Still climbing, the line reached a summit of about 200ft and fell in a deep cutting to the end-on junction with the Midland at Little Bytham.

From Sutton Bridge to Spalding, although little of the trackbed remains, most of the gatehouses are still standing, as are Gedney, Fleet, Holbeach, Moulton and Weston stations. Another welcome survivor is 'Pop Bottle' bridge No 183 near Long Sutton. In Spalding most of the avoiding line embankment has been removed, as have the engine and goods sheds, but the very long Green Lane footbridge No 205 still crosses the site to give a good view of the remains. Spalding station is a shadow of its former self. On the Bourne line all the iron and steel bridges have been removed. Most of the gatehouses still stand, but little remains of North Drove station and Counter Drain has been demolished, although gatehouse No 105A survives, illustrating the later 'domestic' style. Twenty is a private house, but Bourne itself has

Long Sutton
Opened: 3 July 1862
Notes: In 1891 the station was provided with a GN/RSCo-type signalbox by the crossing at the east end, the western yard points being released by Annetts Key. In 1911 it was made a tablet station, but only able to shunt non-passenger trains in the new loop for crossing purposes. The box was replaced by a Midland-type in 1922, with an extension. The western end of the yard then had a ground-frame released from the box. Potatoes and other agricultural traffic was heavy. This traffic including a significant quantity of flowers.
Closed: 28 February 1959 (passengers); 1 May 1965 (goods)
Remains: None

Gedney
Opened: 3 July 1862
Notes: Originally single line, the station was made a passing place in 1897 and supplied with an M&GN type 1a signalbox, originally at the eastern end of the new Up platform, but moved to the crossing at the west in 1926. The waiting shelter was standard M&GN. Goods traffic was mainly potatoes (12-15 wagons a day during the season), hay and other agricultural traffic, coal and later roadstone.
Closed: 28 February 1959 (passengers); 1 May 1965 (goods)
Remains: Fairly complete.

Fleet
Opened: 3 July 1862
Notes: The signalbox of GN/RSCo-type was installed in 1891 and made a tablet post in 1909, having a goods loop only. The yard points at the east end were opened by Annett's Key. Levers working the Clayton fogging device at each distant and home signal were installed in a sleeper-built hut opposite the platform. In 1909 a wharf and dock were constructed as the interchange point with a private narrow gauge light railway owned by Mr A. W. Worth. This line brought in goods from the nearby farms and was latterly operated by petrol-driven locomotives. There were heavy winter loadings of agricultural goods, principally potatoes.
Closed: 28 February 1959 (passengers); 1 May 1965 (goods)
Remains: Fairly complete.

been flattened, except for the enormous GN goods shed, and the M&GN timber shed across the road. Much more of the line to Saxby remains, having considerable earthworks, including Toft Tunnel and Lound Viaduct, and several bridges at Little Bytham.

Below:
Long Sutton in 1959, looking west from the signalbox. The goods loop is on the left, and the goods shed on the far right.
D. Thompson

Below right:
Gedney viewed towards Fleet in c1959. The signalbox was originally at the other end of the Up platform. The crossing gates are genuine M&GN examples.
M&GN Circle

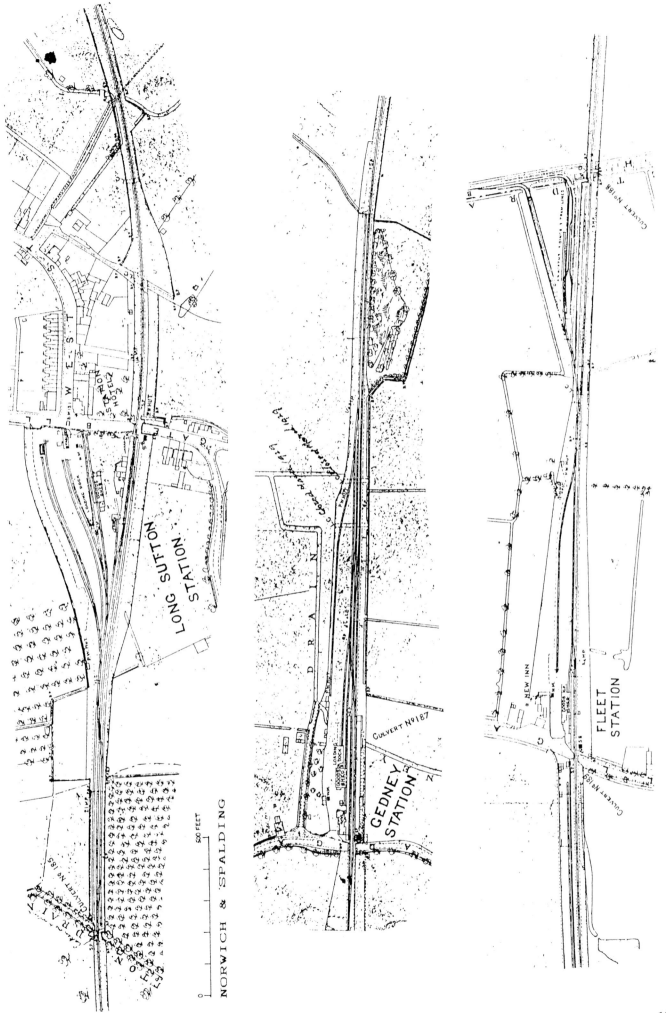

LONG SUTTON STATION

GEDNEY STATION

FLEET STATION

NORWICH & SPALDING

0 ___ 500 FEET

133

Holbeach

Opened: 15 November 1858

Notes: In 1890 the station was made a passing place with a long loop, new platform and timber waiting shelter, and East and West signalboxes of the GN/RSCo-type on brick bases. There was a large panelled brick goods shed and one siding served a large malthouse beyond the yard. Goods traffic consisted of potatoes in large quantities, fruit, flowers and coal.

Closed: 28 February 1959 (passengers); 1 May 1965 (goods)

Remains: Main building survives.

Whaplode

Opened: 15 November 1858

Notes: A single line station with a GN/RSCo-type signalbox installed in 1891 on the east side of the crossing. This was removed c1929. A stationmaster's house was built in 1914 to the new domestic style. Produce was fairly restricted to fruit and flowers loaded on to passenger trains, but the platform could be full of boxes waiting to be loaded.

Closed: 28 February 1959 (passengers); 1 May 1965 (goods)

Remains: Stationmaster's house.

Moulton

Opened: 15 November 1858

Notes: Made into a passing place c1896 with M&GN type 1a signalbox originally at the end of the new Up platform. The box was moved to the crossing in 1926. Passenger traffic was reasonable, the village being only half a mile away. Goods traffic was primarily potatoes, flowers, fruit and sugar beet. Coal was the major inward traffic.

Closed: 28 February 1959 (passengers); 1 May 1965 (goods)

Remains: Fairly complete.

Weston

Opened: 15 November 1858

Notes: There was only a single platform, which could be full of produce during the fruit and flower season. There was a small RSCo gate cabin, which was removed in c1929.

Closed: 28 February 1959 (passengers); 1 May 1965 (goods)

Remains: Fairly complete.

Left:
A general view of Holbeach from the crossing in 1959, showing the timber waiting shelter of 1890, the N&S large station and the goods shed behind it.
D. Thompson

Below left:
The very simple single platform of Whaplode, viewed towards Spalding. The building is a slightly larger version of the standard gatehouse.
D. Thompson

Below left:
Moulton photographed in the Spalding direction in 1959. The signalbox was originally at the far end of the Up platform.
D. Thompson

Below:
The single platform at Weston; the cross gable of the station extension can clearly be seen, with the original building beyond.
D. Thompson

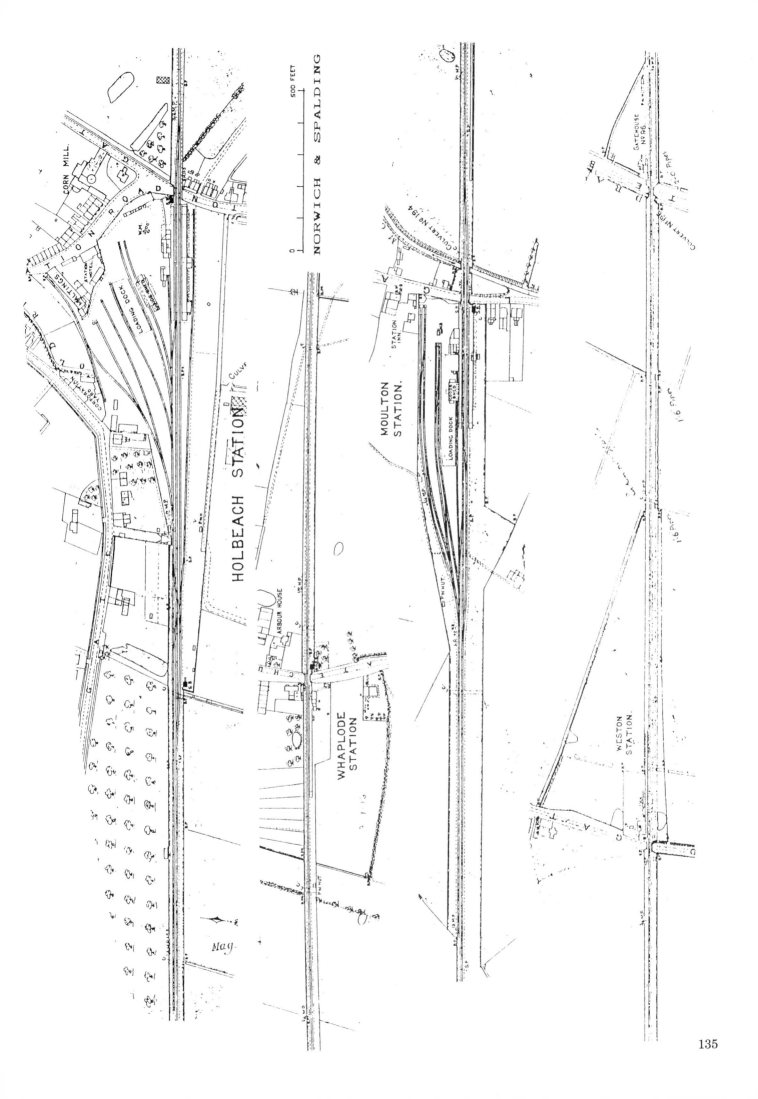

NORWICH & SPALDING

500 FEET

HOLBEACH STATION

CORN MILL.

WHAPLODE STATION

ARBOUR HOUSE

MOULTON STATION.

CULVERT No 194

STATION INN

LOADING DOCK

WESTON STATION

GATEHOUSE No 96

Mag.

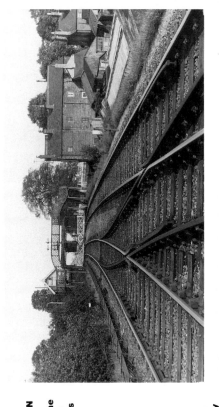

Spalding

Opened: GNR 17 October 1848, N&SR 15 November 1858, S&BR 1 August 1866, M&GN 1 May 1894

Notes: A busy interchange station built by the GN to its standard design of the time. There were several platforms used by the M&GN as follows:

1 & 2 departures to Sutton Bridge and the east;

4 bay at the north used to store M&GN coaches;

6 M&GN arrivals from east or west;

7 departures to Bourne, Saxby and Nottingham.

Goods traffic was heavy: at first principally potatoes, and later flowers, plus fruit, peas, cabbages and sugar beet. Winsover Road crossing at the south end of the station (or Eight Gates as it was known) was the scene of many road hold-ups. There were originally six signalboxes: Nos 1 and 3 controlling the south end of the station with No 2 being the Winsover Road gate box. From 22 February 1922 the six boxes were replaced by three new ones. All boxes were to GN designs.

Closed: M&GN 28 February 1959 (passengers); 5 April and 1 May 1965 (goods)

Remains: Very little of M&GN interest.

Above left:
Approaching Spalding from the east, the line crossed the Welland and the avoiding line branched off at Welland Bank signalbox. There was also a GN-type footbridge. The only feature to survive is the block of houses on the right.
E. L. Back/M. Back

Above:
Spalding station viewed from the south in c1908. M&GN Class C 4-4-0 No 3 is leaving on a local train for Lynn made up of GN, E&M and MR stock. Behind the GE horsebox is a GE train for March via the GN&GEJt. Note the rather archaic signals, and the shunting horse being led past platform No 5.
Author's collection

Above left:
The north end of Spalding shows signalbox No 4 and an interesting variety of stock.
M&GN Circle

Left:
The Spalding avoiding line, converging from the left, and the original alignment on the right joined again at Cuckoo Junction, which was provided with the standard GN/RSCo box, seen here viewed towards Bourne.
E. L. Back/M. Back

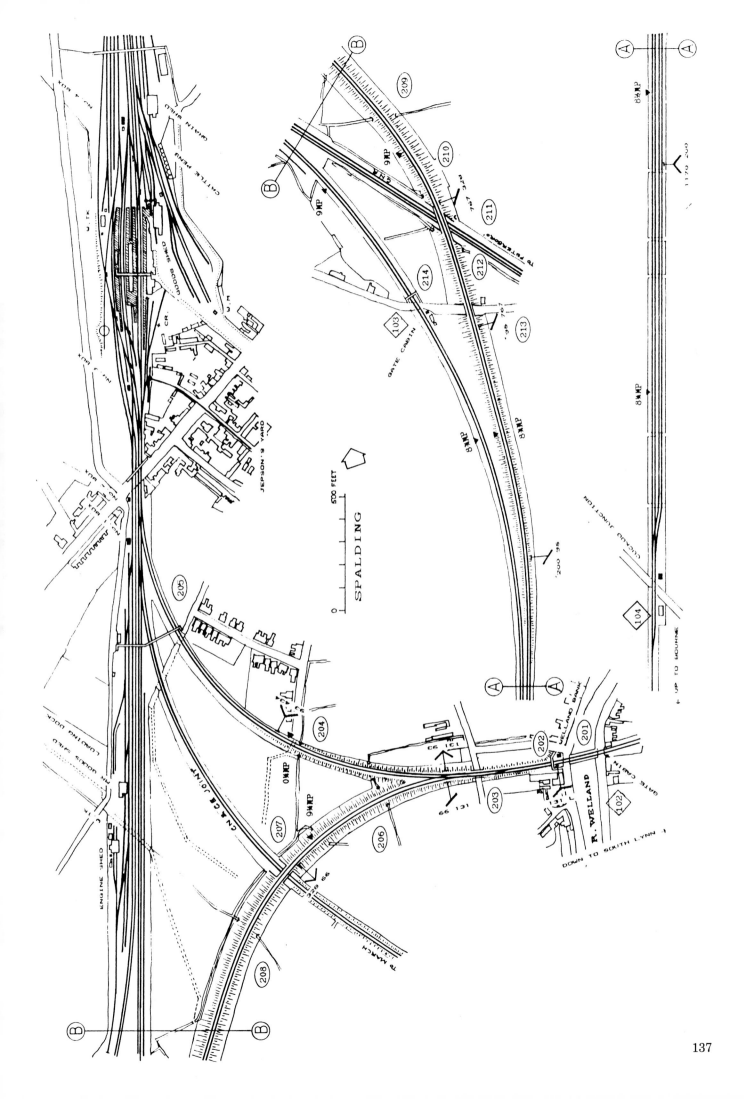

SPALDING

500 FEET

137

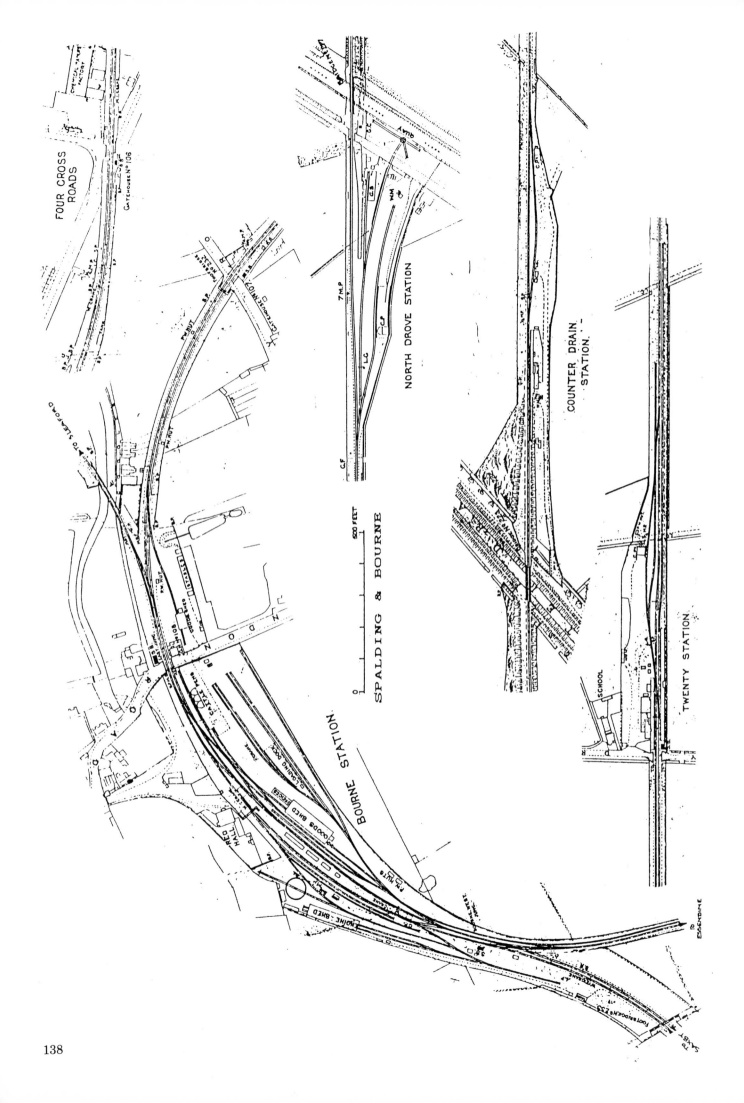

SPALDING & BOURNE

FOUR CROSS ROADS

NORTH DROVE STATION

COUNTER DRAIN STATION.

BOURNE STATION.

TWENTY STATION

North Drove

Opened: 1 August 1866

Notes: On the opening of the Saxby through line the old platform, which had been curved since 1891, was abandoned and a new timber platform and shelter were built. The 1891 signalbox, of GN/RSCo design, was removed in 1924 in favour of a concrete crossing hut opposite. A wharf and siding by the Drain was provided in 1896 and used for barge traffic until c1947. Passenger traffic was very light, but goods traffic was heavy, with large quantities of grain and potatoes, hay and straw, plus fuel oil to the wharf.

Closed: 28 February 1959 (passengers); 5 April 1965 (goods)

Remains: Very little.

Counter Drain

Opened: 1 August 1866

Notes: A standard S&B station with bay window on the platform. The timber goods shed with through siding was demolished in 1925. The GN/RSCo signalbox erected in 1891 by the crossing was removed in 1924. It was replaced by a crossing hut and a tablet-released ground-frame. Gatehouse No 105A was built in 1929 to the domestic style.

Closed: 28 February 1959 (passengers); 5 April 1965 (goods)

Remains: None, except gatehouse No 105A.

Twenty

Opened: 1 August 1866

Notes: A standard S&B station with bay window on the platform, later removed. Provided with a GN/RSCo-type signalbox in 1891, and doubled on 5 June 1893 with new Up platform and timber waiting shelter. This isolated station dealt mainly with agricultural produce — potatoes and sugar beet.

Closed: 28 February 1959 (passengers); 5 April 1965 (goods)

Remains: Main building.

Bourne

Opened: May 1860 (GN); 1 August 1866 (S&B); February 1872 (GN); 1 May 1894 (M&GN)

Notes: The 1894 station at Bourne was GN property. A GN-type footbridge gave access to the platform. The M&GN goods shed was of the timber S&B-type on the east side of London Road. The engine shed was built in 1893 and, having been transferred to the M&GN in 1897, extended in 1898 to hold six locomotives. GN swing water cranes stood on the Up end of the platform and beside the Down end, with a Midland crane beside the Down main line. The turntable was 45ft 0in until 1930 when a 60ft 0in turntable was installed. Bourne East and West boxes controlled the junctions; both were to the GN/RSCo design

To the east of Bourne was Austerby crossing with an E&M-type gate box and Four Cross Roads with a GN/RSCo signalbox and two GN water cranes beside the main line. These cranes were supplied by a water tank. Five miles to the west of Bourne was Little Bytham Junction. At this point the double line singled and became Midland Railway property before crossing the GNR main line. A long refuge siding extended from the junction across the Bytham bridge (MR No 43). The signalbox was of the MR type 2b.

Closed: 28 February 1959 (passengers); 5 April 1965 (goods)

Remains: Goods shed and Red Hall.

Above:

The original platform at North Drove, on which stood the station building, was not used during the M&GN period, and only this timber platform was used, with a shelter provided of the same type as that at Twenty.
E. L. Back/M. Back

Below left:

The small station at Counter Drain, pictured towards Spalding in 1959. The goods loop points can be seen at the end of the platform.
D. Thompson

Below left:

Twenty looking across towards Bourne, showing the typical S&B building (extended) and the GN/RSCo signalbox. Note the concrete nameboard.
D. Thompson

Below:

Bourne viewed from the East box. Note the Red Hall to the right, the enormous goods warehouse on the left dwarfing the station in the centre, and the loco shed and water tank in the distance. The West box is just visible on the far left.
E. L. Back/M. Back

Appendix A: Locomotives and Rolling Stock

Locomotives and Rolling Stock

To gain a detailed picture of this complex subject would require more space than is available, and can be pursued in more specialist publications (see Bibliography). In these notes only a broad coverage of the major classes or types will be given, which should be enough to give the student of the Joint a useful background knowledge. As far as liveries are concerned the reader will find references here which do not appear in the standard published works. This is because they are based on recent research by the Author, and upon information from ex-M&GN men.

Locomotives

The locomotives of the M&GN are a subject full of pitfalls and even well-known authors have come to grief over the ins and outs of Joint motive power. The following summary relies heavily on the work

Below right:
One of the first batch of Class C 4-4-0s delivered in 1894, No 36 is in original condition and sports the 'JTM&GNR' lettering, shunting at Cromer on the Jubilee siding which dates the view to c1897. The water tower has not yet had its roof fitted. To the left are two ex-E&M brake vans, the first (No 7) is lettered 'JT/M&/GN'.
National Railway Museum

Below:
Class C No 18 with extended smokebox fitted in c1910, and No 45 rebuilt with G7 boiler in 1909, at Cromer Beach shed. The buildings behind are the UDC stores on Central Road.
Real Photos/IAL

Bottom right:
Class D 0-6-0 No 58 at Yarmouth Beach in c1925 is almost in original condition, except that a Melton chimney with capuchon has been fitted. The engine is in what may be called the 'intermediate' livery — dark brown with limited lining, but medium sized sanserif letters.
Real Photos/IAL

of Alan Wells and the late Bill Robinson who gathered together all known facts about each engine. A chart is presented for easy reference. (Figs 30/31.)

After the division of responsibilities of the M&GN in which the care of locomotive matters was handed to Derby, the Joint's fleet took on a distinctly Midland flavour. Not only were numbers of the contemporary S. W. Johnson designs delivered but also many ex-E&M engines received Midland-type boilers and boiler fittings. The largest class of engine on the M&GN were the 40 Johnson 4-4-0s with 6ft 6in driving wheels delivered in 1894, 1896 and 1899, known as Class C. Extended smokeboxes and tall Melton-designed chimneys were fitted from 1906 except that Nos 14, 18, 77 & 79 retained their Johnson chimneys for an unspecified time. The class saw several other modifications; two received MR round-topped Class H boilers in 1908, and from 1909-15 eight were rebuilt with MR Belpaire G7 boilers, followed by the two H-boilered locos in 1924/25. All Class C Rebuilds had new cabs, Ramsbottom valves, extended smokeboxes and doors with wheel handle, enclosed splashers and large brass numerals. About 1924 an extra tender coal rail was fitted. Seven others were given MR G6 Belpaire boilers during 1929-31 with new cabs, Deeley smokeboxes and Ross valves, replaced by Ramsbottom valves about 1936. The remainder stayed virtually unchanged. All engines

were given Deeley riveted smokeboxes about 1930, and three of the G7 rebuilds had further smokebox extensions from 1934. Splasher cut-outs were restored in 1935 and a variety of chimneys were tried.

Sixteen Johnson 0-6-0s of the period, M&GN Class D, were delivered in 1896 and 1899. Most remained externally unchanged until the fitting of Deeley smokeboxes. Two were rebuilt with Class H boilers and then they and two others received Class G7 boilers. These Class D Rebuilds had new cabs, Ramsbottom valves, extended smokeboxes with wheel handle door, and large brass numerals. Extra coal rails were fitted to their tenders about 1924. Two were given further smokebox extensions about 1935 and again various chimneys were fitted.

The only examples of GN locomotives were 11 Ivatt 0-6-0s, M&GN Class Da, delivered in 1901. In 1907 extended smokeboxes were fitted and in 1920-27 they were given large diameter boilers and large brass numerals. From about 1930 Deeley smokeboxes were fitted, six of them having the smokebox door offset towards the bottom. Various chimneys were tried about 1935.

Of the ex-E&M locomotives the most well-known and the largest class were the 15 Class A 4-4-0s built by Beyer Peacock & Co of Manchester, delivered between 1881 and 1888. Of the 15, the

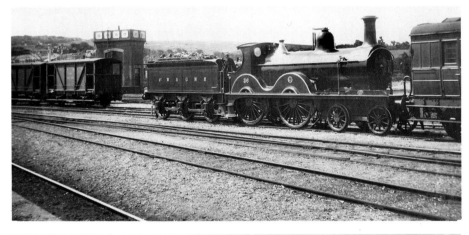

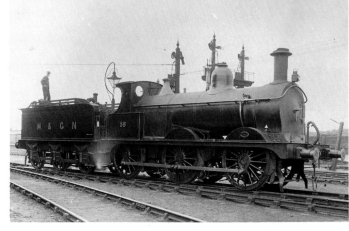

M&GN Locomotives 1910-1936

No	Class	Wheel	Ext Sbox	Reboiler	Notes
1	C	4-4-0	1907		Flowerpot chim c1935
2	C	4-4-0	c1910	1931 G6	
3	C	4-4-0	c1907		
4	C	4-4-0	c1911		Flowerpot chim & ext cab c1935
5	C	4-4-0	c1911		Ext cab c1935
6	C	4-4-0	c1912	1930 G6	
7	C	4-4-0	c1914		Ext cab c1935
8	B	4-4-0T		1894 MC	Loaned to MR 1906-12. Sold 1917
9	AT	4-4-2T			Raked side tanks c1933
9A	B	4-4-0T		1899 MC	Withdrawn 1932
10	B	4-4-0T		1896 MC	Loaned to MR 1906-12. Sold 1917
11	C	4-4-0	c1910		Ext cab c1935
12	C	4-4-0	c1911		Flowerpot chim c1935
13	C	4-4-0	c1908		
14	C	4-4-0	1907		Johnson chim retained for a time
15	MR	0-6-0T			
16	MR	0-6-0T			
16A	–	0-6-0ST			Melton shunter, ex-GY&S *Stalham*
17	C	4-4-0	1907		Ext cab c1935
18	C	4-4-0	c1910		Johnson chim retained for a time
19	B	4-4-0T		1903 MC	Loaned to MR 1906-12. Sold 1917
20A	B	4-4-0T		1903 MC	Withdrawn 1931
20	AT	4-4-2T			Raked side tanks c1933
21	A	4-4-0	c1911	1896 C	Rebuilt 1914. Withdrawn 1936
22	A	4-4-0	c1913	1898 C	Rebuilt 1915. Withdrawn 1936
23	A	4-4-0	c1910	1895 C	Rebuilt 1919
24	A	4-4-0	c1913	1898 C	Rebuilt 1914
25	A	4-4-0	c1920	1906 C	Rebuilt 1920
26	A	4-4-0	c1920	1904 C	Rebuilt 1923. Withdrawn 1936
27	A	4-4-0	c1920	1905 C	Rebuilt 1927
28	A	4-4-0	c1920	1905 C	Rebuilt 1923
29	A	4-4-0	c1914	1906 C	Ext cab & w'bd c1914 W'drawn 1931
30	A	4-4-0	c1914	1906 C	Ext cab & w'bd c1914 W'drawn 1933
31	A	4-4-0	c1914	1907 C	Ext cab c1914 w'bd c1930 Wdn 1933
32	A	4-4-0	c1914	1907 C	Ext cab c1914 w'bd c1930 Wdn 1933
33	A	4-4-0	1908	1908 C	Ext cab & w'bd 1908 W'drawn 1936
34	A	4-4-0	1908	1908 C	Ext cab & w'bd 1908 W'drawn 1936
35	A	4-4-0	1909	1909 C	Ext cab 1909 w'bd c1930 Wdn 1935
36	C	4-4-0	1907	1930 G6	
37	C	4-4-0	c1908		
38	C	4-4-0	c1910		Flowerpot chim 1936
39	C	4-4-0		1908 H	1924 G7
40	B	4-4-0T		1894 MC	Loaned to MR 1906-12. Sold 1917
41	AT	4-4-2T	c1910		Raked side tanks c1933
42	C	4-4-0	c1910		Flowerpot chim & ext cab 1936
43	C	4-4-0	c1911		
44	C	4-4-0	c1911	1930 G6	
45	C	4-4-0		1909 G7	Stvp chim & ext sbx 1934 Wdn 1936
46	C	4-4-0		1915 G7	
47	C	4-4-0	c1908		
48	C	4-4-0	c1911		Flowerpot chim & ext cab 1936
49	C	4-4-0	c1910	1931 G6	
50	C	4-4-0	c1910	1929 G6	
51	C	4-4-0		1915 G7	
52	C	4-4-0		1913 G7	Flowerpot chim 1936
53	C	4-4-0		1910 G7	
54	C	4-4-0		1914 G7	Ross vlvs 1930-33. Tender from 22
55	C	4-4-0		1908 H, 1925 G7	Stvp chim & ext sbx 1934
56	C	4-4-0		1912 G7	Stvp & sbx 1934 Flrpt chim 1936
57	C	4-4-0		1912 G7	Ross vlvs 1930-33 Flrpt chim 1936
58	D	0-6-0			Ext cab c1935
59	D	0-6-0			
60	D	0-6-0			
61	D	0-6-0			
62	D	0-6-0		1906 H,1924 G7	
63	D	0-6-0			
64	D	0-6-0			
65	D	0-6-0			
66	D	0-6-0			
67	D	0-6-0			
68	D	0-6-0		1921 G7	Stvp chim c1935
69	D	0-6-0		1909 H, 1921 G7	Ext sbx & flowerpot chim c1935
70	D	0-6-0			
71	D	0-6-0		1921 G7	Ext sbx & stovepipe chim c 1935
72	D	0-6-0			
73	D	0-6-0			
74	C	4-4-0	c1918		
75	C	4-4-0	c1916		
76	C	4-4-0	c1916		Ext cab 1936

No	Class	Wheel	Ext Sbox	Reboiler	Notes
77	C	4-4-0	c1916	1930 G6	
78	C	4-4-0	c1916		Ext cab & Flowerpot chim c1936
79	C	4-4-0	c1917		Johnson chim retained for a time
80	C	4-4-0	c1919		
81	C	0-6-0	1907	1927 J	Flowerpot chim c1935
82	Da	0-6-0	1907	1921 J	Offset Deeley door
83	Da	0-6-0	1907	1921 J	Flowerpot chim c1935
84	Da	0-6-0	1907	1924 J	Stovepipe chim c1935
85	Da	0-6-0	1907	1926 J	Offset Deeley door
86	Da	0-6-0	1907	1927 J	Stovepipe chim c1935
87	Da	0-6-0	1907	1925 J	Offset Deeley door
88	Da	0-6-0	1907	1920 J	Offset Deeley door Flrpt chim 1935
89	Da	0-6-0	1907	1926 J	Offset Deeley door
90	Da	0-6-0	1907	1926 J	
91	Da	0-6-0	1907	1926 J	Offset Deeley door Flrpt chim 1935
92	Da	0-6-0	1907	1921 J	Offset Deeley door Flrpt chim 1935
93	MR	0-6-0T			
94	MR	0-6-0T			
95	MR	0-6-0T			
96	MR	0-6-0T			No Deeley door
97	MR	0-6-0T			
98	MR	0-6-0T			
99	MR	0-6-0T			

On loan from Midland 1906-1912:

No	Class	Wheel	Ext Sbox	Reboiler	Notes
142		0-4-4T			MR number but M&GN lettering
143		0-4-4T			MR number but M&GN lettering
144		0-4-4T			MR number but M&GN lettering

Reboilering notes:
(Only those affecting appearance are shown)

C	Midland class C boiler		H	large round-topped boiler
G6	small belpaire boiler		MC	special Melton MR-type boiler
G7	large belpaire boiler		J	large GN boiler

Smokeboxes:
Extended smokeboxes where unconfirmed officially are taken as date of first rebuild or estimated from photographs.
From c1927-c1932 all engines received plain riveted smokeboxes and Deeley doors, except Nos 9A, 20A, 96.

Abbreviations

stvp	stovepipe		chim	chimney
flrpt	flowerpot		vlvs	valves
ext sbx	further smokebox extension		ext cab	cab roof extended
w'bd	tender weatherboard		wdn	withdrawn

first four originally had Beyer Peacock chimneys and the following 11 had built-up chimneys and tall domes. All engines had the connecting rods inside the coupling rods. Between 1895 and 1909 all engines were given Midland boilers and fittings with tapered Melton chimneys. Extended smokeboxes were fitted from 1908, some engines having extended cab roofs at the same time. The major rebuilding was of Nos 21-28 between 1914 and 1927 with MR boilers, extra sandboxes on the rear of the splashers, new round window cabs, new straight-sided tenders and large brass numerals. The unrebuilt engines all received tender weatherboards, some at the same time as their extended smokeboxes but others about 1930. Deeley smokeboxes were also fitted from about 1930.

The seven attractive 4-4-0Ts of Class B were delivered between 1878 and 1881. Although all basically the same, three (Nos 10, 19 & 20) were 4in longer at the rear with a coal bunker 3in higher, and there were also some other detail differences. They were all reboilered with a special Melton design having a polished brass dome and safety valve cover based on Midland practice. They were also given Melton tapered chimneys. Class B No 41 was withdrawn in 1904 and thus does not feature in the appended list. Another four were lent to the Midland in 1906, were returned in 1912 and sold in 1917. The two survivors were put on to the duplicate list when their numbers were taken by the Melton Class A tanks.

The three 4-4-2Ts of Class A were officially rebuilds but were actually new engines: No 41 in 1904, No 20 in 1909 and No 9 in 1910. The two later engines had extended smokeboxes and brass numerals but No 41 had an E&M-type number plate and only received an extended smokebox about 1910. From c1930 all had Deeley smokeboxes and from c1933 the side tanks were raked.

Of all M&GN engines the Class MR 0-6-0Ts had the most complex history, supposedly being rebuilds of older engines all but three bought from the Cornish Minerals Railway. Between 1897 and 1902 Nos 1A, 2A, 3A, 11A, 12A, 14A, 15, 16 & 17A were 'rebuilt' but apart from a few wheel-sets they were new engines. All except Nos 15 & 16 were renumbered sequentially Nos 93-99 in 1907. Apart from the Melton tapered chimney the boiler fittings were based on MR practice. From c1930 all but No 96 received Deeley smokebox doors and c1935 coal hoppers were fitted to the bunkers.

The livery of the M&GN was lighter than but not too dissimilar from the E&M 'milk chocolate', being a light brown or ochre. There was apparently no official title but names given to it were 'Autumn Leaf', 'Willow Green' and 'Golden Ochre'. At first it was built up from two coats of yellow ochre and one of raw sienna followed by three coats of varnish. Later the formula was simplified by mixing to a colour board. Frames, wheels and outside cylinders were burnt sienna, a red-brown. Nos 74-80 were delivered ochre all over but were soon repainted. Lining was black, edged with lemon chrome. Tenders which were divided into two panels had the beading painted unlined burnt sienna.

Lettering applied immediately on formation was in the E&M sanserif face being 'M&GNJR' on tenders and tank sides, but only a few ex-E&M engines carried this. The first batch of Midland 4-4-0s delivered in 1894 carried the 'JtM&GNR' required by the RCH and although several locos were relettered thus the normal usage rapidly became just 'M&GN', although the Class A tanks had the name in full, arranged in an arc on the tankside. Letters from 1894 were in gold and seriffed, blocked blue to left and below, shaded black to right and below. The sanserif lettering appears to have been used on some engines as late as 1904. The Device, a circular badge made up of the arms of Norwich, Yarmouth, Lynn and Peterborough inside a garter, appeared on most engines. It was placed on the front or middle splashers of Midland-type engines, but between the 'M&' and 'GN' of the others on tenders or tanks, except for the Class A tanks where the device was under the arc of lettering, and the Class MR tanks where it was above the brass numberplate. The garter colour until 1910 was white, from which time it became blue. The device measured 9.75in wide by 10.75in high.

From c1923 the 'D' and 'Da' classes were painted dark brown (burnt umber enriched with a little vermilion) with limited lemon chrome lining and large sanserif letters on the tender in the same colour. Class MR No 98 was similarly treated. From 1929 the standard livery on all engines was as above but the large tender lettering was now seriffed. The yellow became orange under varnish and cleaner's tallow.

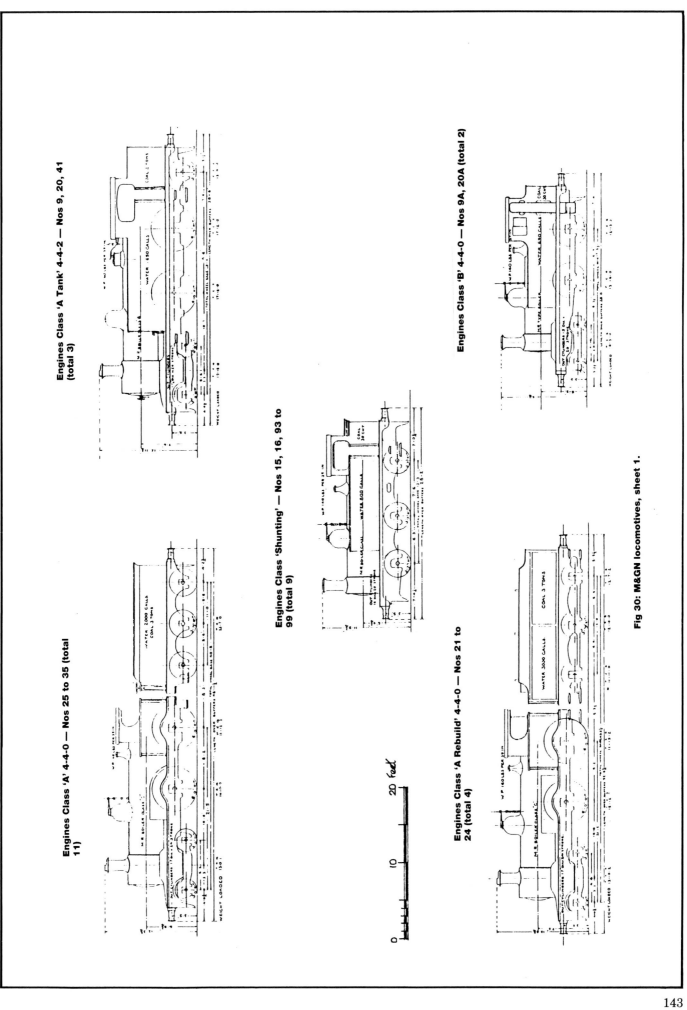

Engines Class 'A Tank' 4-4-2 — Nos 9, 20, 41 (total 3)

Engines Class 'B' 4-4-0 — Nos 9A, 20A (total 2)

Engines Class 'A' 4-4-0 — Nos 25 to 35 (total 11)

Engines Class 'Shunting' — Nos 15, 16, 93 to 99 (total 9)

Engines Class 'A Rebuild' 4-4-0 — Nos 21 to 24 (total 4)

Fig 30: M&GN locomotives, sheet 1.

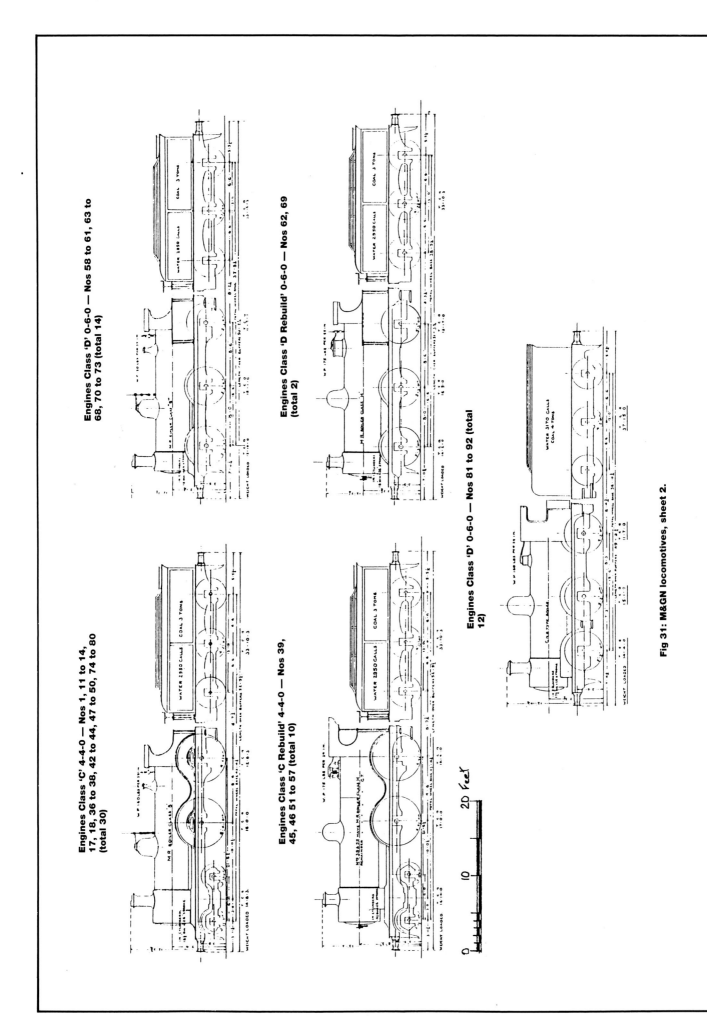

Engines Class 'C' 4-4-0 — Nos 1, 11 to 14, 17, 18, 36 to 38, 42 to 44, 47 to 50, 74 to 80 (total 30)

Engines Class 'D' 0-6-0 — Nos 58 to 61, 63 to 68, 70 to 73 (total 14)

Engines Class 'C Rebuild' 4-4-0 — Nos 39, 45, 46 51 to 57 (total 10)

Engines Class 'D Rebuild' 0-6-0 — Nos 62, 69 (total 2)

Engines Class 'D' 0-6-0 — Nos 81 to 92 (total 12)

Fig 31: M&GN locomotives, sheet 2.

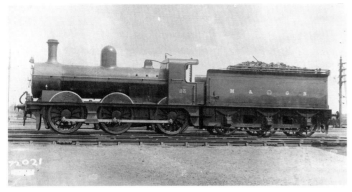

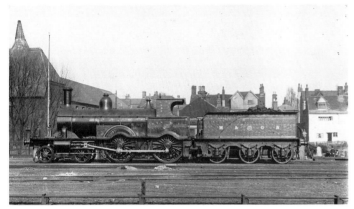

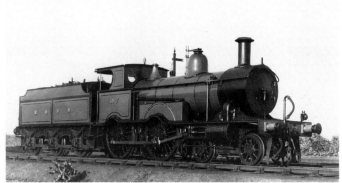

Top left:
Class Da 0-6-0 No 83 as fitted with extended smokebox in 1907, seen here at South Lynn in original livery.
Real Photos/IAL

Top right:
Class Da 0-6-0 No 88 illustrates the type's later incarnation, having been reboilered in 1920. The small brass numerals were replaced with large ones at the same time. From c1930 Deeley smokebox doors were fitted, and some were offset. No 88 is seen in c1933 sporting the final livery.
Real Photos/IAL

Above left:
Class A 4-4-0 No 30 is pictured at Norwich after rebuilding with MR boiler in 1906, but before receiving an extended smokebox in c1914. This engine has had the Beyer Peacock lettering removed from the brass splasher beading, a process all the engines endured sooner or later.
Author's collection

Above:
This is the nearest we get to a colour photo of the original livery. Fortunately Mr Casserley took the time and trouble in 1927 to use a plate treated with the new Panchromatic emulsion, giving correct rendering of Class A No 27 as rebuilt in that year, standing at Spalding shed.
H. C. Casserley

Above left:
Class B 4-4-0T No 10 as rebuilt in 1896 with a special Melton boiler. This engine was originally L&F *Norwich*, delivered in 1880. It was loaned to the Midland in 1906, and is pictured here by Mundesley loco shed in c1902. Note the corrugated iron cladding of this obscure building.
Bucknall collection/IAL

Left:
Class MR 0-6-0T No 1A (from 1907 No 93) shunting in the Down yard at Melton Constable. Note M&GN cattle wagon No 38 visible beyond the engine and the Railway Institute on the skyline.
Lens of Sutton

Passenger Stock

This subject can best be covered in three periods: early (1893-1902), middle (1903-1931) and late (1932-1936). These periods are defined not only by the types of vehicles present, but also by accompanying livery changes.

The stock of the early period was basically the same as that of the E&M, except for some old four-wheel Midland and North London carriages which were immediately withdrawn. There were three groups of carriages. The 'small stock' was all four-wheel arc-roofed with raised beading at the waist only and round-topped windows. There were three luggage brake vans, five thirds, three brake-thirds, 17 composites and one brake-composite. Withdrawals were rapid leaving only the brake vans and probably four of the composites by 1903. The 'large stock' consisted of 16 thirds and eight composites on six wheels and four luggage brakes on four wheels. Beading was conventional with radiused corners throughout, but there was a distinctive high elliptical roof. The 'new stock' was similar although built at Melton from 1892. At first there were two composites and one luggage brake 27ft long, one saloon and one third 30ft long, all on four wheels. Photographic and other evidence shows that two more thirds were also built very similar to the composites. It is believed that the 30ft third became No 56 in 1903, the other two becoming Nos 57 & 58. They were all still four-wheel even in 1909. (Fig 33.)

Livery of the early period was a dark teak finish made by the application of graining in a mixture of burnt umber, burnt sienna and raw umber water colours on a buff base, followed by varnish. A few vehicles were lettered 'M&GNJR' but from 1894 the style officially adopted was 'JtM&GN' in gold sanserif letters apparently blocked red and shaded black. A few vehicles were given plain 'M&GN' in the same lettering. Class marking was in words

and lining was in lemon chrome, fine-lined ultramarine. The device appeared on each first-class door or centrally on thirds.

An agreement with the parent companies ushered in the middle period when the GN and the MR each supplied 70 passenger vehicles and one horse-box. Such an influx demanded a completely new number list and a reconstruction of this is given in the table. After 1903 the Midland appears to have washed its hands of involvement in M&GN passenger stock and all further contributions (103 vehicles from 1906 to 1920) were supplied by the GN. The MR had also transferred rather old stock and withdrawals began less than 10 years after their arrival, leaving about 18 by 1917 when most were sent to France for use by the War Department. (Fig 34/35.)

In contrast the GN had supplied relatively modern vehicles, some of which had corridors, although all were six-wheel. The 24 ex-E&M 'large stock' passenger coaches were also 'rebuilt' from 1906 into a more modern form by the simple expedient of scrapping the body and re-using the six-wheel underframe (or parts from it) with a new body. In this manner were created seven four-compartment composites, nine five-compartment thirds, and from 1915 eight luggage brakes. The elliptical roof profile was preserved. Most vehicles had the standard radiused beading but the brakes were given GN-style beading. Thirteen new luggage brakes were built in 1920-24 to this pattern as replacements for the motley collection of ex-E&M brakes. The seven rebuilt composites were withdrawn in 1926.

The livery for the middle period was basically 'teak' for the ex-E&M vehicles, and varnished teak for the ex-GN vehicles and Melton brakes. The MR vehicles arrived in crimson lake but were refinished in teak within four or five years. Lettering eventually standardised as:

'No' 'MIDLAND &' 'GT NORTHERN' 'No'

in gold sanserif letters blocked blue, shaded black. Where a symmetrical arrangement could not be sustained a plain 'M&GN' in the same lettering was used. Class marking was now in large sanserif numbers and lining was as before.

The final period was characterised by withdrawals of large numbers of the older GN vehicles in 1932 and 1935. The nine rebuilt E&M thirds were all converted to composites in 1933 and increasingly kept back for strengthening purposes only. To compensate for the loss of stock some LNER vehicles were loaned, but in 1935 came the first transferrals of LMS and LNER stock. During the years 1935 and 1936 the LMS transferred 11 composites, eight thirds, seven brake-thirds and one brake-composite of ex-LNWR bogie stock and 12 ex-MR third-class semi-saloons. The LNER transferred 10 NER bogie corridor-thirds and four NER matchboard-sided brake-thirds. The last transferrals to the M&GN proper were five LNWR six-wheel luggage brakes. All these vehicles received M&GN numbers and initials. Following the LNER operational takeover more LNWR bogie corridor vehicles and large amounts of ex-GER bogie corridor vehicles were also transferred.

The livery of this final period saw the adoption of plain 'M&GN' in gold seriffed letters blocked red, shaded black very similar to the LNER lettering, and regarded as 'the thin end of the wedge' at Melton.

Class markings were large seriffed numbers. However, many vehicles were withdrawn in 1935 still carrying the old standard lettering. The stock transferred to the M&GN in 1935/36 was given M&GN lettering but otherwise remained in its LMS/LNER base colour until the application of Stratford brown after 1936. Lining was now plain lemon chrome.

M&GN Passenger Vehicle Number List

M&GN Passenger Vehicle Number List

No	1903	1919 Diagram
1	Saloon 4w EM	–
2	Saloon 4w EM	Saloon MGN
3	Saloon MR	<—
4	Saloon GN	<—
5	Compo 4w EM	–
6	Compo 4w EM	–
7	Compo EM	–
8	Compo EM	Compo MGN
9	Compo EM	Compo MGN
10	Compo EM	Compo MGN
11	Compo EM	Compo MGN
12	Compo EM	Compo MGN
13	Compo EM	Compo MGN
14	Compo EM	Compo MGN
15	Compo 4w EM	Compo GN
16	Compo 4w EM	Compo GN
17	Compo 4w EM	Compo GN
18	Compo 4w EM	Compo GN
19	Lug Compo MR	Compo GN
20	Lug Compo MR	Lav Compo GN
21	Lug Compo MR	Lav Compo GN
22	Lug Compo MR	Lav Lug Compo GN
23	Lug Compo MR	Lav Lug Compo GN
24	Lug Compo MR	Lav Lug Compo GN
25	Lug Compo MR	Third GN
26	Lug Compo MR	Third GN
27	Lug Compo MR	Third GN
28	Lug Compo MR	Third GN
29	Lug Compo MR	Third GN
30	Lug Compo GN	<—
31	Compo GN	<—
32	Compo GN	<—
33	Lug Compo GN	<—
34	Compo GN	<—
35	Compo GN	<—
36	Lug Compo GN	<—
37	Compo GN	<—
38	Lug Compo GN	<—
39	Lug Compo GN	<—
40	Compo GN	<—
41	Compo GN	<—
42	Compo GN	<—
43	Compo GN	<—
44	Compo GN	<—
45	–	Compo GN
46	–	Lav Compo GN
47	–	Lav Compo GN
48	–	Compo GN
49	–	Compo GN
50	–	–
51	Third EM	Third MGN
52	Third EM	Third MGN
53	Third EM	Third MGN
54	Third EM	Third MGN
55	Third EM	Third MGN
56	Third 4w EM	Third MGN
57	Third 4w EM	Third GN
58	Third 4w EM	Third GN
59	Third EM	Third GN
60	Third EM	Third MGN
61	Third EM	Third GN
62	Third EM	Third GN
63	Third EM	Third MGN
64	Third EM	Third GN
65	Third EM	Third MGN
66	Third EM	Third GN
67	Third EM	Third GN
68	Third EM	Third GN
69	Third EM	Third GN
70	–	Third MGN
71	Third MR	Third GN
72	Third MR	Third GN
73	Third MR	Bk Third GN
74	Third MR	Bk Third GN
75	Third MR	Bk Third GN
76	Third MR	Bk Third GN
77	Third MR	Bk Third GN
78	Third MR	Bk Third GN
79	Third MR	Third GN
80	Third MR	(Third GN)
81	Third MR	Third GN
82	Third MR	Corr Third GN
83	Third MR	Corr Third GN
84	Third MR	Third GN
85	Third MR	Corr Third GN
86	Third MR	Corr Third GN
87	Third MR	Corr Third GN
88	Third MR	Corr Third GN
89	Third MR	Third GN
90	Third MR	Third GN
91	Third MR	(Third GN)
92	Third MR	Third GN
93	Third MR	Third GN
94	Third MR	Third GN
95	Third MR	Third GN
96	Third MR	Third GN
97	Third MR	Third GN
98	Third MR	Third GN
99	Third MR	Third GN
100	Third MR	Third GN
101	Third MR	Corr Third GN
102	Third MR	Corr Third GN
103	Third GN	<—
104	Third GN	<—
105	Third GN	<—
106	Third GN	<—
107	Third GN	<—
108	Third GN	<—
109	Third GN	<—
110	Third GN	<—
111	Third GN	<—
112	Third GN	<—
113	Third GN	<—
114	Third GN	<—
115	Third GN	<—

No.	Type		No.	Type		No.	Type	
116	Third GN	<—	163	Bk Third MR	Bk Third GN	210	Brake GN	<—
117	Third GN	<—	164	Bk Third MR	Bk Third GN	211	Brake GN	<—
118	Third GN	<—	165	Bk Third MR	Bk Third GN	212	Brake GN	<—
119	Third GN	<—	166	Bk Third MR 8w	(Bk Third GN)	213	Brake GN	<—
120	Third GN	<—	167	Bk Third MR	Bk Third GN	214	Brake GN	<—
121	Third GN	<—	168	Bk Third MR 8w	(Bk Third GN)	215	Brake GN	<—
122	Third GN	<—	169	Bk Third GN	<—	216	Brake GN	<—
123	Third GN	<—	170	Bk Third GN	<—	217	–	Brake GN
124	Third GN	<—	171	Bk Third GN	<—	218	–	Brake GN
125	Third GN	<—	172	Bk Third GN	<—	219	–	Brake GN
126	Third GN	<—	173	Bk Third GN	<—	220	–	Brake GN
127	Third GN	<—	174	Bk Third GN	<—	221	Cv Car Tk EM	<—
128	Third GN	<—	175	Bk Third GN	<—	222	Cv Car Tk EM	<—
129	Third GN	<—	176	Bk Third GN	<—	223	Cv Car Tk EM	<—
130	Third GN	<—	177	Bk Third GN	<—	224	Op Car Tk EM	<—
131	Third GN	<—	178	Bk Third MR	(Bk Third GN)	225	Op Car Tk EM	<—
132	Third GN	<—	179	Bk Third MR	(Bk Third GN)	226	Op Car Tk EM	<—
133	Third GN	<—	180	–	Bk Third GN	227	–	–
134	Third GN	<—	181	–	Bk Third GN	228	–	–
135	Third MR	(Third GN)	182	–	Bk Third GN	229	Horse Bx EM	<—
136	Third MR	(Third GN)	183	Brake 4w EM	(Brake MGN)	230	Horse Bx EM	<—
137	–	Third GN	184	Brake 4w EM	(Brake MGN)	231	Horse Bx EM	<—
138	–	Third GN	185	Brake 4w EM	(Brake MGN)	232	Horse Bx EM	<—
139	–	Third GN	186	Brake 4w EM	(Brake MGN)	233	Horse Bx EM	<—
140	–	Third GN	187	Brake 4w EM	(Brake MGN)	234	Horse Bx EM	<—
141	–	Third GN	188	Brake 4w EM	(Brake MGN)	235	Horse Bx MR	<—
142	–	Third GN	189	Brake 4w EM	(Brake MGN)	236	Horse Bx GN	<—
143	–	Third GN	190	Brake 4w EM	(Brake MGN)	237	–	–
144	–	Third GN	191	Brake 4w EM	(Brake MGN)	238	–	–
145	–	Corr Third GN	192	Brake 4w EM	(Brake MGN)	239	–	–
146	–	Corr Third GN	193	Brake 4w EM	(Brake MGN)	240	–	–
147	–	Corr Third GN	194	Brake 4w EM	(Brake MGN)			
148	–	Corr Third GN	195	Brake MR	Brake MGN			
149	–	Corr Third GN	196	Brake MR	Brake GN			
150	–	Third GN	197	Brake MR	Brake MGN			
151	–	–	198	Brake MR	Brake MGN			
152	–	–	199	Brake MR	Brake MGN			
153	–	–	200	Brake MR	Brake GN			
154	–	Bk Compo GN	201	Brake MR	Brake MGN			
155	Bk Comp MR 8w	(Bk Compo GN)	202	Brake MR	Brake MGN			
156	Bk Comp MR 8w	(Bk Compo GN)	203	Brake MR	Brake GN			
157	Bk Compo GN	<—	204	Brake MR	Brake MGN			
158	Bk Compo GN	<—	205	Brake MR	Brake MGN			
159	–	Bk Third GN	206	Brake GN	<—			
160	Bk Third MR	Bk Third GN	207	Brake GN	(Brake MGN)			
161	Bk Third MR	Corr Third GN	208	Brake GN	<—			
162	Bk Third MR	Bk Third GN	209	Brake GN	<—			

Key to Symbols

EM	Eastern & Midlands vehicle
GN	Great Northern vehicle
MGN	rebuilt or built by M&GN
MR	Midland vehicle
( )	replacement 1920-24 of vehicle condemned in 1919
<—	as previous column
–	blank number
4w	four wheeled
8w	probable bogie carriage

M&GN Passenger Vehicle Number List, Transferred Stock

M&GN Passenger Vehicle Number List, Transferred Stock

No.	Type	Transferred
5	LNWR Bogie Corridor Composite	1935
6	LNWR Bogie Corridor Composite	1935
7	LNWR Bogie Corridor Composite	1935
8	LNWR Bogie Corridor Composite	1935
9	LNWR Bogie Corridor Composite	1935
10	LNWR Bogie Corridor Composite	1935
11	LNWR Bogie Corridor Composite	1935
12	LNWR Bogie Corridor Composite	1935
13	LNWR Bogie Corridor Composite	1935
14	LNWR Bogie Corridor Composite	1935
15	LNWR Bogie Corridor Composite	1935
57	MR Bogie Corridor Third Saloon	1935/36
58	MR Bogie Corridor Third Saloon	1935/36
59	MR Bogie Corridor Third Saloon	1935/36
62	MR Bogie Corridor Third Saloon	1935/36
66	MR Bogie Corridor Third Saloon	1935/36
67	MR Bogie Corridor Third Saloon	1935/36
68	MR Bogie Corridor Third Saloon	1935/36
69	MR Bogie Corridor Third Saloon	1935/36
79	MR Bogie Corridor Third Saloon	1935/36
93	MR Bogie Corridor Third Saloon	1935/36
97	MR Bogie Corridor Third Saloon	1935/36
99	MR Bogie Corridor Third Saloon	1935/36
103	NER Bogie Corridor Third	1935/36
104	NER Bogie Corridor Third	1935/36
105	NER Bogie Corridor Third	1935/36
106	NER Bogie Corridor Third	1935/36
107	NER Bogie Corridor Third	1935/36
108	NER Bogie Corridor Third	1935/36
110	LNWR Bogie Corridor Third	1935
112	NER Bogie Corridor Third	1935/36
117	NER Bogie Corridor Third	1935/36
120	NER Bogie Corridor Third	1935/36
121	NER Bogie Corridor Third	1935/36
122	LNWR Bogie Corridor Third	1935
129	LNWR Bogie Corridor Third	1935
131	LNWR Bogie Corridor Third	1935
133	LNWR Bogie Corridor Third	1935
137	LNWR Bogie Corridor Third	1935
139	LNWR Bogie Corridor Third	1935
141	LNWR Bogie Corridor Third	1935
151	LNWR Bogie Corridor Brake Compo	1935
170	LNWR Bogie Corridor Brake Third	1935
171	LNWR Bogie Corridor Brake Third	1935
172	LNWR Bogie Corridor Brake Third	1935
173	NER Bogie Corridor Brake Third	1935
174	NER Bogie Corridor Brake Third	1935
175	NER Bogie Corridor Brake Third	1935
176	NER Bogie Corridor Brake Third	1935
177	LNWR Bogie Corridor Brake Third	1935
180	LNWR Bogie Corridor Brake Third	1935
181	LNWR Bogie Corridor Brake Third	1935
182	LNWR Bogie Corridor Brake Third	1935
237	LNWR Luggage Brake (6-wheel)	1936/37
238	LNWR Luggage Brake (6-wheel)	1936/37
239	LNWR Luggage Brake (6-wheel)	1936/37
240	LNWR Luggage Brake (6-wheel)	1936/37
241	LNWR Luggage Brake (6-wheel)	1936/37

Note: Ex-NER corridor vehicles were not fitted with vestibules.

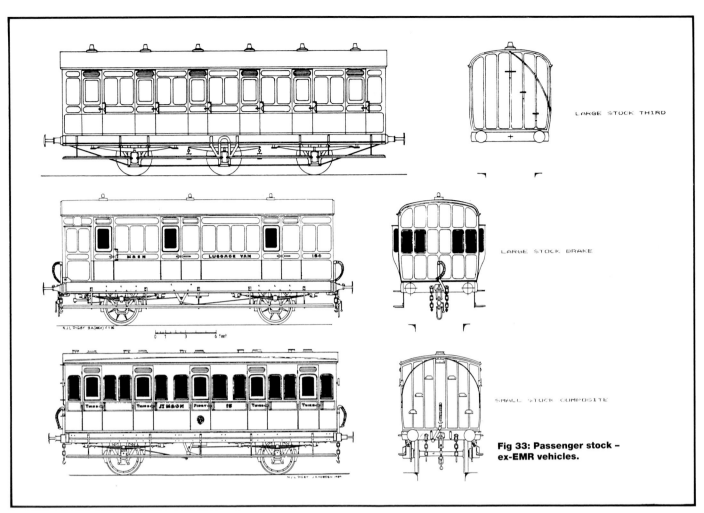

LARGE STOCK THIRD

LARGE STOCK BRAKE

SMALL STOCK COMPOSITE

Fig 33: Passenger stock – ex-EMR vehicles.

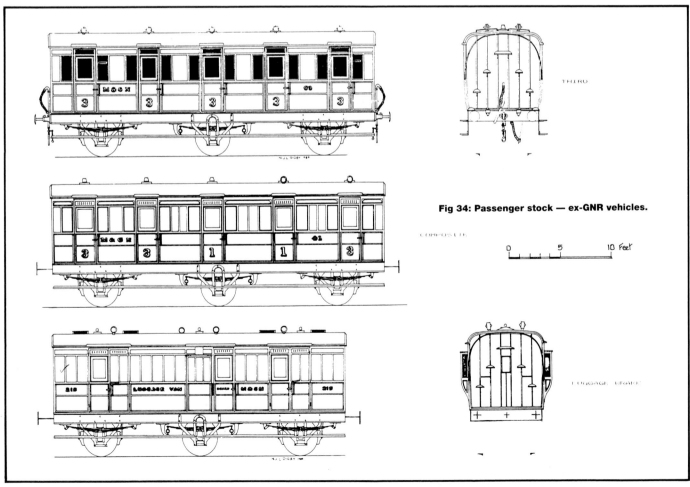

THIRD

Fig 34: Passenger stock — ex-GNR vehicles.

COMPOSITE

LUGGAGE BRAKE

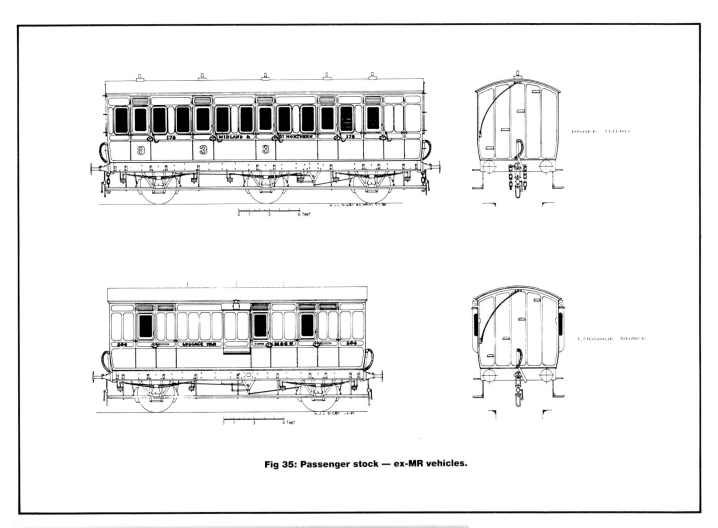

Fig 35: Passenger stock — ex-MR vehicles.

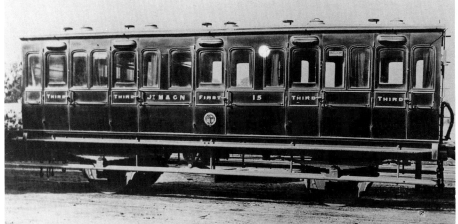

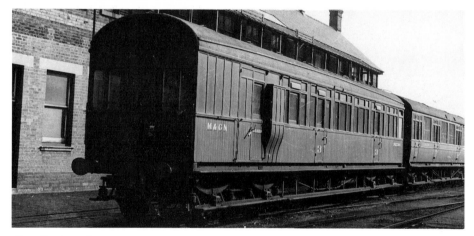

The livery of the E&M appears to have been the same as that of the GNR; a crimson brown known as 'Brown Oxide', with white sanserif initials. Service vehicles appear to have been 'Red Oxide'. The earlier large two-plank letters on open wagons 'E&MRY' gave way by 1893 to 'EASTERN & MIDLANDS RAILWAY' along the top plank. It is believed the box vans and brake vans retained a small version of the earlier lettering.

The first M&GN lettering was small and in the form:

'JTM/&/GN'

along the top plank of open wagons, although the loco coal wagons appear to have had larger two-plank initials with 'LOCO COAL ONLY' in small one plank letters below. Vans and livestock wagons also had small lettering:

'JT/M/&/GN/No.'

between the outside frames. Brake vans had a strange asymmetrical arrangement. By 1900 the normal usage had become plain 'M & G N', still on the top plank, but this was expanded to two plank letters on open wagons by 1910. Box vans, cattle wagons and brakes were lettered with 8 inch initials, box vans and cattle wagons having the initials between the outside frames. Midland pattern cast-iron number plates were attached to the under-frames, replacing the painted underframe numbers used formerly. The official RCH form 'JtM&GN' was used with the number below. Painted body numbers were sometimes omitted from open wagons after the introduction of these number plates, but vans and livestock wagons always had a painted number above the right-hand crossed framing. Brakes had it on the lower right of the body, and by 1923 their lettering was in lemon chrome.

In the main the M&GN appears to have adopted the brown oxide livery of the E&M, with service vehicles painted red oxide. However, during the 'JtM&GN' period there is evidence to suggest that at least some open wagons were grey. This does not seem to have been long-lived, and it was not until the introduction of the Common User system in 1917 that saw M&GN revenue-earning wagons in dark grey. Those included in the system were open wagons and unfitted vans only. After January 1928 when most of the revenue stock was dispersed or scrapped, the remaining vehicles were the brakes (in brown oxide) and the RSV stock (in red oxide). The modern names for the oil-based paints concerned are 'Mars Brown' and 'Indian Red'.

Goods Stock

The M&GN inherited over 700 goods vehicles from the E&M, including 13 brakes, 45 box vans, 136 cattle wagons, 416 open wagons, 23 bolster wagons and 38 coal wagons. There were also various cranes and ballast wagons. Over the next few years 70 wagons were withdrawn, being rather worn, but probably remained in service use. Throughout the ensuing years Melton was constantly withdrawing and renewing stock, although for accountancy purposes most new vehicles were considered as having been 'rebuilt'. In 1928 most of the stock was divided up between the LMS and LNER, leaving only the brakes and service stock still marked M&GN. It would be impossible to cover all the ins and outs of M&GN wagons; all that can be done in the space available is to outline the most readily accessible classes of vehicles. (Fig 36.)

The 10-ton brake vans were perhaps the most distinctive Joint wagons, having outside frames and verandahs at each end. The first block of vans were the old E&M brakes with 21ft 0in body and 12ft 0in wheelbase, and brakewheels outside the verandahs. The remaining brakes were those delivered from 1898 and were shorter (as in the diagram) with the brake wheel inside. Three of the ex-E&M brakes were rebuilt in 1924-26 to 15 tons, and the others were apparently withdrawn between 1933 and 1938.

The box vans were the most widely travelled of Joint stock, being through-piped and some even dual-braked. They were built between 1879 and 1883 and all of them survived to be divided between the LMS and LNER in 1928, apparently after many or all had been rebuilt by 1919.

The cattle wagons were a large group to a uniform design, reflecting the importance of this traffic. Most were built in 1882-83 and had crossed outside framing, very similar to the contemporary GE wagons. Screw couplings and improved springs were fitted from 1904. Again many or most of them had been rebuilt by 1919, as shown in the diagram.

Open goods wagons were roughly equally high-sided (four plank with centre door) and low-sided (three plank with dropsides). Some of the very early wagons appear to have been round-ended, but it is not known how many there were or how long they lasted.

The coal wagons were rather obscure but it seems their sides, although still four plank, were stretched to be 12in higher than the standard high-sided wagon. They were regularly routed between South Lynn and Shirebrook Colliery and were marked 'LOCO COAL ONLY'. Although divided between the parent companies in 1928 it seems some of them were kept for internal storage and movement of coal.

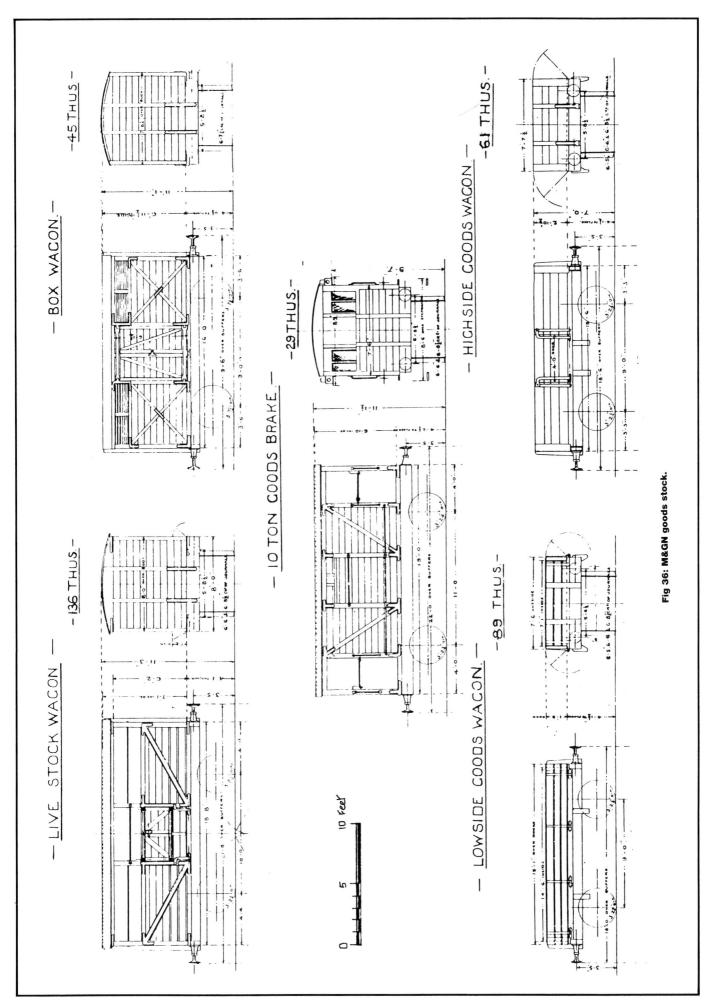

Fig 36: M&GN goods stock.

Right:
The most widely-travelled M&GN vehicles were the vans, and No 550 is seen at Melton having been freshly painted in the early livery on 5 October 1894. Although only hand-braked on one side, No 550 is through-piped for both vacuum and Westinghouse brakes and has screw couplings.
National Railway Museum

Below right:
A high-sided wagon typical of M&GN stock, seen here at Melton c1897 still in the final E&M livery, applied 30 March 1893. The brakes are on one side only and the grease axleboxes bear the lettering 'E&MR A', which survived on many vehicles 50 years later.
National Railway Museum

Bottom right:
A representative selection of low-sided wagons in their latter years in railway service for ballast and loco dirt on the permanent way sidings at Melton in 1937. The origins of the ballast brakes are obscure. It appears that No 13 may have come from the S&DJt in c1931.
H. C. Casserley

Selection of Wagon Numbers in 1919:

E&M Brakes	Nos 1-11
M&GN Brakes	Nos 15-30
Box Vans	Nos 506-550
Livestock Wagons (sample)	
Nos 33, 37, 76, 162, 370, 374, 397, 400, 459	
High-Sided Opens (sample)	
Nos 57, 110, 128, 191, 318, 334, 436, 668, 670	
Low-Sided Opens (sample)	
Nos 47, 112, 172, 242, 307, 421, 499, 551, 598	

Unfortunately, there is very little information regarding wagon sheets. There is no known photograph that clearly shows one and all we really have are descriptions. Presumably the size was approximately the same as other railways, about 21ft x 15ft. During E&M days the name was applied in full, possibly only to the sides, as it would be difficult to fit 'Eastern & Midlands Railway' all round. Numbers would probably have been below the lettering and at each end. Both the E&M and the M&GN sheets were numbered in the hundreds; the amount apparently never passed 1,000. During the early M&GN period it seems the lettering adopted was 'JTM&GNR', but the later standard style was of a white diagonal cross with white corners. Lettering was plain 'M&GN' and probably applied to sides and ends with number below.

There were of course many private owner wagons running on to the Joint, mostly belonging to specific collieries or coal merchants. The largest local merchant was Bessey & Palmer, who had a considerable fleet of wagons based in Great Yarmouth and coal allotments on almost every eastern section station. Vinter was another important merchant, but whether he had a base more local than Cambridge is not known. The firm appears to have had a genuinely large amount of wagons; a series up to a maximum of No 545 appearing in an E&M traffic return of 1885. The reader will note that most of the collieries are from the Nottinghamshire coalfield. Only a selection is given here and illustrations can be found in the PO wagon books noted in the Bibliography.

Colliery/Merchant Letters	Body Colour	Numbers
Annesley	Black	
White		1086
Barnsley Main	Red Oxide	
White		4552
Mansfield	Red Oxide	
White, in arc		4926
Pilsley	Red Oxide	
White, shaded black		4521
Pinxton	Black	
White, shaded red		930
Sherwood	Red Oxide	
White, shaded black		5144
Shirebrook	Red Oxide	
White, shaded black		1847
Bessey & Palmer	Grey	
White, shaded black		30, 34, 51, 361
H. Fulcher	Brown	
White		5
Moy	Red Oxide	
White, shaded black		1851
P. Softley	Grey	
White		11
J. O. Vinter	Red Oxide	
White, shaded black		42-545

Locomotive coal was supplied mostly in MR or GN loco wagons from two or three collieries. The best coal as far as the Joint crews were concerned came from Shirebrook colliery in M&GN loco wagons, regularly routed between the colliery and South Lynn. This coal was supposed to be mixed with the hard coal from the other collieries. South Lynn was considered the loco coal depot for the whole M&GN, supplies for the eastern section depots being relabelled here. There was also a problem of wagon storage, both full and empty, and so several other sidings were pressed into service, particularly Bawsey and at Raynham Park. To save unnecessary movement of supplies, engines leaving South Lynn for the eastern section were encouraged to take as much coal as possible, to avoid coaling at other depots.

152

Appendix B: Signalling and Tablet Operation

Signal Types

Signalling on the western section, even during the M&GN period, owed its origins to the divisions of responsibility of the Bourn & Lynn Joint. Thus all the signalling between Bourne and Sutton Bridge Junction was of the centre-balanced tumbler or 'somersault' type of GNR signal, at first using the contemporary design with the spectacle plate being some distance below the arm. As this type was used on the eastern section from 1893-c1900 it is shown in the accompanying table as MGN:1. (Fig 37.)

The Midland supplied their standard signals between Peterborough and Lynn, beginning with their early slotted-post design and progressing to their standard lower quadrant type with 'figure of eight' spectacle plate by 1897. From photographs it appears that painting of these signals may have followed the MR colour scheme of lemon chrome and venetian red but, unlike the Midland, the arms had a vertical white stripe by 1897 and probably from 1893, 13 years before its use at Derby, due to the GN's responsibility for signalling on the M&GN. The Midland influence extended up to 1901 when the new South Lynn station had several examples of MR types, although by this time the posts were white with black bases to conform with standard M&GN painting. Ground signals on both parts of the western section were mainly the disc type rotating on a vertical axis common to both railways during the early period. There were some examples of the GN miniature 'tumbler' ground signal.

On the eastern section standard Saxby & Farmer slotted-post signals had been used, apparently manufactured at Melton during the E&M period. On the formation of the M&GN the GN introduced their somersault types as the future standard, at first MGN:1 but by about 1900 the spectacle plate usually assumed the more normal position level with the arm, here designated MGN:2. Miniature signals were used extensively, often mounted above one another on the same post. Ground signals were mostly GN rotating disc, although again some tumblers were used. Finials were manufactured from zinc, consisting of a spike and a ball made up from six segments on a hexagonal base, mounted on a square cap. Colours were standardised as white posts with black bases, the black being indented into the white with a semi-circular border. When concrete posts were introduced they were left natural; it was not until the BR era that they were painted white.

There were many distant signals on the M&GN as a number of the manned level crossings were protected by distants. At a few locations, where crossings were close together or their distants coincided with station distants, the two arms shared the same post. With the sidelights on each gatelamp and the crossing distants, the straight fenland sections have been described as an avenue of green lights at night.

After the Grouping there was a move towards modernisation. Concrete posts became the norm and many surviving timber posts lost their finials which were replaced by plain caps. Corrugated steel arms were introduced and by 1931 some new and replacement arms were upper quadrant. Yellow was introduced for distants at about the same time. Route indicators simplified some complex gantries, being lettered screens placed mechanically in front of flood lamps; large cases fronted by ground glass and illuminated from behind by gas or electricity. The screens were stored when the signal was at danger in two ways: the 'vertical' indicator stored them below the flood lamp, and the 'banjo' indicator stored them to one side on arms pivoted on the post below. Metal boxes protected then from the weather. Initial letters were used on the screens, eg 'Y' for Yarmouth, 'N' for

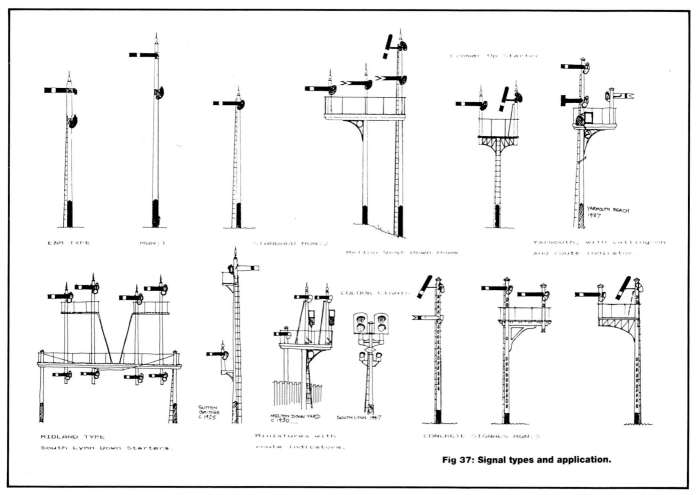

Fig 37: Signal types and application.

Norwich and so on. Experiments in colour-light signalling were carried out in 1932 at Clay Lake near Spalding, in 1933 at South Lynn and in 1939 on the Yarmouth line at Melton East.

Control of double and single line sections

When constructed, the railways of both eastern and western sections were largely single line with few passing places. Over the 1890-1901 period the routes were improved by doubling at several locations. On the whole, the M&GN double lines were controlled on the 'absolute block' system, using GN instruments. Communication between signalboxes was by bell codes, the object being to prevent more than one train being in the section between two boxes on the same line at the same time. No bell code was taken as properly understood unless it was correctly repeated by the signalman receiving it. Each section on either side of the box had an instrument, with dials applicable to Up and Down lines. Their normal position was 'Line Blocked'. Very simply, to pass a train on to the next box (in advance), the signalman would first send one beat of the bell or 'Call Attention'. On receipt of an answer, he would ask if the line was clear by sending the appropriate code. If the section between was clear, the signalman in advance would repeat the code and place his instrument to 'Line Clear', which would repeat on the instrument in the first box. When a train entered the section by passing the starter signal, the 'Train Entering Section' code was sent and repeated, on which the signalman in advance would place the instruments at 'Train On Line'. Once the entire train had arrived at the box in advance, the 'Train Out of Section' code was sent by the signalman there, and on repetition by the first box, he would restore the block instruments to 'Line Blocked'.

Control of trains on the single line was at first by 'Staff and Ticket' in conjunction with simple electric block telegraph systems. The partners in the B&LJt used their own single line systems but the E&M adopted the Tyer's Electric Tablet system which was applied to the whole railway after 1893. By 1898 only Cross Keys bridge and the Yarmouth Union used the 'Staff', and by 1904 only the Union line. King's Lynn Harbour branch was also worked using a staff from the GE box.

By issuing a tablet at one end of a single line section the tablet instrument at the other end was locked, effectively preventing a train from proceeding in the opposite direction. Also by 1921 all tablet instruments had been interlocked with the signals to prevent them being lowered without the issue of a tablet. Very simply, each single line section on either side of the box had a tablet instrument, with indicators for Up and Down trains. The normal position for these was showing 'IN'. Communication was by gong for Down trains and bell for Up trains, activated by pushing the plunger below. A galvanometer needle above showed when the plunger of the instrument in advance was being pushed. Around the plunger was a ring or commutator. The appropriate 'is line clear' code was sent, and when repeated the signalman in advance would continue to push on the plunger, allowing the first signalman to rotate his commutator anti-clockwise, unlock the slide and remove a tablet. His indicator would now show 'OUT', and a single beat on his plunger then changed the indicator in advance to show 'OUT'. The 'train entering section' was sent and returned as the train passed the starter signal. When the train had arrived at the box in advance, the tablet was placed into the instrument there, and the signalman sent 'train out of section', continuing to press the plunger to enable the first signalman to reverse his commutator and push back his slide. He then repeated the 'train out of section' code, emphasising the last beat, restoring the indicator in advance to 'IN'. Finally, the signalman in advance would give one beat on his plunger, restoring the indicator in the first box to 'IN'. The 'call attention' was not used for tablet instruments in 1913, but apparently was introduced later.

The tablets, of gunmetal and brass for the Tyer's No 1 Improved (restoring) instruments, and of aluminium for the Tyer's No 6 apparatus, were engraved with the name of the section and a number, and after withdrawal were fitted into leather pouches. At first the pouches had large hoops for hand exchange but from 1906 the Whitaker automatic exchange apparatus was adopted and these pouches had small, squarish hoops. Some locations during the hand exchange period were provided with receiving posts, there being 26 of these by 1904. The receiver was merely a wooden post, cab height to a locomotive, on which was fixed a metal equivalent of the signalman's arm, bound with cord to slow the pouch and curving round to the rear, sometimes with a wire cage for safety. The receiving point was made more visible by a disc of white card illuminated at night by a lamp. Drivers were required to slow to a maximum of 10mph for all exchanges.

By 1907 the Whitaker automatic apparatus had been installed at most locations, although the N&SJt and some other places retained hand exchange. At Melton East box, a net was provided on a hand exchange post, into which the tablets were dropped; the box was on the wrong side of the line for an automatic apparatus and there was no room on the Up side. The automatic exchangers were a very clever invention. Sets of jaws on the engine and at the lineside engaged with the hoops of tablets held by each apparatus. Exchanges could be carried out at speeds of 40mph or more. The momentum of delivery or receipt of a tablet at the lineside was sufficient to knock a weighted arm over its zenith and the descent of the weight rotated the apparatus out of harm's way via bevel gears. By 1913 there were a total of 22 receiving, 23 delivering and 44 combined exchangers on all lines. All lineside apparatus was on the left hand side of the running direction, and many engines were fitted on both sides to cater for tender-first running. All tank engines (except shunting engines) were thus fitted. The ground apparatus was painted red (post) and white (moving parts).

Above:
The final form of bracket signal installed at Melton, South Lynn and shown here at Sutton Bridge in c1922. The distants refer to Sutton Bridge Junction beyond the station. Note the rod arms for both types of signal, and the slotting arrangements, including switches for electrical repeaters. *Author's collection*

Left:
The only concrete full-sized signalbox was at Cromer. Built of concrete bricks and dressed with concrete blocks, it replaced the old timber box in c1920. *M&GN Circle*

Appendix C: Working Timetable 1910

The timetabling of the M&GN with its numerous junctions and reversals of direction must have been a difficult task, and the rostering of locomotives and coaching sets an absolute nightmare, especially since there were many through services. But there were fixed points, particularly the times of certain express trains and the westbound Class A goods, always known as 'The Fish' and, apart from local passenger trains and roadside goods, an overall pattern is discernible.

Important goods traffic consisted of an easterly flow of trains during the morning and a westerly flow during the afternoon and evening. From very early in the morning a series of fast Class A and Class B goods trains originated from Peterborough and Spalding, carrying the majority of goods and empties for use later in the day from 'foreign' sources to Lynn, Melton, Norwich, Yarmouth and Lowestoft. In the afternoon and evening Class B goods and 'The Fish' would return goods and empties to the west. The important westbound trains often had to be run in two or more portions as the limiting number of wagons over any part of the Joint was 60 and on some parts less than that. In between the major trains were a series of local stopping goods serving the intermediate stations, running according to season.

Similarly, express passenger traffic had a distinct directional flow, this time reversed. Most of the important westbound expresses left M&GN stations in the morning and early afternoon, while their eastbound counterparts did not reach Joint metals until the afternoon and evening.

The oldest express was the King's Cross-Cromer service, introduced in 1887 and running constantly until 1939. Although there were other through coaches from King's Cross (two each way), the crack express always left London at 3.00pm, arriving in Cromer at 7.14pm in 1910. Sets of GN bogie clerestory coaches were introduced in 1908 exclusively for this train, a restaurant car having been added in 1906. The Up working left Cromer at 12.15pm. The main body of the Down train, which also had portions for Spalding and Cambridge, was usually hauled to Peterborough by an Ivatt Atlantic or later a Gresley Pacific, and the Cromer portion also included vehicles for Mundesley, worked forward by a local train. A Norwich coach was detached at South Lynn and followed on the 5.45pm slow train, arriving at 8.04pm.

Although not the oldest, being introduced in 1894, perhaps the most famous M&GN express was the 'Leicester', always thus named despite the fact that its destination was Birmingham. This train ran continuously, except for World War 2, until 1959. The usual pattern was of one train each way during winter, with a second working in summer. The early Down working with portions from Birmingham and Derby passed Little Bytham just after noon, reaching South Lynn at 1.05pm. Here the Norwich portion was left for the 12.20pm Peterborough-Cromer express to pick up eight minutes later, the main train arriving Melton Constable at 1.54pm and Yarmouth at 3.15pm, then working on to Lowestoft. The Norwich portion arrived 3.01pm. The afternoon Down express, the 'Leicester' proper, consisted of through coaches from Birm-

ingham to Cromer, Norwich, Yarmouth and Lowestoft, joined by a portion from Derby, Manchester and Liverpool at Saxby. A restaurant car was added to the latter portion at Nottingham. The train was hauled by an M&GN engine from Leicester (Nos 39 and 55 were the first engines to do so), which took the Norwich portion on from Melton Constable. In 1910 the Down train left Birmingham at 11.48am (the coaches originating at Gloucester) and Derby at 2.30pm, the combined train arriving Melton at 6.25pm. Here was performed one of the complicated movements for which Melton was so famous. The train was divided into Cromer, Yarmouth and Norwich portions as it stood at the Down platform. The train engine drew away with the Norwich portion and two locomotives which had been waiting on the Cromer and Yarmouth lines backed on to their respective portions and departed simultaneously in opposite directions.

The Up working of the main 'Leicester' left Yarmouth, Norwich and Cromer at 9.12am, 9.40am and 9.40am respectively. The famous assembly at Melton depended on the various arrival times. The Norwich train arrived at 10.11am on the Up platform, and the Cromer train at 10.13am on the Down platform and the engine detached. The Norwich train drew forward and set back on to the Down platform to attach the Cromer carriages. Meanwhile the Yarmouth train arrived at 10.20am on the Up platform, the engine being released. The Norwich engine drew the combined train out of the Down platform and set back on to the Yarmouth carriages and departed at 10.30am. Through Cromer-Peterborough coaches were detached at South Lynn and ran as a separate express therefrom. The second 'Leicester' express left Yarmouth and Norwich in the mid-afternoon and combined with a Cromer-Peterborough portion at Melton, which was detached at South Lynn. Once again the complicated combination method detailed above was used, the Norwich engine taking the train. The best Midland Railway stock was used for these trains, later replaced by LMS vehicles, up to 16 bogie coaches being commonplace.

The newest express of the 1910 period was the 'West Riding' from Manchester Victoria inaugurated in 1903, known to M&GN men as the 'Lanky' because of the number of L&Y vehicles in the train (reduced to only one by 1914). It ran daily on weekdays to Cromer and Lowestoft during the summer until World War 1, and a restaurant car was provided in 1909. The L&Y portion left Manchester Victoria at 10.05am and was joined at Wakefield by the GN portion from Leeds, then ran on via Doncaster, Newark, Barkston Junction, Sleaford and Spalding, where M&GN locos took over. The train ran non-stop through South Lynn, arriving Melton 3.19pm, where the Cromer portion was detached. The service was reinstated about 1920 as a Saturdays Only train without restaurant car.

The 'Lime Street' falls outside the period illustrated by the WTT, being introduced in 1923, but is of interest. When it was first run, the vehicles were still in LNWR livery and earned itself the nickname of the 'Ghost' or 'White Train'. It consisted of through coaches from Liverpool Lime Street to Lowestoft with dining car, running to

Nottingham via Stoke-on-Trent and there combining with a portion of through coaches from Manchester (London Rd) to Cromer and Lowestoft. The Down train left Liverpool at 10.50am and Manchester 10.49am, the combined train leaving Nottingham at 1.18pm and arriving Cromer at 4.47pm and Yarmouth 5.14pm. The returning Up train left Yarmouth and Cromer at 11.08am and 11.38am respectively, arriving Nottingham at 3.16pm, Manchester at 5.45pm and Liverpool at 6.00pm. An LMS locomotive hauled the Down train to South Lynn, but an M&GN engine took the Up train back to Nottingham.

Picking their way between the expresses and the fast goods trains were the local passenger services, both long and short-distance. On the western section in 1910 there were four trains each way between Lynn and Spalding, most services working through from Saxby or Bourne, but the last Up service terminating at Spalding. The carriages were through-worked but passengers had to disembark at Spalding while the stock was shunted into another platform. There was also one train each way from Sutton Bridge to Nottingham, hauled in 1910 by a Midland engine to and from Spalding but in later years usually handled by a rebuilt 'Peacock'. The Up working took the Nottingham portion of the 'Leicester'. In addition there was a Tuesdays only service from Lynn to Spalding, attached to the 8.20am Lynn-Peterborough train, the empty carriages returning on the 3.05pm ex-Spalding, and a Saturdays Only train from Spalding to Sutton Bridge, connecting with the 9.20am Peterborough-Lynn service, working back empty coaching stock (ECS) to Spalding. Between Peterborough and Lynn there were six Down trains and five Up, the 4.49pm ex-Peterborough combining with the 4.35pm ex-Bourne at Sutton Bridge and the last Up train detaching from the 6.35pm ex-Lynn and terminating at Wisbech, forming the 7.55am Peterborough train from there the next morning.

Trains on the eastern section were very much more complicated as most included portions for more than one destination and were met by trains from Norwich and Cromer at Melton Constable. There were four Down trains from Lynn at 8.08am, 11.00am, 1.20pm and 5.45pm, the first two with portions for Yarmouth/Norwich/Cromer, the others for Norwich/Cromer and Yarmouth/Norwich respectively. There was also an early service leaving Lynn at 7.45am on Mondays, Thursdays and Saturdays with portions for Yarmouth/Cromer, and a train terminating at Melton on Tuesdays. There were five Up trains to Lynn, all of them through from Yarmouth leaving at 6.55am, 9.30am, 10.45am, 1.45pm and 6.15pm with an additional train for Lynn only at 6.05pm on Mondays, Thursdays and Saturdays. The 10.45am service was only local as far as Melton where a Cromer portion was detached, the train working forward with portions from Norwich and Cromer as an express to Peterborough. Of the others, the trains were made up of carriage sets for Lynn/Cromer, Lynn/Norwich, Lynn, and Lynn/Cromer/Norwich respectively. These sets were detached at Melton and others added from Norwich and Cromer, except the 1.45pm from

Yarmouth to which was added a portion from Norwich only. The complexities of such interchanges can well be imagined and would be impossible to catalogue here. Most movements resembled the method used for the 'Leicester', the differences depending on which train arrived first. The first Up train from Yarmouth was accelerated on Mondays and Tuesdays to an express and left 20min earlier, its connections from Norwich and Cromer likewise being brought forward.

The Cromer and Norwich branches were intensively worked, most trains connecting with the local or express services at Melton, and most trains having through coaches for Norwich or Cromer. There were six Down trains to Norwich having carriages from Yarmouth/Cromer, Lynn/Cromer, Yarmouth/Cromer, Lynn/Cromer, Lynn, and Lynn/Cromer respectively. Two more sets from Cromer were worked through to Norwich by connecting expresses. The seven Up services consisted of Lynn/Cromer, Lynn, Cromer, Yarmouth/Cromer, Lynn, Yarmouth/Cromer and Lynn/Cromer portions respectively. One additional train ran each way to Yarmouth and Cromer on Mondays, Thursdays and Saturdays, and on Saturdays the 5.15pm service ran 10min earlier and was

extended to East Rudham. The Cromer branch had nine Down and 10 Up local trains, all but the last Up service (which terminated at Melton) being through to and from Norwich, Yarmouth or Lynn.

Of the short-distance services the most regular in 1910 was that between Stalham and Yarmouth, four trains each way with one permanently extended to North Walsham, and another on Mondays and Saturdays only. On Wednesdays the last train was extended to Aylsham, returning ECS to Stalham on Thursday mornings.

The N&SJt Mundesley branch was operated concurrently with the GER during this period, there being 11 Down and 10 Up M&GN trains, of which only five ran through to North Walsham Town, the others terminating at Mundesley. The GE ran nine Down and eight Up trains, most running through from North Walsham (GE) to Overstrand, but two terminating at Mundesley. The 3.05pm and 7.20pm trains from Cromer to Mundesley conveyed through coaches from London King's Cross, working back to Cromer on the 7.15am train the next morning. The Lowestoft branch was always operated concurrently and in 1910 there were eight M&GN trains each way, four terminating at Lowestoft North, whereas there

were only five GER trains each way, one terminating at Gorleston-on-Sea. The 3.27pm and 7.30pm trains Yarmouth Beach to Lowestoft conveyed through coaches from the 'Leicester' services, returning to Yarmouth on the 8.15am and 2.0pm trains from Lowestoft Central the next day. The Joint stabled all its coaches at Lowestoft North rather than pay the GE siding rent, running them ECS and collecting them with light engine where necessary.

The final layer of services consisted of the many excursions and special trains not included in the general timetables which had to be squeezed into the few gaps between the normal trains, sometimes following one another at periods of only half an hour or less. At times of high line occupancy, eg summer Saturdays, trains could be queued up at several block posts waiting to pass the bottlenecks where double line changed to single. A notoriously awkward spot was Corpusty where the single line section to Aylsham was particularly long and if four trains were crossed in an hour or perhaps nine in two hours you were doing well.

Fig 38a: 1910 timetable — western section (down).

Train Number		1	2	3	4	5	6	7
		Gds A	Pcls	Goods	Gds B	Goods	Goods	Pass.
PETERBOROUGH	dep.	1 30	2 10		5 10	5 15		6 55
WISBECH	arr.		2 39			7 00		7 27
	dep.		2 41		6 00			7 31
SUTTON BRIDGE	arr.	2 29	2 54		6 17			7 43
Little Bytham	dep.			4 26			6 24	
BOURNE	arr.			4 40			6 40	
	dep.			5 00			6 58	
SPALDING	arr.						7 40	
	dep.			5 18				
SUTTON BRIDGE	arr.							
	dep.	2 30	2 55	5 53	6 18			7 44
SOUTH LYNN	arr.	2 46	3 08	6 10	6 38			8 00
	dep.	4 15		6 50	8 37			8 07
KING'S LYNN	arr.	4 20		6 55	8 42			8 12

Train Number		8	9(SX)	10	11	12	13	14
		Goods	Goods	Goods	Goods	Pass.	Pass.	Pass.
PETERBOROUGH	dep.		7 15	7 30				9 20
WISBECH	arr.		8 19	9 15				10 04
	dep.			9 00	11 10			10 07
SUTTON BRIDGE	arr.		9 18	12 05				10 24
Little Bytham	dep.				6 51			
BOURNE	arr.				7 07			
	dep.				8 05	7 55		
SPALDING	arr.					8 16		
	dep.	7 00			9 55	8 38	9 30	
SUTTON BRIDGE	arr.	8 50			1 20	9 18	10 10	
	dep.		9 30		2 05	9 22		10 26
SOUTH LYNN	arr.		9 55		3 10	9 41		10 45
	dep.		10 30		3 40	9 46		10 50
KING'S LYNN	arr.		10 35		3 45	9 54		10 55

Train Number		15	16	17	18	19	20	21
Description		F.Etys	Pass	Goods	Goods	Goods	Exp.P	Exp.P
		(SX)	(SX)			a.m	p.m	
PETERBOROUGH	dep.	9 35	10 50		11 45			12 20
WISBECH	arr.	10 27		1 40	2 45			12 48
	dep.	10 50			4 10			12 49
SUTTON BRIDGE	arr.	11 20			5 02			1 00
Little Bytham	dep.		10 47		11 06		12 02	
BOURNE	arr.		10 55	11 22			12 10	
	dep.		10 56				12 13	
SPALDING	arr.		11 16					
	dep.		11 35				12 27	
SUTTON BRIDGE	arr.		12 18				12 51	
	dep.	11 32			5 40		12 52	1 01
SOUTH LYNN	arr.	12 35			6 12		1 05	1 13
	dep.						1 23	
KING'S LYNN	arr.						1 28	

Train Number		22	23	24	25	26	27(SX)	28
		Pass.	Goods	Exp.P	Goods	Pass.	F.Etys	Exp.P
PETERBOROUGH	dep.	12 30					2 15	2 38
WISBECH	arr.	1 09					3 57	
	dep.	1 12						3 08
SUTTON BRIDGE	arr.	1 29						3 18
Little Bytham	dep.			1 07	1 57			
BOURNE	arr.			1 23	2 05			
	dep.			2 55	2 28			
SPALDING	arr.				2 49			
	dep.		1 00	1 58	3 45	3 05		
SUTTON BRIDGE	arr.		4 10		3 44			
	dep.	1 31		2 23	10 10	3 47		3 19
SOUTH LYNN	arr.	1 55			10 55	4 08		
	dep.	2 00		2 35		4 10		3 31
KING'S LYNN	arr.	2 05		↓		4 15		↓

Train Number		29	30	31	32	33	34	35
		Goods	Pass.	Exp.P	Pass.	Exp.P	Pass.	Goods
PETERBOROUGH	dep.		3 05			4 40	4 49	
WISBECH	arr.		3 44			5 08	5 27	
	dep.		3 47			5 10	5 32	
SUTTON BRIDGE	arr.		4 04			5 21	5 48	
Little Bytham	dep.		2 50		4 12			
BOURNE	arr.	3 06			4 20			6 05
	dep.			4 23	4 35			7 20
SPALDING	arr.				5 00			
	dep.				5 35			
SUTTON BRIDGE	arr.			4 27	6 14			
	dep.	4 08		5 01	6 20	5 22		
SOUTH LYNN	arr.	4 25		5 13	6 39	5 34		
	dep.	4 30		5 33	6 42	5 48		
KING'S LYNN	arr.	4 35		5 38	6 47	5 51		

Train Number		36	37	38	39	40	41	42
		Pass.	Pass.	Goods	Goods	Goods		
PETERBOROUGH	dep.	7 30		10 45				
WISBECH	arr.	8 09		12 06				
	dep.	8 13		12 22				
SUTTON BRIDGE	arr.	8 29		12 40				
Little Bytham	dep.		8 03		9 32	11 24		
BOURNE	arr.		8 10		9 48	11 40		
	dep.		8 15			1 15		
SPALDING	arr.		8 35					
	dep.		9 00					
SUTTON BRIDGE	arr.		9 39			2 05		
	dep.	8 30	9 40	12 50		3 17		
SOUTH LYNN	arr.	8 46	9 58	1 10		4 23		
	dep.	8 50	10 00	10 17				
KING'S LYNN	arr.	8 55	10 05	10 22				

Fig 38b: 1910 timetable — western section (up).

Train Number		43	44	45	46	47	48	49
		Goods	Goods	Goods	Pass.	FruitA	Goods	Pass.
KING'S LYNN	dep.	3 00					6 30	7 05
SOUTH LYNN	arr.	3 05					6 35	7 10
	dep.	3 18				6 40	7 40	7 12
SUTTON BRIDGE	arr.	3 40				7 31	8 05	7 27
	dep.						9 40	7 28
SPALDING	arr.							8 12
	dep.							8 36
BOURNE	arr.						2 00	8 57
	dep.			5 00	6 30		2 15	9 14
Little Bytham	dep.			5 19	6 51		2 50	9 34
SUTTON BRIDGE	dep.	3 42				7 33		
WISBECH	arr.	3 56				8 20		
	dep.	4 06			7 55	8 30		
PETERBOROUGH	arr.	4 52				8 35	9 27	

Train Number		50	51	52(SX)	53	54	55	56
		Pass.	Goods	ECS	Exp.P	Pass.	Goods	Exp.P
KING'S LYNN	dep.	8 20			9 56			
SOUTH LYNN	arr.	8 25			10 01			
	dep.	8 26	8 30		10 05			11 18
SUTTON BRIDGE	arr.	8 43	10 50		10 20			
	dep.			10 20			10 30	11 23
SPALDING	arr.			10 50			11 10	
	dep.						11 38	11 55
BOURNE	arr.						11 59	12 08
	dep.						12 22	12 12
Little Bytham	dep.						12 33	12 20
SUTTON BRIDGE	dep.	8 44	11 50		10 23			
WISBECH	arr.	9 00	12 40		10 34			
	dep.	9 03	1 25		10 36			
PETERBOROUGH	arr.	9 46	6 50		11 10			

Train Number		57	58	59	60	61(SX)	62	63
		Exp.P	Goods	Pass.	Pass.	FruitA	Exp.P	Goods
KING'S LYNN	dep.		12 25	12 45	1 11			
SOUTH LYNN	arr.		12 31	12 50	1 16		↓	
	dep.	11 27	2 00	12 52	1 19		1 25	1 43
SUTTON BRIDGE	arr.	11 38	4 33	1 12	1 33	2 20	2 00	
	dep.		5 30		1 37			2 30
SPALDING	arr.				2 15			7 05
	dep.				2 58			
BOURNE	arr.		8 20		3 21			
	dep.		8 35					
Little Bytham	dep.		8 53					
SUTTON BRIDGE	dep.	11 33			1 14	2 31	2 21	
WISBECH	arr.	11 50			1 35	3 00		
	dep.	11 51			1 42	3 46	2 11	
PETERBOROUGH	arr.	12 19			2 30	4 49	2 43	

Train Number		64	65	66	67	68	69	70
		Pass.	Exp.P	Pass.	Goods	Exp.P	Exp.P	Pass.
KING'S LYNN	dep.	2 56		3 50		4 50		
SOUTH LYNN	arr.	3 01		3 55		4 55		
	dep.	3 02	3 33	3 58		5 00	5 06	
SUTTON BRIDGE	arr.	3 21		4 20			5 20	
	dep.		3 47	4 24		5 12		
SPALDING	arr.		4 10	5 07				
	dep.			5 15				5 50
BOURNE	arr.			5 32		5 55		6 12
	dep.			5 35		5 59		
Little Bytham	arr.					6 07		
SUTTON BRIDGE	dep.	3 22			4 40		5 22	
WISBECH	arr.	3 38			6 20		5 33	
	dep.	3 40			6 30		5 38	
PETERBOROUGH	arr.	4 22			7 10		6 15	

Train Number		71	72	73(SX)	74(SX)	75	76	77
		Goods	Pass.	FruitA	FruitA	Goods	Goods	Pass.
KING'S LYNN	dep.		5 50					6 35
SOUTH LYNN	arr.		5 55					6 40
	dep.		5 56		5 20			6 41
SUTTON BRIDGE	arr.		6 17		5 37			7 01
	dep.						7 12	7 03
SPALDING	arr.						9 15	7 45
	dep.					7 15		
BOURNE	arr.	5 55	7 20			7 55		
	dep.					8 05		
Little Bytham	arr.					9 22		
SUTTON BRIDGE	dep.		6 18					7 15
WISBECH	arr.		6 35			6 52		7 30
	dep.		6 40		6 50	7 02		
PETERBOROUGH	arr.		7 26			7 38	7 45	

Train Number		78(SX)	79	80	81	82	83	84
		FruitA	FishB	Goods	FishB	FishA	Goods	Goods
KING'S LYNN	dep.		6 40	7 10			10 35	10 55
SOUTH LYNN	arr.		6 45	7 15			10 40	11 00
	dep.		7 35	7 50	9 55		10 55	11 25
SUTTON BRIDGE	arr.		7 55					
	dep.			8 24	10 03		11 15	11 45
SPALDING	arr.					12 00		
	dep.						12 25	
BOURNE	arr.				9 50			12 45
	dep.				10 00			1 00
Little Bytham	arr.				10 10			1 10
SUTTON BRIDGE	dep.		7 55			10 11		
WISBECH	arr.					10 25		
	dep.	7 15	8 37	8 40		10 27		
PETERBOROUGH	arr.	8 35	9 30	10 45		11 05		

Fig 39c: 1910 timetable — eastern section main line.

Train Number		85	86	87	88	89	90	91
		Gds B	Pass.	Pass.	Goods	Cattle	Goods	Goods
KING'S LYNN	dep.	2 00	a.m			(SO)		
SOUTH LYNN	arr.	2 05						
	dep.	3 25					5 30	7 15
MELTON CONSTABLE	arr.	4 41					9 55	8 40
	dep.	5 05			6 40			8 55
NORWICH CITY	arr.	6 00					8 10	10 06
MELTON CONSTABLE	dep.	4 50			5 50			
NORTH WALSHAM	dep.	5 32			7 55			
STALHAM	dep.	5 45	6 40	8 20	8 35			
YARMOUTH BEACH	arr.	6 30	7 20	9 00	11 27			

Train Number		92	93	94	95	96	97	98
		Pass.	Pass.	Pass.	Goods	Pass.	Pass.	Pass.
KING'S LYNN	dep.		7 45	8 08		(SO)	(SX)	
SOUTH LYNN	arr.		7 50	8 13				
	dep.		7 55	8 18	8 35			
MELTON CONSTABLE	arr.		8 55	9 23	10 40			
	dep.	8 45		9 39		10 35	11 17	
NORWICH CITY	arr.	9 27		10 36		11 23	11 47	
MELTON CONSTABLE	dep.		9 05	9 36	11 00			
NORTH WALSHAM	dep.		9 35	10 16	12 35			11 30
STALHAM	dep.		9 51	10 29	12 51			11 44
YARMOUTH BEACH	arr.		10 20	11 10	2 27			12 22

Train Number		99	100	101	102	103	104	105
		Goods	Pass.	Exp.P	Exp.P	Pass.	Pass.	Exp.P
KING'S LYNN	dep.		11 00	p.m			1 21	
SOUTH LYNN	arr.		11 05				1 26	
	dep.	9 40	11 10	1 10	1 18		1 35	2 05
MELTON CONSTABLE	arr.	11 50	12 15	1 54	2 12		2 40	3 19
	dep.	12 55	12 40		2 25		3 13	
NORWICH CITY	arr.	2 42	1 26		3 01		4 03	
MELTON CONSTABLE	dep.		12 35	2 03		2 30		3 23
NORTH WALSHAM	dep.		1 12	2 33		3 08		3 50
YARMOUTH BEACH	arr.		2 10	3 15		4 03		4 27

Train Number		106	107	108	109	110	111	112
		Exp.P	Exp.P	Pass.	Exp.P	Pass.	Goods	Pass.
KING'S LYNN	dep.					5 45		
SOUTH LYNN	arr.					5 50		
	dep.	3 31	5 18		5 40	5 46	6 10	
MELTON CONSTABLE	arr.	4 15	6 02		6 28	6 59	8 20	
	dep.	4 32	6 12			7 12	9 00	8 08
NORWICH CITY	arr.	5 05	6 45			8 02	10 45	8 59
MELTON CONSTABLE	dep.	4 30	6 07			7 10		
NORTH WALSHAM	dep.	4 58	6 35	7 05		7 44		
STALHAM	dep.	5 10	6 46	7 20		7 59		
YARMOUTH BEACH	arr.	5 43	7 13	7 58		8 38		

Train Number		113	114	115	116	117	118	119
		Goods	Goods	Pass.	Pass.	ECS	Pass.	Pass.
YARMOUTH BEACH	dep.		5 10	6 55		7 40	(SO)	8 35
STALHAM	dep.		7 45	7 36		8 08		9 16
NORTH WALSHAM	dep.		10 45	7 50		arr.		9 29
MELTON CONSTABLE	arr.		1 15	8 25				arr.
NORWICH CITY	dep.			7 45			8 35	
MELTON CONSTABLE	arr.			8 32			9 16	
	dep.				8 47			
SOUTH LYNN	arr.				9 56			
	dep.	1 35			10 04			
KING'S LYNN	arr.	1 40			10 09			

Train Number		120	121	122	123	124	125	126
		Exp.P	Exp.P	Goods	Goods	Pass.	Exp.P	Pass.
YARMOUTH BEACH	dep.	9 12	9 30			10 45		
STALHAM	dep.	9 27	10 13			11 29		
NORTH WALSHAM	dep.	9 50	10 32			11 47		
MELTON CONSTABLE	arr.	10 20	11 09			12 23		
NORWICH CITY	dep.	9 40	10 15		11 15	11 50		1 30
MELTON CONSTABLE	arr.	10 11	11 06		4 20	12 37		2 01
	dep.	10 30	11 25	11 35			1 02	
SOUTH LYNN	arr.	11 15	12 30	5 55				
	dep.	11 25	12 35				1 42	
KING'S LYNN	arr.	11 30	12 40				↓	

Train Number		127	128	129	130	131	132	133
		Exp.P	Pass.	Exp.P	FishB	Gds B	Pass.	Cattle
YARMOUTH BEACH	dep.	1 32	1 45	2 45	2 55			(SO)
NORTH WALSHAM	dep.		2 28	3 05	3 55			
MELTON CONSTABLE	arr.	2 41	3 21	4 00	5 20			
NORWICH CITY	dep.		2 18	3 15			4 05	5 15	5 20
MELTON CONSTABLE	arr.		3 07	3 46			5 10	5 57	6 35
	dep.	2 50	3 30	4 08	5 50	6 00		
SOUTH LYNN	arr.		4 35	4 55	7 10	8 10		
	dep.	3 32	4 43	5 04	8 20	8 55		
KING'S LYNN	arr.	↓	4 48	5 09	8 25	9 00		

Train Number		134	135	136	137	138	139	140
		Pass.	Pass.	FishB	Gds B	Goods	Pass.	Pass.
YARMOUTH BEACH	dep.	5 20	6 24	6 35			9 00	
STALHAM	dep.	6 04	7 05	7 03			9 40	
NORTH WALSHAM	dep.	6 17	7 20	8 00			arr.	
MELTON CONSTABLE	arr.	arr.	7 58	8 36				
NORWICH CITY	dep.		7 05		8 05	9 20		
MELTON CONSTABLE	arr.		7 52		8 55	10 16		
	dep.		8 09	8 46	9 15	10 35		
SOUTH LYNN	arr.		9 16	9 46	10 30	12 48		
	dep.		9 24					
KING'S LYNN	arr.		9 30					

Fig 39d: 1910 timetable — Cromer and N&SJt (down).

Train Number	141	142	143	144	145	146	147
	Goods	GEPass	Pass.	GEPass	GEPass	Pass.	Pass.
MELTON CONSTABLE dep.	5 25	a.m				8 35	
SHERINGHAM dep.	6 40			7 34		9 10	
				C			
NORTH VALSHAM dep.							
North Valsham GE dep.			7 05	7 15	8 20		
MUNDESLEY dep.					8 47		T
OVERSTRAND dep.			7 15	7 28	8 58		9 16
CROMER BEACH arr.	6 50	arr.		7 38	arr.	9 20	9 26

Train Number	148	149	150	151	152	153	154
	GEPass	Pass.	GEPass	Pass.	GE Gds	Pass.	Goods
MELTON CONSTABLE dep.		9 36		10 35			
SHERINGHAM dep.		9 34	10 15		10 59	10 45	
		C				C	
NORTH VALSHAM dep.							
North Valsham GE dep.				10 04			
MUNDESLEY dep.				10 17		11 02	11 10
OVERSTRAND dep.		arr.		10 28		11 15	11 42
CROMER BEACH arr.			10 25	arr.	11 09	11 25	11 52

Train Number	155	156	157	158	159	160	161
	Pass.	GEPass	Goods	GEPass	Pass.	Pass.	Pass.
MELTON CONSTABLE dep.		p.m	10 45		12 21	12 50	
SHERINGHAM dep.			12 45	12 36	12 56	1 13	
			C				
NORTH VALSHAM dep.							1 02
North Valsham GE dep.		12 02					
MUNDESLEY dep.	11 40	12 14					1 17
OVERSTRAND dep.	11 53	arr.					1 30
CROMER BEACH arr.	12 03		12 33		1 06	1 24	1 42

Train Number	162	163	164	165	166	167	168
	GEPass	GEPass	Exp.P	GEPass	Pass.	Pass.	Pass.
MELTON CONSTABLE dep.			2 17			2 55	
SHERINGHAM dep.	2 14	2 28	2 42			3 30	
		arr.	C				
NORTH VALSHAM dep.							2 59
North Valsham GE dep.	1 22						
MUNDESLEY dep.	1 36				2 59		3 12
OVERSTRAND dep.	1 59				2 58		3 32
CROMER BEACH arr.	S		2 51		3 08	3 39	3 42

Train Number	169	170	171	172	173	174	175
	Exp.P	GEPass	Pass.	Pass.	GEPass	Pass.	Pass.
MELTON CONSTABLE dep.	3 22					6 06	
SHERINGHAM dep.	3 47					6 30	
NORTH VALSHAM dep.							6 27
North Valsham GE dep.		4 22			5 50		
MUNDESLEY dep.		4 37		5 23	6 02		6 41
OVERSTRAND dep.		4 48		5 36	arr.		6 54
CROMER BEACH arr.	3 57	arr.	4 45	5 46		6 40	7 06

Train Number	176	177	178	179	180	181	182
	GEPass	Exp.P	Pass.	GEPass	Pass.	GEPass	
MELTON CONSTABLE dep.		6 35			8 12		
SHERINGHAM dep.		7 03		8 00	8 36		
					C		
NORTH VALSHAM dep.			7 50				
North Valsham GE dep.	6 46					8 39	
MUNDESLEY dep.	7 00		8 04			8 52	
OVERSTRAND dep.	7 11		8 17			9 03	
CROMER BEACH arr.	arr.	7 14	8 27		8 46	arr.	

Fig 39e: 1910 timetable — Cromer and N&SJt (up).

Train Number	183	184	185	186	187	188	189
	GEPass	Goods	ECS	GEPass		Pass.	Pass.
CROMER BEACH dep.	a.m	7 30	8 00	8 25		8 45	8 50
OVERSTRAND dep.		7 37	7 53	8 40			9 01
MUNDESLEY dep.		7 50	8 35	arr.			9 16
North Valsham GE arr.		8 02			T		
NORTH VALSHAM arr.			9 00				9 28
					C		
SHERINGHAM dep.			8 00		8 33	8 54	
MELTON CONSTABLE arr.			8 35		arr.		9 20

Train Number	190	191	192	193	194	195	196
	GEGds	GEPass	Exp.P	GEPass	Pass.	Pass.	Pass.
CROMER BEACH dep.			9 40		10 35	11 50	
OVERSTRAND dep.		9 30			10 49		
MUNDESLEY dep.		9 43			11 00		
North Valsham GE arr.		9 55			arr.		
NORTH VALSHAM arr.							
		C		C			
SHERINGHAM dep.	9 25		9 50	10 14	10 44		11 59
MELTON CONSTABLE arr.	arr.		10 13	arr.	11 14		12 29

Train Number	197	198	199	200	201	202	203
	Pass.	Exp.P	GEPass	GEPass	Pass.	Pass.	Exp.P
CROMER BEACH dep.	12 00	12 15			1 40	1 47	2 00
OVERSTRAND dep.	12 11	12 32				1 58	
MUNDESLEY dep.	12 26	12 47				2 10	
North Valsham GE arr.		12 59					
NORTH VALSHAM arr.	12 36					2 20	
				C			
SHERINGHAM dep.	p.m 12 28		1 10		1 49		2 09
MELTON CONSTABLE arr.		12 48	arr.		2 19		2 37

Train Number	204	205	206	207	208	209	210
	GEPass	GEPass	Goods	Pass.	Pass.	S	Pass.
CROMER BEACH dep.			2 15	2 50	3 05	S	3 20
OVERSTRAND dep.			2 25		3 16	3 29	
MUNDESLEY dep.		2 20	arr.		3 28	3 44	
North Valsham GE arr.		2 32		arr.		3 58	
NORTH VALSHAM arr.							
	C						
SHERINGHAM dep.	2 14			4 00		3 07	3 31
MELTON CONSTABLE arr.	arr.			5 20			3 58

Train Number	211	212	213	214	215	216	217
	Pass.	GEGds	GEPass	GEPass	Pass.	Pass.	GEPass
CROMER BEACH dep.	4 10					5 10	5 20
OVERSTRAND dep.	4 20	4 30		5 07	5 22		
MUNDESLEY dep.	arr.	5 06		5 20	5 38		6 13
North Valsham GE arr.		5 26		5 32			6 25
NORTH VALSHAM arr.					5 50		
		C					
SHERINGHAM dep.		4 43				5 29	5 52
MELTON CONSTABLE arr.		arr.				5 52	

Train Number	218	219	220	221	222	223	224
	Pass.	FishB	Pass.	GEPass	Pass.	Pass.	GEPass
CROMER BEACH dep.	6 18	6 40	6 53		7 20	7 23	
OVERSTRAND dep.			7 12		7 31		7 52
MUNDESLEY dep.			7 25		7 42		8 07
North Valsham GE arr.			7 37		arr.		8 19
NORTH VALSHAM arr.							
					C		
SHERINGHAM dep.	6 29	7 05			7 19	7 33	
MELTON CONSTABLE arr.	6 54	7 32			arr.	7 59	

Train Number	225	226	227	228	229	230	231
	GEPass	Pass.					
CROMER BEACH dep.		10 30					
OVERSTRAND dep.							
MUNDESLEY dep.							
North Valsham GE arr.							
NORTH VALSHAM arr.							
		C					
SHERINGHAM dep.	9 04	10 39					
MELTON CONSTABLE arr.	arr.	11 05					

NOTES:

Gds/Fish/FruitA	Express Goods, Fish or Fruit train
Gds/Fish/FruitB	Fast Goods, Fish or Fruit train
Pcls	Express perishable traffic train composed of coaching stock.
F.Etys	Fruit empties.
ECS	Empty coaching stock.
SO	Saturdays only
SX	Saturdays excepted
W	May stop at Four Cross Roads to take water.
C	To/from Cromer Junction GE.
S	To/from Sheringham via Overstrand.
T	To/from Trimingham.
G	To/from Gorleston.
↓	Train runs through station.
10 47	Small numbers denote passing times only, trains do not stop.

Fig 39f: 1910 timetable — N&SJt to Lowestoft.

Train Number	232	233	234	235	236	237	238
	Goods	Pass.	GEPass	Goods	Pass.	Pass.	ECS
YARMOUTH BEACH dep.	7 00	8 10			9 35	10 47	11 30
Yarmouth Southtown dep.	a.m		9 20				p.m
Lowestoft North dep.			8 35	9 44	10 42	11 14	11 55 12 15
LOWESTOFT GE arr.	7 30	arr.		9 50	10 50	11 20	arr. 12 23

Train Number	239	240	241	242	243	244	245
	GE ECS	GEPass	Pass.	Pass.	GEPass	GEGds	Pass.
YARMOUTH BEACH dep.			2 25	3 27			4 40
Yarmouth Southtown dep.	12 33	1 00			3 36	3 40	
Lowestoft North dep.	G	1 24	2 50	3 49	4 00	5 37	5 02
LOWESTOFT GE arr.		1 30	arr.	3 55	4 06	5 45	5 08

Train Number	246	247	248	249	250	251	252
	Pass.	GEPass	Pass.				
YARMOUTH BEACH dep.	7 30		8 56				
Yarmouth Southtown dep.		8 32					
Lowestoft North dep.	7 57	8 56	9 15				
LOWESTOFT GE arr.	8 03	9 02	arr.				

Train Number	253	254	255	256	257	258	259
	GEPass	Pass.	Pass.	GEPass	GEGds	Pass.	GEPass
LOWESTOFT GE dep.	7 43	8 15		11 46	11 50	12 35	
Lowestoft North dep.	7 50	8 23	10 00	11 53	12 20	12 43	G
Yarmouth Southtown arr.	8 13			12 17	1 45		1 22
YARMOUTH BEACH arr.		8 50	10 26			1 10	

Train Number	260	261	262	263	264	265	266
	Goods	Pass.	GEPass	Pass.	Goods	Pass.	GEPass
LOWESTOFT GE dep.	1 05	2 00	3 10		5 10	5 25	6 46
Lowestoft North dep.	1 20	2 07		3 55		5 32	6 53
Yarmouth Southtown arr.			3 41				7 17
YARMOUTH BEACH arr.	2 15	2 30		4 21	5 40	5 58	

Train Number	267	268	269	270	271	272	273
	ECS	Pass.	Pass.				
LOWESTOFT GE dep.	8 20						
Lowestoft North dep.	8 26	8 30	9 50				
Yarmouth Southtown arr.							
YARMOUTH BEACH arr.		8 56	10 15				

Glossary

Glossary

Abutment	Vertical brick end support of a bridge from which the arch springs or on which joists rest.
Annett's Key	Key kept in signal box frame to release distant points by hand.
Arch	*Elliptical*: a compound curve having five centres. *Flat*: plain lintel of vertical or splayed brick. *Gothic*: simple pointed arch. *Segmental*: curved into a segment of a circle. *Semicircular*: half-circular, round-headed. *Tudor*: Pointed compound arch.
Arts & Crafts	Popular informal type of architecture incorporating Elizabethan details, dating from the 1870s and revived many times.
Ashlar	Thin facing blocks of stone laid in very regular courses with very small joints between.
B&LJt	Bourn & Lynn Joint Railway
BR	British Railways
Bargeboard	Timber board covering ends of roof timbers on a gable. Often decorative.
Beading	Small section timber strips or plates covering joints in boarding on buildings or coaches, often imitated in metal castings.
Boarding	*Close*: vertical timber boards butted together with no pronounced jointing. Often tongued and grooved, otherwise joints beaded. *Lapped*: horizontal overlapping boards of special section to enable them to lie flush. *Weather*: simple horizontal overlapping boards.
CNR	Central Norfolk Railway
CR	Caledonian Railway
Canopy	Roof over platform or entrance supported on columns or cantilevered from building.
Capital	Enlargement at top of column, usually to a Classical order, eg Tuscan: a plain tapering column with a capital of several rings of increasing size.
Casement	Window hinged to frame.
Castellated	Having an edge resembling castle battlements.
Chert	Nodules of flint-like stone.
Corbelled	Brick or stonework brought out from the face of a wall in small steps.

Cornice	Upper part of building or wall, standing proud and often decorated classically.
Cupola	Small tower mounted on roof, often open with a leaded roof and weathervane.
Dentils	Course of brick or stonework below cornice with regular gaps between, literally resembling teeth.
Device	Unofficial 'coat of arms' of an organisation.
Dormer	A window or decorated gable with small pitched roof subsidiary to the main roof.
Down Line	On the M&GN from the west to Norwich, Yarmouth, Lowestoft and Cromer.
Dressings	General name for decorative edges to openings etc
E&M	Eastern & Midlands Railway
Eastern Section	The lines east of South Lynn.
Elizabethan	General term for the architecture of the later 16th century, which the 'arts & crafts' copied.
Facia	Eaves board on which the guttering is fixed.
Finial	Building: a carved batten or turned post fixed at the apex of bargeboards. Often decorative. Signal: turned wood or fabricated metal decoration finishing off signal or other posts.
Frieze	Decorated strip below cornice.
GC	Great Central Railway
GE	Great Eastern Railway
GN	Great Northern Railway
GW	Great Western Railway
GY&S	Great Yarmouth & Stalham Railway
G&SW	Glasgow & South Western Railway
Half-hipped	Hipped roof with small gabled ridge extension, often a louvred vent or half-timbered area.
Half-timbering	Timbers applied to a wall to imitate Elizabethan construction, with brick or stucco infilling.
Herringbone	Brickwork arranged in alternating diagonal courses, often between half-timbering.
Island	Platform entirely surrounded by tracks, approached by footbridge or subway.
Italianate	Literally, influenced by Italian Renaissance architecture, itself based on classical Roman.

Jackarch	Small brick or concrete arch between cross-girders under plate girder bridges.
Joist	Loadbearing wooden, iron or steel beam.
KLDR	King's Lynn Dock & Railway Co
L&F	Lynn & Fakenham Railway
L&SB	Lynn & Sutton Bridge Railway
L&Y	Lancashire & Yorkshire Railway
LMS	London, Midland & Scottish Railway
LNER	London & North Eastern Railway
LNWR	London & North Western Railway
Lantern	Large louvred ridge-top ventilator.
Lintel	Beam or flat arch of brick, etc, over opening.
M&GN	Midland & Great Northern Joint Railways
M&E	Midlands & Eastern Railway
MR	Midland Railway
Matchboard-sided	Specifically the flat-sided NER coaches clad in small vertical boards.
Monopitch	Roof pitched in one direction only, 'lean-to'.
Mullion	Vertical part of window frames.
N&S	Norwich & Spalding Railway
N&SJt	Norfolk & Suffolk Joint Railway
NER	North Eastern Railway
Occupation	Bridge or crossing for convenience of landowner whose land is divided by the railway.
Office	Used as general term for second design of Wilkinson & Jarvis station.
PW&S	Peterborough, Wisbech & Sutton Railway
Panelled	Brick wall in which areas of lesser thickness form a regular pattern, often with a window.
Pantile	Typical Norfolk overlapping 'S' section clay tile.
Parapet	Weather-resisting capping to wall of building or bridge. Often stone, concrete or special brick.
Pavilion	Used as general term for first and third designs of Wilkinson & Jarvis station, consisting of two cross-gables divided by central portion.
Pediment	Representation in stone or brick of low-pitch gable end of classical temple, over windows, doors or porticoes.

159

Pendant	Feature hanging towards ground.
Pier	Support for bridge of several spans, or for wall.
Pilaster	Square column to classical order as part of wall.
Plinth	Decorative thickening of wall at base.
Podium	A solid base on which a building is elevated above the surrounding ground level.
Portico	Classical porch, usually with four or six columns and pediment above.
Quoin	Corner blocks or bricks standing proud of wall level or in different colour material.
RC	Reinforced Concrete
RCH	Railway Clearing House
RIJ	Rolled iron joist.
RSCo	Railway Signal Company
RSV	Railway service vehicle.
Raking post	Diagonal bracing post in fencing.
Rock-faced	Concrete block finished in random, uneven relief.
Rubbed brick	Soft bricks rubbed together to form splayed brick arch with very fine joint lines.

Rustic	In the context of iron castings usually means an imitation of nature, eg rough wood.
S&B	Spalding & Bourne Railway
S&DJt	Somerset & Dorset Joint Railway
S&F	Saxby & Farmer
Sash	Sliding window of building or signalbox.
Serif	Decorative features on each letter of typeface. *Sanserif*: without the above, plain letters.
Shear-legs	Assembly of three posts with block and pulley at apex. Used for lifting locos and tenders.
Sill	Lower part of window or door frame, or bottom frame member of wooden building.
Soffit	Board under eaves.
Spandrel	Cast-iron right-angle and arched bracing, often with decoration, eg initials of railway.
Staff	Single-line token.
String course	Course of brick or stone in wall in relief or in different colour.
Stucco	Plastered wall, also 'pebble-dashed'.

TMO	Traffic Manager's Office
Tablet	Metal single-line token.
Terracotta	Fired clay in special moulded shapes.
Transom	Horizontal bar of window frames.
Up Line	On the M&GN, from Cromer, Lowestoft, Yarmouth, Norwich and South Lynn to the west.
Valance	Decorative edging to canopy.
Vestibule	Corridor connection between coaches.
W&J	Wilkinson & Jarvis Ltd, contractors.
WD	War Department
Western Section	Lines west of South Lynn.
Whitaker Apparatus	Automatic tablet exchanger invented by the S&DJt Locomotive Superintendent Alfred Whitaker.
Wing Walls	Outspread retaining walls of a bridge.
Y&NN	Yarmouth & North Norfolk Railway

Bibliography

M&GN Circle Bulletin; Editor: Mick Clark, M&GN Circle
A Short History of the M&GN; Ronald H. Clark, Goose & Son
The M&GNJR; A. J. Wrottesley, David & Charles
The M&GNJR; John Rhodes, Ian Allan
Scenes from the M&GNJR; Ronald H. Clark, Moorland
Norfolk's Railways Vol 2: M&GN; Handscomb & Standley, S B Pubs
The Melton to Cromer Branch; S. C. Jenkins, Oakwood Press
Midland Style; R. E. Lacey, HMRS
Locomotives of the M&GN; Alan Wells, HMRS/M&GN
Midland Railway Carriages Vol 1; Lacey & Dow, Wild Swan
The Signal Box; Signal Study Group, OPC

Forty Years of a Norfolk Railway; William Marriott, M&GNJRPS
Britain's Railway Liveries; E. F. Carter, Starke
Trains Illustrated Annual 1960; G. Freeman Allen, Ian Allan
Modeller's Sketchbook of PO Wagons; A. G. Thomas, Model Ry Mfg

M&GN Circle Archives
Norfolk Record Office
Public Record Office
House of Lords Records
National Railway Museum Records

History of M&GN Rolling Stock; Hobden & Watling, unpublished
The Signalling of the M&GN; Michael Back, unpublished

Rear cover, top:
Class AT 4-4-2T No 41, after receiving an extended smokebox in c1910, is seen at Yarmouth Beach. The other two engines had cut-out brass numerals. Note the 'banjo' route indicators on the starter signals, and the two water tanks in the background, with the loco sand dryer adjacent. *Real Photos/IAL*

Rear cover, centre:
A general view of Melton Constable from the east in c1961. From left to right are the carriage, wagon & paint shop, the fitting shop, the drawing office, Melton East box with loco depot behind and the station. Note the early concrete signal with ironwork bracket, and the M&GN water crane.
E. Tuddenham

Rear cover, bottom:
Hillington viewed up the 1 in 100 gradient towards Massingham. Beyond the original pavilion building is the brick tariff shed with one of the new 'arts & crafts' waiting rooms nearest the camera. *M&GN Circle*

Front cover, top:
A coloured postcard of 'C' class 4-4-0 No 53, this was one of a series produced by the Locomotive Publishing Co. *Author's collection*

Front cover, bottom:
Class A 4-4-0 No 26 hustles a short passenger train towards Peterborough in the 1920s. Note the single line tablet catcher on the side of the tender.